THE LITERATURE OF CRIME AND DETECTION

An Illustrated History from Antiquity to the Present

UNGAR WRITERS' RECOGNITIONS SERIES

Mystery Writers

Arthur Conan Doyle by Don Richard Cox
Raymond Chandler by Jerry Speir
P. D. James by Norma Siebenheller
The Murder Mystique:
Crime Writers on Their Art edited by Lucy Freeman
Roots of Detection:
The Art of Deduction before Sherlock Holmes
edited by Bruce Cassiday
Sons of Sam Spade:
The Private Eye Novel in the 70s by David Geherin
Rex Stout by David R. Anderson
Dashiell Hammett by Dennis Dooley
Michael Innes by George L. Scheper
The American Private Eye:
The Image in Fiction by David Geherin
John le Carré by Peter Lewis
13 Mistresses of Murder by Elaine Budd
The Secret of the Stratemeyer Syndicate:
Nancy Drew, The Hardy Boys,
and The Million Dollar Fiction Factory
by Carol Billman
Dick Francis by Melvyn Barnes

The Literature of Crime and Detection

An Illustrated History from Antiquity to the Present

Waltraud Woeller and Bruce Cassiday

UNGAR · NEW YORK

1988
The Ungar Publishing Company
370 Lexington Avenue, New York, N.Y. 10017

Originally published as *Illustrierte Geschichte der
Kriminalliteratur*
Copyright © 1984 by Edition Leipzig

English translation by Ruth Michaelis-Jena
and Willy Merson.
Additional material and American adaptation
Copyright © 1988 by Bruce Cassiday

Printed in the German Democratic Republic

Library of Congress Cataloging-in-Publication Data

Woeller, Waltraud.
    The literature of crime and detection.

    Translation of: Illustrierte Geschichte der
Kriminalliteratur.
    1. Detective and mystery stories—History and
criticism. I. Cassiday, Bruce. I. Title.
PN3448.D4W6413   1987   809.3′876   86-16040
ISBN 0-8044-2983-9

Contents

Introduction

The literature of crime and detection has a long history. It can be traced back to antiquity and is found in medieval tales of horror, the Pitaval collection of *Causes Célèbres* of the seventeenth century, and the Gothic novel of the eighteenth century. However, the genre in its many variations gained wide popularity only in the nineteenth century, when well-known writers began using it as a medium. Since then Edgar Allan Poe, Arthur Conan Doyle, Agatha Christie, Edgar Wallace, Dashiell Hammett, Georges Simenon, Friedrich Dürrenmatt, and Maj Sjöwall and Per Wahlöö, to mention a few, have become famous practitioners, providing tales of detection and adventure, the "hard-boiled" private-eye story, the psychological tale of crime, and the *roman policier*.

The crime story, to its many addicts the "whodunit," is approached by the reader with varying expectations. One may see in it a carefully disguised chess problem, the solution of which is anticipated with pleasure, while another may be fascinated by exciting lawsuits and the diversity of crimes and criminals. Still others like taking part, at least in their imagination, in a police hunt through streets and over rooftops. The reader of the crime story will, in fact, choose his reading by the title, the author, the hero, or even simply by the picture on the dust jacket.

This variety of taste and the many types of crime fiction that exist side by side are by no means new phenomena. The literature of crime has covered a wide spectrum from the very beginning. When did it all begin? Was it with Edgar Allan Poe in the first half of the nineteenth century, in antiquity, or in the Bible with Cain's murder of Abel?

One would be doing less than justice to this branch of writing by limiting research solely to crime and murder wherever it was to be found in books, the theater, or in oral tradition. Helen of Troy was carried off by Theseus; Siegfried of the *Nibelungenlied* was treacherously murdered. In these ancient sagas and epics the crime stands only as the beginning, the prelude to the catastrophe. The story then proceeds to lay bare the limits of human endurance. In contrast, crime fiction is written chiefly to entertain, a perfectly legitimate purpose that need not produce merely worthless hack writing. It relies on the creation of tension in the reader, tension that arises from the unraveling of the mystery and the picking up of clues, at the same time supplying the reader with an intellectual exercise in the thrill of finding the solution. Tension may increase without the loss of emotional interest.

At the same time moral issues may be raised in the way an offense or crime is presented and in the description of the culprit, his background, and his dilemma. Properly expounded, crime and punishment will satisfy the reader's longing to see justice done. In the crime story it is man who punishes evil, while in myth and legend the penalty is always exacted by the gods, fate, or the furies.

Emotional elements may come into play in many different ways. Through the years man has been fascinated by the dark side of life, by horror, and by murder. In preliterate days he witnessed crime and murder on the stage, and later, as a reader, he gained insight into the whole range of human emotions through the literature of crime. Seeing crime and punishment enacted fulfills a deep-seated desire, apparent even in the play of children; the scale of emotions includes chills, horror, and fright—the *mysterium fascinosum et tremendum*. The demoniac knows no limits of law and order that may at times appear problematical to man.

Human society sets up norms—varying in time and place—as to what is objectionable or wicked and as to what constitutes crime. The man who offends against these norms is singled out as a culprit. Once doubts arise as to the validity of a set of values, social protest follows. This raises the question of whether or not a branch of writing mainly concerned with entertainment and the pleasure of suspense should be weighted down with problems. From this point of view Dostoyevski's *Crime and Punishment* cannot be considered a crime story. Apart from the murder of the old moneylender the author concerns himself with man's guilt, how he bears it, and how he eventually atones for it—problems that lie beyond the scope of entertainment for its own sake.

In spite of certain demarcations in its definition and in its development the subject remains so diverse that the present book can only deal with literature in the narrative print form. An exception is the dramatic form when, before the rise of general literacy, crime was presented to the public through action on the stage. Comic books and serial publications have been excluded from consideration since these tend to reflect inhumane attitudes and merely masquerade under the label of "crime fiction" to exploit sex and violence. To repeat: when did the literature of crime begin? The answer may well be when man no longer believed gods and demons caused evil; when man held himself solely responsible for his good or wicked deeds. Only then could his guilt and his crime be investigated and judged. This change in values came about through the work of the Greek philosophers.

Thus it seems logical to begin the history of this particular branch of literature with antiquity. It is a view shaped by Dorothy Sayers in her lecture "Aristotle on Detective Fiction" given at Oxford in 1935. In it she said: "What in his [Aristotle's] heart of hearts he desired was a Good Detective Story; and it was not his fault, poor man, that he lived some twenty centuries too early." The term "detective story" describes only one form in the wide spectrum and long history of crime fiction.

The detective form does not seem to have existed in the Middle Ages when literacy was limited almost solely to the clergy and writing for entertainment alone was rare. Entertainment was then provided by tales told aloud, not set down in the written word. In faded documents, however, those centuries do supply evidence that can be interpreted as pertinent to the subject of crime fiction. It must be stressed once again that the genre did not fully develop and diversify until the nineteenth century. Scholars and literary critics were slow in paying attention to it, believing that it did not deserve study. The first serious consideration occurred in Britain where certain crime writers spoke up for their own works, among them G. K. Chesterton and Dorothy Sayers. Their ideas about structure, function, literary merit, and other aspects prove to be as varied, and even as contradictory, as their writing; this continuing variety in critical judgment poses some problems today, but at the same time adds ongoing interest to the subject.

Interest in the subject of crime, of course, goes beyond fiction. A general interest in criminology is part of the study of the social scientist. How is a crime investigated? How is the identity of the culprit determined beyond a doubt? How is he brought to trial? How is he convicted? How is he punished? The present book will not go into full details of legal documents or cite codes of law, yet its illustrations tell their own tale: pictures of prison walls, of interrogations, instruments of torture, court scenes, portraits of philosophers, advocates, judges, and offenders. They also depict the many different facets of crime fiction, showing authors and the heroes of their novels, pamphlets, and drawings.

Others show bindings and book jackets. In selecting what to include, it became clear that the early period provided the most pictorial material, which was, after all, natural at a time when literacy was limited. These pictures are often remarkable in their artistic quality. With the rise of literacy, however, a flood of popular printed books appeared, and the pictorial content diminished. In the twentieth century the situation changed again when a great wealth of visual matter came on the market, not so much in the form of books as in the mass media of films and television, both of which thrived on the subject of crime. Early and present-day illustrations are witness to the fascination that crime in its many forms has always exerted on the public. In the famous detective tradition of Sherlock Holmes, this book will consider all the facts and hope to come to some kind of conclusion.

Many thanks are due to Professor Horst Kunze, Emeritus Director of the Staatsbibliothek Berlin, for the constant interest he has taken in my work. I am also indebted to my son, Matthias Woeller, for his continued support.   —WALTRAUD WOELLER

ANTIQUITY

"And could you say," asked Theagenes,
"how and with what motive he committed this murder?"

—Heliodorus

The literature of crime and detection begins in the fifth century B.C., when both art and literature were flourishing. Philosophy had separated from myth and religion; the citizen of the Greek city state, not the god or the hero, had become the focal point of most artistic expression. The plays of Aeschylus, Sophocles, and Euripides were part of this development. The attention of the average Greek citizen could be easily gripped by these popular dramas—tragedy as well as comedy. The intellectual life of the city state was carried on by public debates and discussions; drama, turning words into action, was accessible to everybody. Whether one's interests lay in politics, science, or the arts, the average person wanted to be entertained, and plays fulfilled this need. It is therefore understandable that in some plays there are elements of suspense which, combined with the question of crime and guilt, make them important to the literature of crime. Indeed early beginnings appear in mythology and the Homeric epics; these eventually led to the Greek novel.

Plays were often based on material from mythology, but with the mythical figures turned into mortals, topical allusions were common. Instead of an uncritical belief in fate, the question of personal guilt soon arose.

In Aeschylus's *Oresteia*, Orestes avenges the murder of his father Agamemnon by killing his mother Clytemnestra and her lover Aegisthus. The Erinyes (Furies), three fearful winged maidens, goddesses of fate and revenge, pursue Orestes, constantly encouraged by the ghost of his murdered mother. Apollo advises Orestes to flee to Athens and ask Pallas Athena for protection and justice. Athena, however, does not want to decide Orestes' fate on her own. She wants the people of Athens to judge whether he is

guilty or not. The concept of trial by jury was thus introduced in Greek literature. The Erinyes represent the prosecution. Apollo is both counsel for the defense and witness at the same time—a most reliable witness, for as a god and worker of oracles, he cannot lie. Twelve chosen citizens of Athens form the jury, and Athena herself is the judge. She decides in Orestes' favor and acquits him. All the facts are carefully considered: Orestes does not deny having murdered his mother, but was he not driven to the deed by Apollo? Did Clytemnestra kill Orestes' father or not? Orestes has produced as evidence the cloak bloodied by the sword of Aegisthus; he could not have done otherwise because no prosecutor or judge would have dared to act against the queen. The case of Orestes shows clearly how crimes are to be dealt with: the question of guilt should be considered carefully in public, weighing all the details before pronouncing a verdict. When the oracle guided Orestes to the jurisdiction of the city state, it underlined this historical development. Trial by jury thus became authorized with the members of the jury drawn by lots from a representative assembly of the people.

When Sophocles dramatized the Oedipus legend, he borrowed from ancient myths the fascination—the demoniac attraction—of the evil deeds committed unwittingly by Oedipus. As predicted by the oracle, Oedipus has killed his father, Laius, King of Thebes. He solves the riddle of the sphinx, overcomes her, and frees the city. When the Thebans make him their king, without questioning the fate of Laius, he marries Jocasta, his mother, ignorant of his true relationship to her. So he adds incest to the crime of murder. He is then forced to investigate the killing of Laius, an outbreak of plague having indicated the existence of an unexpiated outrage. As

King of Thebes, he leads the investigation and unmasks himself as the murderer of his father and the husband of his mother. Oedipus might therefore be called the ancestor of the detective hero since, as soon as he learns of a crime, he begins his investigations—leading to the shocking discovery that *he* is the guilty man.

Greek drama taught the general public to think logically and to seek a critical understanding of the world. To reach a wide audience, character motivation was clearly and dramatically exposed. Of course Greek drama was never a "thriller" in the modern sense, but its concern with crime provided suspense, in itself a dramatic element. Even at that time inspiration for the playwright came directly from public legal proceedings.

Around 400 B.C., especially in political discussions, the art of speaking and the ability to hold an audience became crucially important to success. Demosthenes' oratory in the law courts aroused great public interest. It was the elegance of his expression, his sagacity, and the logical accuracy of his evidence that attracted attention. The lawsuits themselves contained interesting and often odd elements: legacy hunting, insurance fraud, and barratry (the sinking of ships with all hands on board).

In Roman antiquity and during the first century B.C. Cicero's speeches were quickly copied and circulated so that those who had not heard him in person could at least read his deliberations and enjoy them. He became known through two notorious lawsuits. One was against the governor of Sicily, the infamous Gaius Verres, in the year 71 B.C.; the other the defense of Sextus Roscius of Ameria in 80 B.C.

Verres had looted art treasures on a large scale, conducted illegal grain deals, and was responsible for a number of murders. Cicero, as representative of the Sicilian cities, brought charges against him, and as a result of a brilliant opening speech and the evidence of witnesses succeeded in sending him into voluntary exile. A further speech that Cicero then could not deliver was later published and makes good reading to this very day.

Sextus Roscius was accused of patricide, a crime usually punished by sewing the culprit into a sack and drowning him. Cicero revealed that two relatives had arranged for Roscius's father to be murdered and the blame attached to the son in order to seize the family fortune. The case ended in an acquittal.

The business of book selling goes back as far as about 500 B.C. Atticus, a friend of Cicero, became famous as a publisher in Rome. It is interesting to note that Cicero actually envisaged a book that could be put together by the use of separate metal letters. The boom in manuscript sales came during the era of Imperial Rome, when even remote provinces were supplied with scrolls and editions sometimes ran to as high as a thousand copies.

In the first century B.C. a few educated Romans built up huge private libraries. One such in Herculaneum was owned by the poet Philodemus and contained 1,803 scrolls. The first public library was founded in the fourth century B.C. in Heraclea and soon Rome could boast of as many as twenty-eight. The biggest library of antiquity was in Alexandria, with 500,000 scrolls, while that of Pergamum contained 200,000. This meant that a great variety of reading matter had begun to circulate, much written for entertainment. It was then that the early crime story made its appearance, written for an educated and leisured audience. Although the literary critics of the time did not take the crime story seriously, its appeal was general and widespread.

The Golden Ass by Lucius Apuleius, the Platonic philosopher and rhetorician of the second century A.D., belongs to this literature. It contains some stories written solely for entertainment, free of philosophical reflections. Some of them do in fact represent an early form of crime fiction. Apuleius's intention was to entertain with "delectable matter." In the preface to his work he states: "I will set forth unto you a pleasant Grecian jest. Whereunto, gentle reader, if thou wilt give attendant ear, it will minister unto thee such delectable matter as thou shalt be well contended withal."

The tenth book starts out with a crime story. A widower has remarried and his new wife very soon casts her eyes on her almost grown-up stepson, who rebuffs her advances. Her love turns to hate, she determines to get rid of him at any price, and to this end she sends a slave to procure a lethal poison. It is not the virtuous youth who drinks the poisoned cup, but his twelve-year-old stepbrother, and the opportunistic woman immediately accuses her stepson of murdering her child.

After the funeral the unhappy father accuses his son of murder in court. The man's grief and distress persuade the council to put the youth to death by stoning—without even a trial. Fearing that this may lead to a riot, the authorities request a trial to hear the evidence before pronouncing a verdict. The prosecutor is called forth first and then the accused. The advocates are asked to plead their cases briefly, without resorting to lengthy preambles or appeals to the compassion of the people. When the speeches have been made, it is decided to seek further definite proof of the truth and verify the reliability of the accusations.

A certain slave was said to be acquainted with the manner of the youth's death. He tells a fabricated tale, presenting it as the truth. The youth, he says, called him and ordered him to kill the stepbrother, at the same time promising a large reward for keeping the deed secret. Refusing to carry out the murder, the slave was threatened with death. In the end, he says, the accused administered the poison to the boy with his own hand. The scoundrel, visibly trembling, relates all this with the appearance of complete truth.

None of the council members now believes in the innocence of the youth. Verdicts are about to be placed in the bronze urn when suddenly one of them, a well-respected physician, covers the urn with his hand, preventing the others from voting. He then addresses the assembly and says: "I will not be party to the commission of a second murder. The accused stands condemned by false accusation. I shall tell you the true story. This good-for-nothing slave came to me not so long ago and asked for some quick-acting poison, needed, he said, for a sick man. I knew he was lying, so I gave him a potion for which I refused to take his money, making him instead put the price in a pouch and seal it with his own seal. Here is the same pouch. You can verify the seal yourselves."

The court attendants then seize the slave and on his finger find an iron ring whose seal tallies with that on the pouch. The slave remains unrepentant. Even trial by fire brings no confession.

The physician then says: "I cannot tolerate that you should condemn this innocent youth to death. Nor will I allow this wretched slave to make a mockery of the courts and escape punishment for his crime. I shall therefore give you infallible proof of what I have told you. I gave a potion to this man because I knew that if I had refused, I would have made it easier for him to commit his crime. He might have bought the poison from someone else or executed his deed by the sword or in some other manner. What I gave him was an infusion of mandrake, a well-known narcotic inducing a deathlike sleep. If the boy has really drunk my potion he should still be alive, in a deep sleep. If he met his death in some other way, then you must look further for the cause."

Those assembled go to the boy's grave and when the father lifts the coffin lid he finds his son alive,

Socrates, condemned to death, drinks a cup of poisonous hemlock to carry out the ancient Greek form of the death penalty. Woodcut from a painting by J. Louis David.

In Greek antiquity the Erinyes (Furies) pursue criminals and punish them, particularly those guilty of murder. Their faces are represented as having fixed merciless stares, their heads surrounded by snakelike hair.

A relief from Marcus Aurelius's column, representing a Roman court scene held in public.

stirring from a deathlike sleep. Delighted, he embraces him and presents him to the assembled people. With the boy still wrapped in his winding sheet they return to the court. The crimes of the wicked slave and the even more wicked wife have been exposed. The stepmother is sent into lifelong exile and the slave is crucified. All agree that the physician should keep the gold pieces as a reward for his prudence in not supplying the poison.

Another story that might be called an example of early crime fiction is one told by Herodotus in the second book of his *History*. It concerns the treasure house of Rhamsinitus, Ramses III, the builder of the pavilion of Medinet Abu at Thebes. The king builds a treasure house of stone and the architect leaves one stone loose, well adjusted, so that nobody notices. He entrusts the secret to his two sons who plunder the treasure at will, until the older is finally caught in a snare. The younger son cuts off his brother's head to keep his identity unknown, and continues to outwit the king. In the end he marries the king's daughter. The motif of the "master-thief" is widespread in the folktales of the world.

The romantic stories that flourished as early as Greek antiquity feature one recurring theme: the separation and eventual happy reunion of faithful lovers after endless adventures in distant lands that often involved crimes. Heliodorus, the sophist of the third century A.D., considered to be the best of the romance writers, published *Aethiopica (The Ethiopian Story)*, which in ten books describes the adventures of Theagenes and Charicleia. Sex and crime are the main attractions of the book. Theagenes, Charicleia, and Cnemon find a young Greek woman murdered in a brigands' den in Egypt. "Judging by the sword we found at the scene of the murder," says Theagenes, "the culprit must be Thyamis. It belongs to him; I recognize it by the eagle—his symbol—on the hilt. Can you now tell me," he asks, "how, when, and why he committed the deed?"

In the story the crime is overshadowed by adventure; the reader's main concern is the final reunion of the lovers, a happy ending that in spite of many objections over the centuries is still popular with the reading public.

In antiquity the crime motif alone was not sufficient material to sustain a novel. Yet it did supply the plot for a short story in Apuleius's *Golden Ass*. The reader's interest in these stories is prompted by intellectual curiosity, a wish to investigate and arrive at a logical and just conclusion. Apuleius himself ironically expressed this desire: "I am not curious," he said, "but I should like to know everything."

FROM THE MIDDLE AGES TO THE SIXTEENTH CENTURY

O! gentlemen; see, see! Dead Henry's wounds
Open their congeal'd mouths and bleed afresh.

—Shakespeare, *King Richard the Third*

The impulse to learn and investigate was not as strong during the Middle Ages as it was in antiquity. Then man searched for a clear understanding of the universe; now he accepted a divine order. Any attempt to study and comprehend this order was considered sinful and the work of the Devil. Nobody doubted that the Devil was the cause of all evil, and to listen to his promptings and blandishments led a man to commit foul deeds. Such ideas are clearly reflected in the miracle stories of the period. In the first half of the thirteenth century Caesarius, prior of the Cistercian monastery of Heisterbach in the Rhineland, collected hundreds of these, all showing that it was not intellect and human effort, but a miracle that discovered or prevented evil. The purpose of these particular tales was to edify, not entertain.

At the beginning of the Middle Ages not many people outside the circles of the clergy were able to read and write and so practically all literature preserved from antiquity was kept in the monasteries. These works, either in the original or in copies, were not used as a point of departure for new ideas; they provided accepted facts. About the year 1200 a process of secularization set in. The lay population was seized by a desire to study and learn, although haltingly at first. In contrast to religious asceticism, troubadours and minnesingers composed love songs and political poetry. Ancient heroic ballads from the time of the Migration of Nations were turned into epics by churchmen and these spoke openly of violence and described in great detail the appearance and armament of the hero. If someone committed manslaughter he did not conceal the deed. It was clear for everyone to see. These epics, though dealing with crime, bear no relation to the literature of crime and detection.

When at the time of the Renaissance the economic situation of the middle classes improved, they proudly began to develop their own culture with a definite leaning towards antiquity. The most important event in this progress was the invention of printing in 1448. In the fifty years that followed, some forty thousand books were published with an estimated total of eight million copies—about two hundred copies per book. This low number of copies per edition made these books expensive, meaning that only the rich could buy them. There were, however, many ways of amassing a goodly collection. In 1462 Jacob Püterich von Reichertshausen, a learned Munich patrician, reported that he had built up his library by borrowing, stealing, and, if it was the only way, buying.

For every book there was an appreciable number of people who got to know its contents by having it read or related to them. These people might be members of a family, friends, or others too poor to afford to buy. Only Luther's Bible reached an edition of a thousand copies, a number quite common during the time of the Roman Empire. Alongside religious tracts and ecclesiastical pamphlets, stories written for entertainment now began to appear.

Broadsheets illustrated by woodcuts became very popular. Their favorite subjects were horrifying details of the appearances of comets, great fires, murders, and other wicked deeds. One main feature of this ever-increasing use of pictorial material—directed mainly at an illiterate public—was the reproduction of the portraits of criminals. The culprit was usually represented as a monster, as one who had made a pact with the Devil. The link between crime and punishment however was missing, nor was there any allusion to the detection and final conviction of

In Diebold Schilling's *Schweizerchronik*, a "chronicle" of crime in the early sixteenth century, Hans Spiess is forced to undergo the famous "bier" test. Brought to his murdered wife's coffin in the cemetery at Ettiswyl in 1503, he watches as her dead body begins to bleed. Found guilty, Spiess is charged with murder, made to confess under torture, and is then broken on the wheel.

A pamphlet showing the torture and execution of Hans Reichart, a glazier in Dietfurt, Germany. Pictorial material outweighs written text.

Also from *Schweizerchronik*: the "water" test, an ancient ordeal supposed to prove guilt or innocence.

Punishment was seen as a deterrent to crime—hence its harshness. Drawing and quartering, from a woodcut *c.* 1514 in Livy's *History of Rome*.

Preparation for the "penal question." From the Bamberg criminal code, the predecessor of the *Carolina*.

From the *Lay Mirror* of 1512. Other forms of execution, all performed in public, were meant to destroy the criminal completely.

Tools of execution and torture. In order to keep the criminal working, so-called *Ehrenstrafen* (punishments to humiliate him) were inflicted.

the criminal. These points did not lend themselves to pictorial representation, of course; but above all they did not seem to interest the public.

Incidents of ordeal by fire, water, or other means occurred in many legends and folktales: a flower might turn into a bleeding limb when a murderer was about to pick it from the grave of someone he had secretly killed. A dead man's bone made into a shepherd's pipe might unmask the felon. Undetected crimes were expected to be punished by an Act of God. Crime was not dealt with as a separate incident; it was part of a miraculous happening and atonement was seen as an expression of divine justice. Even a historically established criminal case might be turned into a tale. *Bluebeard*, in Charles Perrault's collection *Contes de ma Mère L'Oye*, is an example. This story was based on the accidentally discovered crimes of Giles de Rais in the first half of the fifteenth century. He lured more than two hundred young people and children to his castle in Brittany where he cruelly murdered them.

Interest in crime did therefore exist, demonstrating itself in various ways. Although it had not yet established its own specific literary idiom, it found its way into the traditional forms of story telling. How then did matters stand, outside the popular tales of miracles, with regard to crime, detection, and punishment? The legal process was based on an accusation made by a person who believed himself wronged, against a person believed to have committed the wrong. Both parties were equal in the eyes of the law and both were expected to provide sponsors to vouch for them. The courts had difficulty in pronouncing a verdict unless the culprit was caught red-handed.

Detection played a part in lawsuits, with the searching for evidence such as murder weapons. As an example, one might consider the time grass took to rise again after being trampled down. But it was still difficult to reach a verdict. Severe crimes would be dealt with by ordeal of fire, water, "legal combat," or that of the "bier." For the accused much depended on which form of ordeal was chosen. Ordeal by water gave the accused no chance. Should he succeed in keeping afloat in spite of fettered hands and feet, he was guilty; he was innocent if he drowned.

Shown below are the infamous mask and cage.

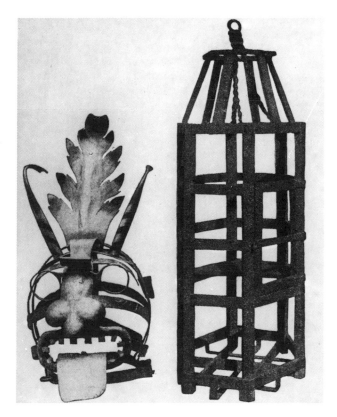

The test of the "bier" was a dramatic one. The victim became in effect the witness against the culprit; his wounds were expected to bleed as the accused approached him. The sixteenth-century *Schweizerchronik* by Diebold Schilling contains a report on Hans Spiess, a murderer, under the title "Von einem wunderbaren Mordhandel" ("A Tale of an Amazing Murder") that went as follows:

In the year 1503 Hans Spiess, a soldier, whoremonger, gambler, and debaucher, lives on a farm in the parish of Ettyswyl near Lucerne. One night in the Haymonth (June) he suffocates his wife in bed and in the morning leaves the house as usual. Suspicion rises against him and he is arrested at Willisau and severely tortured. He does not confess. Twenty days after her burial in the cemetery at Ettyswyl it is decided to disinter her body. The suspected husband is to be brought before the laid out corpse on a bier. Naked, and with his head shaven, he is to lay his right hand on the corpse and swear a solemn oath to

God and all the saints that he is innocent of her death. The gruesome scene is set. As the man looks at the body, the woman begins to retch and foam at the mouth. As he approaches the bier to swear the oath, she changes color and blood begins to stream from her body. The man falls on his knees, confesses his guilt, and begs for mercy. Hans Spiess, however, is not pardoned; instead, he is broken on the wheel.

In the thirteenth century, "inquisition" replaced the ancient procedures of accusation. Inquisition—an official inquiry into a crime—was originally used in the persecution of heretics. Through the influence of scholasticism, which regarded the archaic and dubious ordeals by water or fire as contradictory to logic, the method of inquisition became more generally adopted. The inquisitor was prosecutor, examining magistrate, and judge—all in one. He endeavored to extract a confession from the accused; then, if he failed, he resorted to torture. Often the mere display of the instruments of torture was sufficient to obtain

A felon is taken to prison. Woodcut, 1523.

Execution by a mechanical axe, in use as early as the sixteenth century. Woodcut by Lucas Cranach the Elder.

18

a confession. The terror was all the greater, since the trial was held in secret. The inquisition aroused fear and anguish and because of its inflexibility, interest in the final verdict was negligible. There could be no dialogue between prosecution and defense. No defense existed; the pros and cons could not be weighed. This procedure was used in many witch trials. Where the crime was clearly motivated by a pact or even a "love affair" with the Devil, and the suspect was convicted prima facie of being a witch, there was little opportunity for a work of literature on crime to develop.

Lesser offenses, supposed to be settled among the people, were dealt with in a magistrate's court. These were offenses such as fraudulent bankruptcy, dealing in counterfeit coin, or disputes over wills. The magistrates, untrained in law, tended to depend on ordeals in doubtful cases.

By the mid-sixteenth century something resembling crime fiction made its appearance. In Germany a collection of merry tales—the *Rollwagenbüchlein* by Jörg Wickram, a town clerk of Burgheim in Alsace— appeared in 1555. It contains "a cruel and horrific tale" concerning a double murder committed at an inn. Everyone present is arrested; and each is to be interrogated under torture. The investigator in charge of the case, however, decides otherwise. An experienced man, he carefully examines all the suspicious circumstances and advises the officials in charge not to deal too hastily with those arrested. In his opinion the innkeeper himself has murdered his wife and then committed suicide; his theory proves correct. The story ends with a caution: beware of false accusations and over-hasty action.

Many of the merry tales of the fifteenth and sixteenth centuries included indictable acts: disappearance without paying for food and drink, fraud, adultery, slander, and damage to property. But in this sort of writing these acts are seen from a comic point of view. There are no victims, simply people being bettered and exposed to ridicule. The cunning of the rogues amuse the listeners and readers who admire their guile, their tricks, and their intrigues. Life and death do not enter the plot.

In 1532 the *Carolina (Constitutio Criminalis Carolina)* was published in the Holy Roman Empire. It was an attempt to consolidate the many different interpretations of the law throughout the Empire. Torture was to be restricted, though not completely abol-

Title page of the *Carolina*, the *Peinliche Gerichtsordnung* of Emperor Charles V.

ished, and it could still be used in conjunction with other legal practices. At the same time princes, electors, and the estates were assured that their traditions would continue. The inquisition remained part of legal procedure until well into the seventeenth century, with its total secrecy in private sittings. The vacuum created by absolute secrecy caused speculation and suspicion, but it was not material for which writers were looking.

In Elizabethan London the situation was entirely different. There, in an atmosphere of economic security, the citizen held his head high and wanted to know about his country's history and what was going on in the world. He appeared determined, above all, to gain a certain amount of control over the administration of justice. Drama was the ideal medium to present problems to a wide public; like the plays of antiquity, situations connected with crime were enacted on the stage. The citizens of London thronged the theaters and playhouses, including the illiterate and those who could not afford books.

This development can be seen clearly in the works of Shakespeare. In the early historical plays the lust for power, ambition, murder, and intrigue are essential ingredients of the plot. In the comedies, such as *The Merchant of Venice*, legal matters play an important part. Murder is at the center of *Hamlet* and *Macbeth*. In *Hamlet* the murder has been committed before the action begins and the play is concerned with the effects of the crime, the question of revenge, and how justice is to be effected. But equally the play concerns itself with the idea of how great a burden of conflict and guilt can be borne by a man. It is this that separates Shakespeare's plays from the literature of pure crime.

In an almost medieval manner *Macbeth* presents the demoniac temptation of murder, and shows how, once the deed is committed, it leads inevitably to further foul actions. Shakespeare's aim was not merely to relate tales of horror; it was to lay bare the whole range of human passions by raising them to dramatic heights. The wide public that frequented the theater wanted drama made visible with dagger and sword, witches and ghosts:

> Thoughts black, hands apt, drugs fit and time agreeing:
> Confederate season, elso no creature seeing.

These words of Lucianus, nephew of the Player King in Shakespeare's *Hamlet*, describe to perfection a situation often encountered in the crime writing of later centuries.

Although Shakespeare was a man of the theater whose plays were written to be acted on the stage, they were undoubtedly also read by the wealthy and the literate few. On the continent of Europe English strolling players popularized his work, though mostly in bowdlerized forms. The Thirty Years' War, however, drove these actors away and for a long time his plays were forgotten.

THE SEVENTEENTH CENTURY

Parliament instructed the judiciary
to make a thorough search in the town
and the neighboring countryside.

—Georg Philipp Harsdörffer

Early in the seventeenth century René Descartes's dictum, *Cogito, ergo sum*—I think, therefore I am—expressed the philosophical creed of rational thought. Everyday life, however, was still far removed from rational thinking.

In fact, the seventeenth century was marked by sharp contrasts. In England the Habeas Corpus Act came into being (1679), a writ preventing the imprisonment of a person on suspicion only. On the continent, nevertheless, proceedings against witches, founded mainly on suspicion, continued. Alongside the academies of science and art, astrology and alchemy flourished. Opulent baroque culture existed hand in hand with dire poverty and lawlessness. By and large literature used courtly life as a model. It produced amorous and heroic novels, tragedies dealing with matters of state, and obsequious prose paying homage to princes and the nobility. Drinking songs and pastoral novels were also in vogue. At the same time the seventeenth century saw the rise of the popular novel. The contrasts to be found in language and literature were also apparent in painting, sculpture, and music.

About that time a new and irrational type of evildoer appeared: the vampire, a gruesome being that attacked innocent sleepers, sucking their blood. For centuries the notion of a nocturnal demon devouring souls or hearts had been restricted to folklore and reported only in chronicles, tales, and legends. It was not until the nineteenth century that the vampire emerged from the twilight to turn up in horror stories and later, in the twentieth century, in films. It has survived to this day as a subject suited to certain crime writers.

Another particularly interesting phenomenon of the seventeenth century is the picaresque novel. Its hero is the *picaro*, a rogue and braggart, with his origin in the *novela picaresca* of Spain. He is one of the underprivileged, managing to gain a place on the fringe of society by his quick wit, his cunning, and his trickery. The Thirty Years' War established him as the typical representative of the flotsam and jetsam of battles, famines, and plagues. Examples of the figure are the hero of the German writer Grimmelshausen's novel, *Simplicissimus*, and Bertolt Brecht's *Mother Courage*. Being poor and deprived led the *picaro* easily into a life of adventure and vagabondage, and, as a matter of course, into crime. Highwaymen and imposters, degenerate descendants perhaps of Robin Hood, also played their part in the seventeenth-century romances.

In 1608 Thomas Dekker's *The Bellman of London*, with the subtitle, *Bringing to the Light the Most Notorious Villainies Now Practised in the Kingdom*, gave a lively account of the London underworld. The book presented a picture of morals and manners that proved entertaining and amusing to a reader. There was nothing specially new in this interest in rogues, which after all was in the long-established tradition of merry stories and tall tales.

In France in 1630 Jean Pierre Camus, Bishop of Belley, published the *Amphithéâtre Sanglant* in which he retold a number of stories heard on his travels, on pilgrimages, and in meetings with important people. The title—translated loosely as *The Bloody Lecture Hall*—was sensational, but ecclesiastical ardor and moralizing were ingredients of all the tales. His book became the model for a German collection, *Der grosse Schauplatz jämmerlicher Mordgeschichte (A Gallery of Horrible Tales of Murder)* published after 1649 by a Nuremberg legal man, Georg Philipp Harsdörffer. Many tales of murder were represented in this work.

It was actually the beginning of a new literary form—the case history, presented as a short story. Harsdörffer, however, instead of the sober legal term *Mord* used purposely the more flamboyant *Mordgeschichte* (murder story). If Harsdörffer in the structure and title of his collection was close to Camus, he also consciously absorbed scientific ideas—for example, the "Theater of Anatomy," a large lecture hall where scientists presented experiments in medicine and natural history to an avid public.

Harsdörffer's own background made him the proper writer to present crime, detection, and punishment in a literary form. A well-traveled patrician, trained in the law, he was also a respected poet. In Nuremberg he founded several groups of pastoral poets, well-known throughout Germany. His stories set out to create a feeling of tension, with the author himself urging the reader on to a satisfying ending. The supernatural was usually an important element, even if it impaired the stories' credibility.

In *Das Gespenst (The Ghost)* the ghost helps to find and convict a murderer, in an intriguing mixture of the rational and the supernatural. It is retold in shortened form here:

"Once upon a time, in the capital of Sweden, a butcher fell in love with a pretty servant girl. Being a good girl, she was not willing to give in to her admirer's sinful desires. Of course, if the butcher were to be widowed, he could take her as his lawful wife.

To the man's distress, his good lady showed no signs of leaving this world. Being anxious to remedy the situation, he had a coffin made and killed his wife with a chopper while she was asleep. He put her quickly into the coffin, announcing that she had died of the plague. He then married the servant girl, confident that no one save the murderer would know about the crime. However, shortly afterwards a terrifying ghost came to the house of the newly married couple and eventually drove them out. The old house then stood empty while at the same time the butcher was much troubled in his conscience.

"It so happened that an Imperial Diet was to be held in Stockholm and an aristocratic widowed lady arrived in the city. There was a shortage of accommodation, so she was offered a room in the butcher's empty house. Being a God-fearing woman she accepted readily, despite rumors that the house was haunted. Around midnight the ghost entered the lady's bedroom. She turned her face to the wall and prayed. On the following night, when it became obvious that the ghost meant her no harm, the widow spoke to it, saying: 'All good spirits praise the Lord, our Master.' The ghost replied: 'I am a good spirit and I praise the Lord, our Master.'

"The lady, thus encouraged, ventured to ask the ghost how she came to be in this empty house.

"At that the ghost related the whole story of her murder, insisting that she could not find rest until the murderer had received his just deserts."

The seventeenth century and its wars brought misery and distress to the people of the Holy Roman Empire, with roving soldiery raiding and pillaging the countryside and committing murder. Scene shows typical robbery with violence; etching by Hans Ulrich Frankh.

Georg Philipp Harsdörffer, Nuremberg patrician and poet, and collector of tales of murder. Contemporary engraving.

Title page of *Grosser Schauplatz jämmerlicher Mordgeschichte (A Gallery of Horrible Tales of Murder)*.

Table of contents of the third part of *Grosser Schauplatz jämmerlicher Mordgeschichte*.

Up to this point the story is quite credible, but what follows is pretty hard to believe.

"The lady," the story goes on, "pulled a signet ring off her finger, threw it into the split skull, and bound the two parts with her shawl. The ghost then disappeared and next day the widow reported the whole matter to the authorities. Nobody really believed her tale but, well aware of the integrity of the lady, they agreed to open the grave of the butcher's wife who had supposedly died of the plague. When they did so, to their amazement, the shawl and the ring were discovered on the corpse."

The supernatural belief in ghosts and the rational search for proof and evidence—the ring and the shawl—were combined in this story. The reader, who felt an agreeable chilling of the spine and saw law and order prevail at the end was both entertained *and* instructed.

It was the town dweller who, after the hard years and privation of the Thirty Years' War, longed for security yet at the same time looked for things that were exciting and intriguing. He wanted this without any effort on his part; indeed it was armchair adventure he desired. Yet he *was* receptive to new ideas in science and natural history.

Another of Harsdörffer's stories, *Die Erscheinung der Geister (The Appearance of the Ghosts)* is not simply concerned with the supernatural but deals also with the question of an alibi. Briefly it runs like this:

An aristocratic gentleman in France, estranged from his wife, strangles her and to hide his crime consults a sorcerer who, through magic, arranges for the dead woman to be seen around for several days after her death. The cunning husband goes on a journey and when he returns finds his wife dead. The corpse discovered in the house, however, is evil-smelling and decaying and naturally the rumor goes around that all is not well. Eventually suspicion falls on the husband, who is then arrested. He confesses and is broken on the wheel. The sorcerer manages to flee the country but he too is caught and burnt alive.

Neither deception nor magic can interfere with the uncovering of a crime and its perpetrator or can keep justice from prevailing. This is reassurance, and at the same time, warning to the reader.

When dealing with the subjects of torture and the bier test Harsdörffer was more a lawyer than a storyteller. While torture and ordeals persisted well into the eighteenth century, more and more voices, including those of the legal profession, began to express doubts about their use. They cited cases where guilt was successfully proved along with doubtful ones, and they demanded that precise evidence be furnished instead of convicting on mere conjecture.

Harsdörffer's first literary collection was followed by a second, *Grosser Schauplatz Lust- und Lehrreicher Geschichte (A Grand Gallery of Entertaining and Instructive Tales)* (1653). Again it was the murder story that

satisfied author and reader alike. The collection began with an exciting tale of robbers being chased on foot and horseback, given the innocuous title of "Das glückselige Almosen" ("The Lucky Alms"). Another story deals with a case of subtle theft, "Der subtile Kirchenräuber" ("The Crafty Church Robber"). In the center of a church a robber pretends to die of the plague. Worshippers and clergy at once flee the place in terror and a little later watch with relief as the dead man is carried out in a wooden box by his friends. In fact, it is the church silver being removed in the "coffin" under the very eyes of the congregation! The end of this "merry" tale again underlines the desire for justice to be done: the robber who has feigned death is actually dead of the plague, and his companions meet their fate on the gallows.

He also tells a traditional French story, used again fifty years later by François Gayot de Pitaval in his *Causes Célèbres*. It has nothing to do with the supernatural but concerns the disappearance of a merchant and the detection and punishment of a murderer by a blind witness.

An Italian merchant, who has spent some time in England, is about to return home. He writes to his friends, telling them to expect him in six months' time. With his servant, a Frenchman, he travels from London to Rouen, from where he is to continue to Paris. With him he has his ledgers, promissory notes, and money. In the vineyards near Argenteuil his servant attacks and robs him. A blind man passing with his dog asks the servant on horseback who it is he can hear moaning by the roadside. The murderer tells him it is a sick man and rides on. In Lucca the merchant's friends wait for him in vain, and in the end send out a messenger to try to obtain news of his whereabouts. The latter discovers that the merchant has indeed traveled from Dieppe to Rouen, but after that has vanished. A petition is made to parliament, instructing the judiciary to search the town and neighboring countryside thoroughly. The judiciary, a man called Bigot, grows suspicious of a merchant who has opened a big shop in Lucca only eight months before; he arrests him. Further investigations are carried out on the road to Paris, and it comes to light that a body has been found on the hillside near Argenteuil. At that very moment, by chance, a blind man comes to the judiciary, begging for alms. Overhearing talk of a murder, he remembers some months

earlier resting in a vineyard and hearing the sounds of someone in distress; he remembers asking a passing horseman who it was moaning. The judiciary, having first concealed the blind man, asks the prisoner to speak. The beggar immediately recognizes the voice and confirms that it belonged to the man he met near Argenteuil.

When the prisoner realizes what is happening, he complains that he is being falsely accused, and that in any case it is unfair to call a blind man as a witness. Twenty men are then brought in and, along with the prisoner, asked to speak in turn. On each occasion the blind man recognizes the voice he has heard at the scene of the murder. At that the suspect is threatened with torture and a priest called who urges the man to confess. Eventually he does so, his conscience no longer able to bear the burden of his guilt.

This murder mystery was solved actually through factual investigation by the people and the police and, although chance did play a part, elements of the supernatural did not intrude. The main feature of the tale was the confrontation of the guilty man by a witness, leading to his punishment. It was always stressed that this sort of story was "true." Presented in this fashion, such collections of tales were attractive to mind and emotions alike.

It was fitting that this particular tale should take place in France, for there, especially in Paris, police administration developed rapidly in the seventeenth century. In a period of despotism, that city had grown into the economic, cultural, and social center of the country. It was overcrowded, and social tensions were ever-increasing, to the extent that part of the city was actually in the hands of bands of criminals who terrorized the population. The dark streets and narrow crowded lanes spelt immediate danger. Much of the aristocracy was corrupt, with fascinating and bizarre deaths occurring frequently. Rumors about *poudre de succession*—succession by gun powder—were common and even the court was not exempt from attempted or successful murders by poison.

In 1667 the Haute Police was set up in the city with the Lieutenant Générale de la Reynie at its head. New measures for the improvement of civic order included police raids, street lighting, and the closing at 10 P.M. of restaurants and public houses. The most

Relation

Oder Beschreibung so Anno 1669. den 23. Martij in der Römischen Reichs-Statt Augspurg geschehen / von einer Weibs-Person / welche ob grausamer vnd erschröcklicher Hexerey vnd Verkreniungen der Menschen / wie auch wegen anderer verübten Vbelthaten durch ein ertheiltes gnädiges Vrthail von eim gantzen Ehrsamen Rath / zuvor mit glüenden Zangen gerissen / hernach aber mit dem Schwerdt gericht / der Leib zu Aschen verbrennt ist worden.

Erstlich hat Anna mit Namen Eberlehrin / gewese Kindtbeth-Kellerin von Augspurg gebürtig / gut vnd betrohlich aufgesagt vnd bekändt / daß sie vor vngefähr 13. oder vierzehen Jahren / sich mit dem bösen Geist / als er damahlen bey einer Hochzeit in Manns-Gestalt zu jhr auff den Tantz / vnd hernach in jhr Hauß kommen / dergestalt in ein heimlichen Pact vnd Verbündtnuß eingelassen / das sie nit allein demselben sich gantz vnd gar ergeben / sondern auch der Allerheyligisten Dreyfaltigkeit abgesagt / dieselbe verlaugnet / vnd dise zuevor Mündtliche gethane all zuegrausame vnd höchst Gottslästerliche Absag vnd Verlaugnung / auff begehren deß bösen Feinds / nach dem er selbige selbst zu Papier gebracht / vnd jhr die Hand geführt / auch so gar mit jhrem Blut vnderschriben vnd bekräfftiget / von welcher Zeit an sie mit dem laidigen Sathan auch manches mahlen Vnzucht getriben: Deßgleichen auf antrib desselben durch eine von jhme empfangnes weisses Pülverleins wenigist 5. Personen / vnd darunder 4. vnschuldige vnmündige Kinder elendiglich hingerichtet / vnd vmbs Leben gebracht / nit weniger habe sie jhren leibeignen Bruder durch ein dergleichen jhme im Trunck beygebrachtes Pülverlein verkrümbt / vnd dardurch sowol demselben als andern Menschen mehr / die eintweders an jhren Leibern Knipffel oder sonsten grosses Kopffwehe bekommen / zu mahlen dem Vieh durch Hexerey vnd zauberische Mittel geschadet / auch darunder zwey Pferdt gar zu schanden gemacht / Ferners habe sie auch nit allein durch grausam fluchen vnd schwören mit zuthun deß bösen Feinds etliche Wetter gemacht / darunder eines zu Guntzburg eingeschlagen / vnd grossen Schaden gethan / sondern auch vermittelst Nächtlicher Außfahrens zu vnderschidenen mahlen bey den Hexen-Täntzen vnd Ver-

samblungen sich eingefunden / vñ darbey dem bösen Geist mit Kniebiegen vnd dergleichen solche Ehr bewisen die sonsten GOtt dem Allmächtigen allein gebühre. So hat sie auch über daß noch weiters auff gesagt vñ bekändt / daß sie in Zeit diser jhrer mit dem bösen Feind gehabten gemein vnd Kundtschafft einsmahls vngebeicht das Hochwürdige heylige Sacrament deß Altars empfangen vñ genossen / auch sich vnderstanden / nit allein durch jhr vergifftes Teufflisches Pulver vñ anders / zwey Weibs-Personen vnfruchtbar zumachen / bey deme es aber ausser einer nit angangen seye / sondern auch ein Mägdtlein vnd einen jungen Knaben zu den Hexen-Täntzen mit genommen vnd verführt.

Ob welcher vnd anderer verübter vilfältiger schwerer vnd grausamer Vnthaten / vnd Verbrechen halber ein Ehrsamer Rath mit Vrtheil zu Recht erkandt / daß jhr Eberlehrin obwolen sie denen Rechten nach lebendig verbrennt zu werden verdient hette / dannoch auß Gnaden allein mit glüenden Zangen am Auffführen drey Griff gegeben / vnd sie bey der Richtstatt mit dem Schwerdt vnd blutiger Hand vom Leben zum Todt hingerichtet / auch der Cörper zu Aschen verbrandt solle werden.

A   Die Abführung ab dem Tantz / vnd in Anna Eberlehrin Behausung Einführung von dem Teuffel.
B   Die Außfahrung Nächtlicher weil mit dem bösen Feindt.
C   Die Beywohnungen der Hexen-Täntzen.
D   Die Hexischen Zusamenkunfften vnd Teufflische Malzeiten.
E   Verhörung vnd Außsag wegen jhrer verübten Hexereyen.
F   Verführung zweyer jungen vnschuldiger Kinder / als eines Knaben vnd Mägdlein.
G   Anna Eberlehrin Außführung zu dem Gericht / vnd wie sie mit glüenden Zangen gerissen wird.
H   Die Hinrichtung vnd Verbrennung zu Aschen jhres Leibs.

Zu Augspurg / bey Elias Wellhöffer Brieffmaler / bey vnser L. Frawen Thor.

Pamphlet discussing the "danger" of witches. Woodcut, 1669.

Scene of an execution from *Les Misères et les Malheurs de la Guerre (The Miseries and Horrors of the War)* by J. Callot, 1633.

A criminal is taken to the place of execution. Copperplate, 1669.

Le Marquis d'Argenson, lieutenant Général of the Paris Police in 1720.

spectacular case in the world of the aristocracy happened in 1676. Marie Madeleine d'Aubray, Marquise de Brinvilliers, was executed in the Place de Grève after being found guilty of poisoning her father and her two brothers. She had first experimented with the effectiveness of arsenic on guests and on paupers in the local hospitals. When she was threatened with arrest, she fled the country and eventually reached a monastery near Liège in Belgium. The lieutenant of police trailed her and, disguised as an amorous priest, lured her from an apparently safe refuge. Madame de Sévigné, the great letter writer, expressed at the time a fear that the scattering of the Marquise's ashes might well infect others with similar thoughts on the efficacy of poisoning. In fact, the germ did spread rapidly. In 1679 Madame Monvoisin was arrested "in the King's name" for conducting a lucrative business in the concoction of poisonous potions. Her customers included members of France's grandest families. However, it was only with the Revolution that such notorious cases became public knowledge.

Since the mid-thirteenth century, the administration of French law lay with Parliament in Paris. There the legal men of the middle classes formed the majority. After the seventeenth century trials for witchcraft ceased. This was partly due to objections by philosophers and natural scientists, but it was equally the entrepreneurial spirit of the expanding middle classes that found such trials obsolete and a waste of time and money. Cases involving poison, however, continued to be strictly dealt with though it was not until the eighteenth century that poisonings provided raw material for the writer. Before that stories and rumors of such horrific happenings flourished, but the actual case files simply gathered dust in the archives of the courts. A German legal expert, Matthias Abele von und zu Lilienberg, however, learned of the existence of this material and decided to bring it to the notice of the reading public. The first edition of his *Metamorphosis und seltsame Gerichtshändel (Metamorphosis and Unusual Law Cases)* was published in 1651 and reprinted five times by 1685. It was translated into Dutch, French, and English and a sequel appeared under the doubtful title *Vivat ... Unordnung (Long Live Disorder)* (1673)!

If legal documents, rumor, and gossip provided a basis for early crime writing, the activities of the world of fashion also contributed. In the seventeenth century the solving of riddles and the unraveling of

Marie Madeleine Marquise de Brinvilliers, notorious Parisienne poisoner of her father and two brothers, during the time of Louis XIV.

conundrums had become popular party games, and much of the writing of the period concerned itself with the play of the intellect and tests of ingenuity. Formerly, in the "merry" tales, trickery and getting the better of someone provided the attraction; now it was the solving of problems and the breaking of riddles that increased in popularity. Looking at things in detail and from new angles now became an intellectual exercise.

In the Middle Ages the riddle had been much cultivated, and in the Orient it had an even longer history. It might be worthwhile to consider, for a moment, this phenomenon. Riddles are found in the popular writing of the Ming Dynasty in China (1368-1644). A collection of tales, *Chin-Ku-Chi-Kuan*, was published between 1632 and 1644. The texts were cut in wood and then printed. Tale 36, *A Five Year Old Is Received by the Son of Heaven*, deals with the young son of a prince. He is sharp enough to escape a robber who is about to kidnap him. He puts secret marks on the man, leading to his eventual identification and the arrest of his whole robber gang. An earlier version of a tale of identification survives from the Yuan Dynasty (1280-1368). It is the first to use the motif of the "chalk circle." Judge Pao Cheng solves a complicated case simply by applying logic and human understanding. The tale begins with a poisoning, false accusations, and attempted child substitution. The judge observes closely the behavior of those implicated and invents the "trial of the chalk circle" as a means of identifying the child's real mother. It is an essential ingredient of popular literature that the high and mighty also should get their just deserts and not escape punishment. The motif of a legal dispute between the mothers goes back, of course, to the judgment of Solomon in the Old Testament and is deep-rooted in Oriental tradition.

In China, however, this particular kind of writing did not develop further and eventually died out. In seventeenth-century Europe no definite crime fiction existed either. Yet the forerunners of such writing were making an appearance in the form of murder stories, the recounting of legal cases, legends of ordeals and, as we have already seen, even in folktales.

While there was a pillory and gallows in or near many towns, only bigger ones could afford jails and prisons. The *Zuchthaus* at Bamberg, Germany; the towerlike building contains a torture chamber. Copperplate, 1627.

The growing circle of new readers included many who were interested in crime although few writers yet took up the subject seriously. There was among them, however, a German novelist, Johann Beer, who wrote a story in the style of the older *Volksbuch* (popular romance, or chapbook) in 1698. A chapbook, incidentally, is the modern name for a popular type of literature of the seventeenth and eighteenth centuries, circulated by itinerant dealers or chapmen, consisting of pamphlets of tales, ballads, tracts, or stories. These were usually sixteen pages or twenty-four pages long, and sold from a penny to sixpence in England. The subject of Beer's *Volksbuch* was the murder in 1085 of the Count Palatine, Friedrich von Gosek, who was slain while hunting. The murderer was never found, but rumor, legend, and ballad surrounding the case blamed the Landgrave Ludwig of Thuringia for the deed. It was said he was driven to it by the Count Palatine's wife. One fact is certain: Ludwig did marry the widow.

This subject of murder for love gave Beer a reading public that, even centuries later bought his tale in cheap little chapbooks at markets and fairs. The *Volksbuch* tradition is clearly visible in the woodcuts

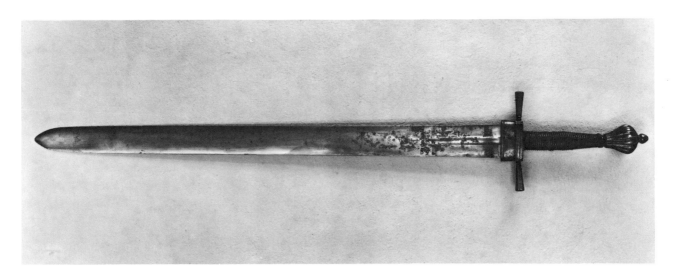

Executioner's sword from the Kulturhistorisches Museum, Dresden. In 1601 the Saxony councilor, Dr. Nicolaus Krell, was executed with this sword in the *Jüdenhof* in Dresden.

made by Beer himself, illustrating the more dramatic moments of the story.

In spite of the growth of rationalism there lingered still a strong belief in supernatural powers and magic that kept rational crime writing to a minimum. If in some of the works of Harsdörffer and Abele the supernatural was firmly excluded, an Augustine monk and preacher, Abraham à Santa Clara, returned to the theme of the bier test. He tells how in 1585, while hunting near Vienna, a nobleman notices that his dog has dug up some bleached bones that appear to be human. He takes them home and orders an armorer to make them into a handle for his hunting knife. Hardly has the armorer touched the bones than they begin to bleed. In a fit of alarm, the terrified man reveals that the bones are those of a fellow-workman whom he killed in a quarrel while they were traveling together as journeymen. He himself buried the body at the place where the bones were found.

Between 1686 and 1695 this story appeared in print under the title *Judas der Erzschelm (Judas the Archvillain)*. As a provincial prior of the Augustines and court preacher in Vienna, Santa Clara could not afford to be skeptical about miracles. His sermons, published much later, were addressed to a public that included many illiterates, all of whom believed in the miraculous. Indeed they kept hoping that a miracle would happen and drive out the besieging Turks.

Most tales of crime in the seventeenth century were directed at a public that wanted the age-old tradition of the "goodies and the baddies," stories in which crime is detected and punished, virtue rewarded, and law and order always prevails in the end. It is a tradition that continued well into the eighteenth century.

THE EIGHTEENTH CENTURY

*In the whole history of man
there is no more interesting chapter than the one dealing
with his aberrations.*

—Friedrich Schiller

During the eighteenth century the middle classes made their political and economic demands felt with ever-increasing insistence, a movement that culminated in the French Revolution and greatly influenced writing and philosophy. The literature of Rationalism and Enlightenment, even romantically sentimental prose, no longer took the courtly life as its model. Writing directed at a middle-class public praised middle-class virtues, contrasting them with the loose morals of the court and the intrigues of the fashionable world. It was a situation that could well have led to the development of crime fiction—but the time was not yet ripe. The stern and bleak conception of virtue that the highly moral weeklies upheld did not consider the revelation of crimes and intrigues at court to be desirable material for the reading public. There were few books of popular instruction or entertainment. Interest was limited to philosophical treatises and only travel books and romantic fiction were free from moralizing.

The switch to Rationalism brought with it a taste for a traditional form of entertainment: the solving of puzzles. This was reflected, for example, in Voltaire's *Zadig* (1750; first version 1747) concerning the adventures of the Prince of Serendip, a figure previously introduced into French literature by d'Herbelot de Mailly.

There was also a tendency to pay attention to apparently insignificant and unimportant matters. This can be seen in Defoe's *Journal of the Plague Year* (1722) in which he describes in great detail how the citizens of London, mainly from the poorer districts, watched skeptically, full of distrust and foreboding, the growing lists of dead, deaths often ascribed to other diseases. When a careful investigation was demanded, it was discovered that the plague had come

to the city as early as 1665. In the introduction Defoe quoted this date as circumstantial evidence of the manner in which the government had deliberately deceived the people.

The French philosopher Denis Diderot gave a sense of direction to all branches of literature by stressing the need for the arts to honor virtue and expose vice. The German writers of the sturm und drang movement were in the forefront of this trend when they dealt openly with subjects hitherto seldom discussed. Depravity, seduction, and child murder turned up again and again, less perhaps in prose than in ballads and plays, which had an immediate appeal to the reader's or listener's emotions. The material was often taken from historical cases, as for example Goethe's story of Margaret in *Faust*, who is modeled on Susanna Margareta Brand, executed for child murder in Frankfurt. Such writers set out boldly to shock their audience into rebellion against existing social conditions.

The German writer Schiller's early play, *The Robbers*, was subtitled *In Tyrannos* and took as its source an eighteenth-century legal case. Schiller knew about the existence of gangs of robbers as recorded in the so-called *Akte Butlar* between 1734 and 1736. It was essential to the concept of his play that these records gave proof of an aristocratic family's connection with a hired band of robbers. Legacy hunting, slander, violence, and murder were all exposed in the action of the play. These crimes, including the attempted murder of a father and brother, are perpetrated by a wicked aristocrat, Count Franz von Moor, while the "noble" head of the robber gang tries to see justice done by taking the law into his own hands.

This moving and exciting style of writing leaves no room for uncertainties. The position of the characters is stated in detail at the outset: the seducer-slanderer is an aristocrat, possibly even a courtier; while the seduced-betrayed is a poor girl.

An early type of crime fiction now made its appearance, namely, Pitaval's *Causes Célèbres*, which became an immediate best seller.

The Pitaval Story

*I have taken care to arrange the material in such a way
that the reader cannot spot at once how a case will end
and what verdict will be pronounced.*

—François Richer

The criminal elements forming an important part of the literature of the sturm und drang in Germany whetted the appetite of the reading public, but it was the legal profession, in search of new values, that discovered and popularized the "case history."

François Gayot de Pitaval, an advocate at the parliamentary court of Paris, was a compiler of criminal records, continuing the work done by Harsdörffer in Germany in the seventeenth century. The first volume of his collection of cases—*Causes Célèbres et Intéressantes (Famous and Interesting Cases)*—appeared in 1734.

Ever since the fourteenth century reports of legal proceedings had been turning up spasmodically in European chronicles. It was Pitaval who pieced together the more memorable cases extracted from historical files. His collection proved of interest both to the legal expert and to the casual reader. Most of his cases had attracted attention in their time—either because of the gravity and violence of the crime, or the difficulty of tracing the culprit and proving guilt. Pitaval's material went back to the sixteenth century and included many strange and remarkable proceedings such as those concerning a certain Martin Guerre. In a corner of the southwest of France, Guerre, an immature and disgruntled young farmer, leaves his family and disappears to serve as a soldier in foreign parts. Ten years later a man arrives in the village, announcing himself as Guerre. Though somewhat changed, he is accepted as Guerre by everybody, including his wife. Eventually rumors surface that the returnee is an imposter and an inquiry is begun. At the critical moment the real Guerre appears and proves his identity. The false Guerre is hanged.

Most of Pitaval's material reflected the manners of the time of Louis XIII, XIV, and XV, with the proceedings against Marie Madeleine d'Aubray, the Marquise de Brinvilliers, of such special importance that it became known to history as the "Poison Affair."

Naturally these were cases that did not add glory to the reputation of the Paris police, although they certainly supplied food for thought to both the legal profession and the general public. Accused people were often condemned, perhaps even to death, on the flimsiest of grounds. One case of circumstantial evidence almost condemned a postilion to death, while others involved the use of torture, the leaving of innocent people crippled, or the thirst for revenge resulting in mass hysteria as in the case of the unfortunate Father Urban Grandier. Judicial murder ended the life of one poor woman who was convicted of having killed her baby merely on the evidence of hasty and ill-conceived investigations.

Literary critics, at times slow to accept the new, but well aware that they were witnessing the emergence of a new literary genre, persistently attacked Pitaval and his case histories. They did not take exception to the subject matter but to his presentation. In spite of all the criticism, however, the twenty volumes of Pitaval's collection were avidly read. The interest inherent in the material overcame its awkward style of presentation. François Richer, also an advocate in the parliamentary court, said of the work: "Few books have been as eagerly received and at the same time sharply criticized as the legal cases collected by Monsieur Gayot de Pitaval. Everyone able to read wanted to have them." When he edited Pita-

Pamphlet showing the interrogation, conviction, and execution of a child murderess. The presentation is easily comprehensible even to the illiterate.

val's work, Richer tried to improve the style by making it more lucid. He wanted to increase the reader's emotional involvement and intensify the feeling of tension. "I have," he said, "taken care to arrange the material in such a way that the reader cannot spot at once how a case will end and what verdict will be pronounced. He will remain in a state of uncertainty during the development of the action and in that way, I believe, each case will become more gripping, with the attention of the reader captivated to the end. Since the outcome is uncertain and the result in balance, the reader will remain curious up to the final page." With these words Richer clearly announced the purpose of the crime story and set its basic structure and technique.

Between 1772 and 1778 the revised edition of Pitaval's *Causes Célèbres* was published in twenty-two volumes in Amsterdam. Part of the work's immediate success, even in the early form containing as it did too much legal matter, can be attributed to the pro-

cess of French law. It presented lawsuits that had been dealt with by the parliamentary court in Paris, in which justice was meted out equally to the highborn and to the common man, and seemed to have been applied fairly.

In reality, however, things were somewhat different. The dreaded *lettres de cachet*, issued by the French king, were still in use. These warrants made it possible for anyone to be arrested and imprisoned in the Bastille without investigation and without knowledge of family or friends. Louis Sébastien Mercier, social historian and member of the Académie Française, devoted several chapters of his *Tableau de Paris (The Paris Scene)* to the subject of French justice. He described the gloomy dungeons of the Bastille and other prisons, the executions in the Place de Grève, and said that the book relating all the cases of innocents condemned still remained to be written.

In this climate *Trente-Cinq Ans de Captivité (Thirty-Five Years in Prison)* by Jean Henry Masers de Latude was bound to find many readers and to exert considerable influence on the public's attitude toward justice. As a young artillery officer, Latude, illegitimate son of one of France's most noble fami-

Arrest by France's infamous *lettre de cachet*.

Removing the dead from prison. Contemporary engraving.

A French doctor, Joseph Ignace Guillotin, presents a model of his machine for execution to members of the National

Convention. The horrendous machine was named after him. After a painting by J. C. Hertrich.

33

Queen Marie Antoinette was closely connected with the scandalous Queen's Necklace Affair.

The case of the Chevalier de Sirven, also taken up by Voltaire, shows him once more fighting against suspect witnesses, arbitrary justice, and intolerance, matters that deeply concerned him. Clearing up an individual case was to him secondary to the wider human issue. The clamor of the public for true justice was to find its climax in the storming of the hated Bastille, the signal for the start of the French Revolution. All philosophers agreed that torture was against the dignity of man and should be abolished once and for all. The treatment of prisoners, too, should be more humane, and witch trials abolished.

In Prussia after the accession to the throne of Frederick II in 1740, torture was done away with and other countries followed; France did so in 1789. However, the *Constitutio Criminalis Theresiana*, established in 1769 by the Empress Maria Theresa, retained torture and even provided as a sort of appendix to the act a display of pictures of the instruments and methods used. Subtle torture tactics continued in most forms of corporal punishment, including starvation and solitary confinement in dark rooms.

Given these circumstances, the reading of legal cases and the detection of crime became almost the duty of the citizen, as well as a fascinating pastime.

Strangely enough, one of the most spectacular cases of the eighteenth century, the so-called Queen's Necklace Affair, had not yet been dramatized by writers. The whole case, involving "Madame la Comtesse" Valois de la Motte, an adventuress, was a rogue's comedy, material suitable to be played out by a *picaro*. The La Mottes, husband and wife, were a pair of rascals, possibly blue-blooded, who succeeded in persuading the Prince Cardinal de Rohan, a wealthy, vain, and profligate man, to purchase a precious diamond necklace that had originally been intended for Madame Dubarry, the favorite of Louis XV, but remained unsold after the king's death. With the gift of this necklace, the La Mottes maintained, Rohan would win the favor of Marie Antoinette. His Eminence, quite unsuspecting, enjoyed his moment of happiness in the shrubberies of Versailles, not with the Queen but with a little Parisian dressmaker. When the story eventually came out in 1786, the name of Marie Antoinette was never mentioned, although everyone knew that the charges, made against La Motte and the Cardinal, were really being made against her. With her reputation, a fraud of this kind seemed quite credible. The Ancien Régime

lies, had sought to secure Madame de Pompadour's favor by revealing to her a plot to poison her. The plot was discovered to be of his own contriving and he was sent to the Bastille in 1749 where he remained for some thirty years.

Voltaire, known for his zeal in fighting fanaticism, took up the case of Jean Calas, a French protestant and well-respected tradesman in Toulouse, who became the victim of a judicial murder. One evening in 1761 Calas's eldest son, Marc Antoine, a youth addicted to gambling and fits of deep melancholy, was found hanged in his father's warehouse. There was not a shadow of doubt that the young man had committed suicide, but his father, because of his religious beliefs, was accused of murder. Arbitrary action by the state, fired by religious fanaticism, confirmed the verdict and the wretched man was executed in 1762. Voltaire succeeded in taking up his case, which by then had gained importance beyond the personal to become one of basic human rights. He succeeded in the eventual rehabilitation of the dead man's family.

Title page of *Constitutio Criminalis Theresiana*, of the Empress Maria Theresa.

Illustration from the *Theresiana*, showing the use of thumbscrews in torture.

Stringing up the delinquent.

Birching. Contemporary illustration.

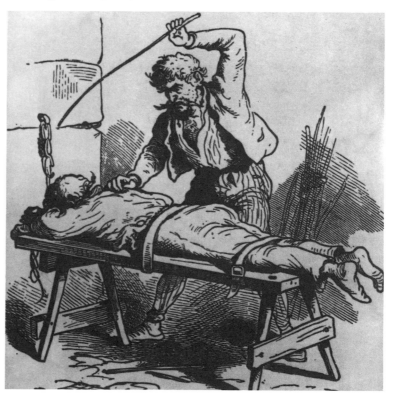

Pamphlet showing the execution of two guilty women outside the gates of Leipzig.

August Gottlieb Meissner, author of crime-story collections.

stood truly exposed. Caricaturists and pamphleteers seized delightedly on this spicy scandal and pamphlets defending the accused appeared in print before the trial even begun. Bookshops were besieged and the indignant as well as the merely curious flocked to Paris from the provinces. Huge crowds gathered in front of the Palais de Justice and the Cardinal found himself in the Bastille where some of the others involved in the affair had already been lodged. During the trial it became clear that the whole transaction was a trick: the messages from the Queen had been forged. In May the proceedings came to a close when, to the delight of the crowds, the Cardinal and the midinette were acquitted. La Motte was branded on each shoulder with the V—for *voleuse* (thief)—and condemned to life imprisonment. Her husband, who had fled to England, was sentenced in his absence to the galleys for life.

The Queen's Necklace Affair was more than just a criminal case: it was a political matter, the lightning before the storm. At the time, however, it proved too serious and too topical a subject for light fiction. Only in the second half of the nineteenth century did Alexandre Dumas père use it as the theme of one of his novels, and when Goethe wished to dramatize political events of the recent past he incorporated the subject in a comedy, *Der Grosskophta (The Grand Master)*. It also appeared rather belatedly in the *New Pitaval* in 1858.

Pitaval's collection of criminal case histories grew more and more popular and in due course was translated into a number of languages. The German edition of 1792 carried an introduction by the writer and poet Friedrich Schiller that makes interesting reading today. "We find," he says, "in this collection a number of legal cases each sufficiently interesting to form the subject of a novel and at the same time each has the advantage of being factual. People are seen here in difficult situations, each capable of holding any reader's attention. The anticipation right up to the eventual unraveling of the plot provides an intellectually satisfying pursuit. Hidden motives take

Execution on the *Rabenstein* (gallows). Copperplate by D. Chodowiecki.

Sitting of the Berlin Civic Courts. Copperplate by D. Chodowiecki.

Capture of the Bavarian, Matthias Klostermeyer, in 1771.
From a contemporary copperplate.

Pamphlet showing the public burning of a thief and
arsonist in Berlin in 1786.

on a new aspect when freedom, life, and property are at risk, and in that way a judge gains a deeper insight into men's hearts and minds." Schiller also suggested that there might well be a sequel to the series. He stressed that the most important feature of *Causes Célèbres* was that they were true stories. Readers, it appeared, preferred fact to fiction. The collection commanded respect from even the most unimaginative reader, its fascination has lasted to the present day.

By the end of the eighteenth century Pitaval's work had established itself as a definite category of crime writing. Schiller's interest in it led him to work in this medium himself, and in 1792 he republished a crime novella, *Der Verbrecher aus verlorener Ehre (Lost Honor Makes a Criminal)*, previously published anonymously. The story is based on a case history from his home country, Swabia, and tells the story of an innkeeper, Friedrich Schwan (1729-60). Schiller had heard the tale from his Stuttgart teacher Jakob Friedrich Abel who in 1787 published a lengthy biography of the unfortunate man; another German writer, Hermann Kurz used the subject for a novel in 1854.

Although he did not alter the established facts, Schiller avoided writing a Pitaval-like case history. Instead he created a new style, the crime novella. What concerned him was not the legal procedure, nor in fact any purely legal problem. He looked at the question from a moral and ethical point of view, asking the simple question, "Who is guilty?" His overwhelming concern was with the motives for the deed and not the discovery and punishment of the evildoer.

Contempt for human beings, indifference, and a soulless legal machinery had excluded Schwan from society—a society on which he determined to avenge himself. Schiller dwells on the period preceding the crime, while the crime itself, its discovery, and punishment, he treats only briefly. The reader is seen as the overall judge. Schiller limits his concern to the motivation behind the culprit's descent from mere poaching to murder itself and approaches the question of crime and punishment through the study of the man's life prior to his commission of the deed.

While he was editing Pitaval, Schiller conceived the idea of a play to be called *Die Polizey (The Police)*. Actually the concept of the play was more suited to crime fiction than to the theater. The hero was to be a lieutenant of the Chambre Ardente, the French supreme court, which dealt with serious crime, and where the punishment was, appropriately enough, burning at the stake. Many prominent families were involved in the crimes that the hero sought to clear up; the whole of Paris in fact was to be investigated. The project was never finished but in its draft form it anticipated the structure and plot of Eugène Sue's *Les Mystères de Paris*.

The German reader who wanted to be entertained and to be acquainted with important questions of the time found what he wanted in *Skizzen (Sketches)* by August Gottlieb Meissner, published in fourteen parts between 1778 and 1796. An academic, and later ecclesiastical councillor, Meissner based his crime-story solutions on rational thought. He attacked the jurisdiction of the courts and the practice of torture, maintaining that the establishment would rather see ten innocents tortured than one evildoer escape. Thumbscrews and other instruments of torture, he said, too often did their diabolic work on bodies of the accused who had over and over maintained their genuine innocence. His intention was to shock his readers into an awareness of the social ills of the time, to expose in particular the way "justice" was done, and the fact that torture was still used to extract confessions. In one story he related how an innocent girl was accused of child murder and left a cripple for life as a result of relentless torture. The real murderess was discovered by chance through gossip at an inn and the alertness and intelligence of the innkeeper and his wife. A servant girl had in fact killed her illegitimate child. The question then arose: had *she* committed the deed out of shame, the fear of losing her job, or was perhaps her employer implicated in the crime? A short story could not really answer all these questions.

To serve the steadily growing public interest, it seemed advisable for writers of the period to stick to a limited number of characters and problems in a novel or a play.

Schiller's early plays followed that advice in a manner comprehensible to all. He expressed what the common man in Germany had to endure and the feelings he was as yet too inarticulate to put into words.

The Robber Tale

In the dark reaches of the forest ...

—Christian August Vulpius

The ever-increasing reading public provided a receptive audience for the novel, thereby creating a veritable boom in fiction, a type of literature little regarded up to that time. In Germany the enthusiasm for Schiller's early play about the noble robber chief, Karl Moor, heralded a flood of light reading matter about robbers, not all of it published as books but some printed in small chapbooks, or pamphlets, in serial form. Even the well-known Romantic poet, Ludwig Tieck, was caught up in this wave and contributed a hair-raising tale about poachers and highwaymen. The plot of these effusions was always similar: robbers ambushed a stagecoach, killed the men, and made off with the women and the money.

The best seller of the period was *Rinaldo Rinaldini*, the story of a robber chief, told in nine volumes, the first published in 1799. It was written by the Weimar librarian Christian August Vulpius, Goethe's brother-in-law.

While on a journey, Vulpius came across an Italian chapbook relating Rinaldo's deeds. The *Journal de l'Europe* had also reported on Rinaldo who was indeed a real person living in Italy as head of a robber band. Rinaldo and his followers were not just brigands; half of their operations were amorous adventures. Time and again Rinaldo would encounter damsels in distress whose virtue he protected; or perhaps they would be noble ladies who wanted to be loved. His deeds were all virtuous and he was presented as a thorough gentleman. These same harassed, charming ladies were to turn up in updated form in the novels of Edgar Wallace and others in the early twentieth century. Rinaldo remains the noble hero throughout the exciting plot of *Rinaldo Rinaldini*, midst the goings-on of secret societies and political intrigues that hold the reader enthralled. At the final denouement this gentleman robber is revealed—surprise!—to be of noble birth himself. In a very short time the book was reprinted in five authorized editions and was translated into a number of European languages.

The success of the robber tale depended largely on the tradition of "taking from the rich to give to the poor," the tradition inspired by Robin Hood. In popular literature such a man was never considered to be a criminal. Whatever befell him, he had the sympathy and admiration of the reader. The plot with the daring hero, his comrades, the heroine in need of protection, the villain and a father figure in the background—all these elements were developed in such tales eventually to find a lasting place in crime fiction. Its favorite locations—castles, ruins, underground vaults, and secret passages—provide the setting not only for "robber tales" but for the Gothic novel that was to establish itself in the eighteenth century.

The robber in folklore differs considerably from the robber in the "robber tale." In tales, ballads, and songs he does not help the poor but appears as a pitiless, violent criminal who drags young maidens into his lair and attacks defenseless people in the forest to rob and murder them. Legends about "murder inns" are full of tension, recounting deeds of robbery committed with violence. In the lonely countryside, in deep impenetrable forests, travelers disappear without trace. There is only one "inn" to provide shelter. There the innkeeper robs the travelers, murders them, and makes their bodies disappear by means of cunning mechanical contraptions. It is a combination of chance and a certain traveler's acute observation that brings to light the innkeeper's crimes in the end. In the case of the *Robber Bridegroom*, a folktale, the innkeeper-murderer is convicted through the courage of the kidnapped maiden who presents the severed finger of a murdered girl as evidence of the crime. In other versions of the tale, the culprit is caught through the alertness and vigilance of the girl's grandmother.

All folktales and legends have one thing in common: the unmasking of the evildoer and his capture. The hero is the man who successfully renders him harmless. Physically such heroes are generally weaker than the criminal—like the young girl, the old woman, or the traveler in the "murder inn" story—

"Rinaldo Rinaldini" in the arms of the beautiful "Rose."
A late illustration of 1870/80.

but morally and spiritually they are superior. This is
a comforting thought to the "underdogs" (and readers) who feel themselves to be in the right.

At all times some writers are bent on honoring
virtue and exposing vice wherever they find it. Denis
Diderot, already mentioned, editor of the famous *En-
cyclopédie*, wrote a powerful story, *La Religieuse (The
Nun)*, in which he exposed the evils of convent life.
His *Le Neveau de Rameau (Rameau's Nephew)*, too, laid

bare the follies and corruptions of society. Yet the
constant praise of virtue can be boring in the long
run, and literature preoccupied with vice is always
more profitable and certainly more entertaining—
provided of course virtue reassuringly triumphs in
the end. The tales of robbers and brigands fall into
this pattern, often with chapters drenched in noble-
mindedness.

The deepest and most interesting insights into
dens of vice and crime were, however, to be found in
the Gothic novel. Gothic, a word originally signifying
a barbarian, had found a new meaning.

The Gothic Novel

*The aspect of the vault, the pale glimmering of the lamp,
the surrounding obscurity, the sight of the tomb.*

—Matthew G. Lewis

In 1764 Horace Walpole, the parliamentarian, surprised the English reader with *The Castle of Otranto*. Disguising it as a translation from the Italian and disregarding all literary rules and all criticism, Walpole intentionally wrote his novel in contrast to the formal Classicism of the time. Although the action is placed in the twelfth century, he did not set out to write a historical novel. His characters, the castle with its dungeons and subterranean passages, the churches of the graveyards—all these set the scene for the unexpected to happen and for ghosts to appear.

The Castle of Otranto was different from later Gothic novels in that it was a slim volume, although filled with dramatic incident. What it did not have, and later Gothics did, were detailed descriptions of characters, scenery, castles, and villages. Despite its

Horace Walpole.

promise, it turned out to be less gruesome than many of its successors. Perhaps the drama was almost overdone. In an essay on Walpole, Sir Walter Scott remarked that a certain mystic darkness over everything seemed to conjure up visions of the supernatural. Matthew Lewis used this same twilight atmosphere in his 1796 novel *The Monk*, the story of Ambrosio, a zealous Capuchin seduced by Matilda, a lustful woman disguised as a novice monk. Sexual desire for her overcomes him, and, guilt-ridden, he turns to crime, killing his mother, ravishing his sister, and bringing disgrace upon all close to him. In the end he is not convicted and punished by an earthly power; it is the Devil himself who abandons, outwits, and destroys him.

Lewis's figure of the Devil appears more convincing than the incidents of *The Castle of Otranto*. His concept of this fiend is closely related to that of legend and folklore. Lewis's Devil corrects social injustice and provokes the secretly wicked in such a way that they commit crimes they have only dreamed of. Matilda, the seductive beauty clad in a monk's habit, is a true creation of hell.

A subplot tells the story of the wicked abbess of Santa Clara who is charged with murder, leading to the discovery of her victims in mausoleums, vaults, and musty dungeons. It may seem strange that Lewis, like Walpole, chose Spain for the setting of his novel. One would have thought that England, with her crumbling abbeys and castles, would have provided an excellent background for mysterious and horrific adventures. By placing the story in Spain, however, Lewis provided the protestant reader with an added attraction. The horrifying events and blood-curdling crimes of the monk and the abbess were all laid at the door of the Church of Rome, with the evil power of the Spanish Inquisition still lurking in the background. With the excitement of the publication of *The Monk* went the conviction that here was edifying reading, which was not boring, but which, in fact, was very thrilling.

Illustration for a French edition of Ann Radcliffe's Gothic
novel *The Italian* (1797).

Public hanging at Tyburn, London.

Ann Radcliffe's novel, *The Italian*, published in 1797, was in the same vein. Here too are monks, priests, inquisitors, dark vaults, secret tribunals, and a rugged dark countryside. There are frightening apparitions and a heroine rescued from terror. As in Lewis's book, everything is explained rationally at the end as part of a plot set up by criminals. The denouement is typical of the light fiction of the period, a solution similar to the same author's *The Mysteries of Udolpho* (1794). Mysterious happenings at a castle in the wildest part of the Appenines, a murdered aunt, corpses (including fake ones made of wax), are revealed to be the perpetration of a gang of criminals. The heroine, sobbing and frequently fainting, eventually manages to escape and fall into the arms of her lover, whom she happily marries. The apparition at the Castle Mazzini turns out to be not a ghost but a real woman, the aristocratic owner's wife, said to be dead but in fact imprisoned in a vault under the deserted south tower. The law is not involved. The wicked couple—the marquis and his mistress—meet with violent deaths, leaving the noble family stunned by their horrible deeds and the tricks played by fate.

If the eighteenth-century language of the Gothic novel seems old-fashioned and complicated at times, in its plot and colorful background the Gothic is still the forerunner of much future crime writing. Ann Radcliffe, for example, is masterful in creating an atmosphere of terror when she describes how a young couple tries to escape through narrow, low passages where they cannot walk upright. They come to a heavy, iron-clad door, which the hero manages to force open. And there they see a huge, dark vault, full of corpses, miserable victims of bandits. Incidentally, the term "mystery story," which is still in use today, dates back to the Gothic tradition.

GIN LANE.

Gin curfed Fiend, with Fury fraught,
Makes human Race a Prey.
It enters by a deadly Draught.
And fteals our Life away.

Virtue and Truth, driv'n to Despair.
It's Rage compells to fly.
But cherishes, with hellish Care.
Theft, Murder, Perjury.

Damn'd Cup! that on the Vitals preys.
That liquid Fire contains.
Which Madness to the Heart conveys.
And rolls it thro' the Veins.

William Hogarth's engravings show the same
critical view of contemporary English justice as,
for example, Godwin's novel *Caleb Williams*.
This is Gin Lane, a hotbed of vice.

The English Gothic gained international popularity, yet similar works in other countries remained largely confined to local interest. Only the novels of the German writer Christian Heinrich Spiess appear to have exerted influence on English crime fiction. Behind them lay a sociological rebellion against *Kabinettsjustiz*, the high-handed judicial system by which a prince could intervene without consultation in any legal proceeding. In the mid-nineteenth century, J. W. Appell, a German literary historian, could rightly say that there was revolt against the corrupt state of the courts in Germany and extortion by the princes. If in novels superiors who squeezed the last penny out of the sorely tried peasant were dismissed and banished from the country, high-living aristocratic rogues unmasked, and maltreated innocents reinstated in triumph, the real meaning for the contemporary reader was quite obvious. Many a poor devil took great comfort in these highly colored pictures of wickedness in high places and its well-deserved and crushing defeat in the end.

The Pitaval case histories developed in France, but the *Newgate Calendars* were an English phenomenon. Newgate Prison stood at the West Gate of the old city of London. The earliest prison there (1218) was built into a niche of the "new gate," hence the name. The *Calendars* contained accounts of legal cases, not taken from files, but written down on the spot from the evidence taken from the criminals.

In earlier days Tyburn had been the place of execution, but nasty scenes attending the procession of criminals from Newgate Prison to the gallows saw the need for a change and in 1783 they were erected in front of Newgate. Forerunners of the *Newgate Calendars*, or as they were subtitled, *The Malefactors' Bloody Register*, were the *Tyburn Calendars*. Spectators at executions tended to be absorbed in the criminals' "last words," with the result that clergymen who attended the convicts reported verbatim their confessions, which then appeared in print. The best-known practitioner of this squalid art was the Reverend Paul Lorraine, one of whose tales began with the words: "The crimes related here are great and true."

The literary manner of presenting these sensational events bore great similarity to that of the detective story. Some incidents were ideal; Dick Turpin was captured when one of his former teachers recognized his handwriting—that is, strictly through detection and deduction.

Executions took place at Newgate eight times a year. Spectators congregated in great numbers. It was a meeting place for the common people as well as elegant ladies and gentlemen. As a stern warning, even children were brought along to witness the cruel spectacle. In good weather many people spent the night in the open, when pickpockets availed themselves of the many opportunities offered by the unwary. To secure a good view, those with money bought window seats to be able to watch in comfort; inns and public houses did a roaring trade.

During the eighteenth century the *Newgate Calendars* were the most extensive reports on crime published anywhere. There were five volumes, forerunners of the Newgate novel. Scenes in which the criminal got the better of his captors, and perhaps even escaped, were read with special delight, the criminal becoming as popular as the cunning *picaro* of the seventeenth century.

The heroes of the *Calendars* lived on into the nineteenth century, still heroes of the London street urchins. Besides Dick Turpin, the highwayman, horse-thief, and murderer, there was Jack Sheppard, also a thief and a highwayman who gained notoriety when Daniel Defoe visited him in prison and later wrote tracts about him. Sheppard was born into a family of carpenters, a trade he followed successfully at first. Then he fell into bad company and was committed to prison for robbery. He escaped several times, but his luck deserted him in the end and he was hanged at Tyburn in 1724, in the presence, it is said, of two hundred thousand spectators. Claude Duval, born in Normandy, became known for his daring deeds on England's highways and through a satiric ode Samuel Butler wrote about him.

Jonathan Wild, another infamous criminal, became the subject of Henry Fielding's powerful and ferociously satiric novel, *The Life of Jonathan Wild the Great*. It can be said that Wild was the first man to organize London's underworld. After imprisonment for debt and for consorting with criminals, he became a receiver of stolen goods—a fence, in modern terms—and then a betrayer of thieves who refused to share with him—a stool pigeon, as it were. The purpose of Fielding's work was to expose the difference between "greatness" as distinct from "goodness." In the novel he relates the life and career of a rogue from his birth to his final arrival at the "tree of glory"—the gallows.

THE REWARD OF CRUELTY.

Behold the Villain's dire disgrace!
Not Death itself can end.
He finds no peaceful Burial-Place;
His breathless Corse, no friend.

Torn from the Root, that wicked Tongue,
Which daily swore and curst!
Those Eyeballs, from their Sockets wrung,
That glow'd with lawless Lust!

His Heart, expos'd to prying Eyes,
To Pity has no Claim:
But, dreadful! from his Bones shall rise,
His Monument of Shame.

Designed by W. Hogarth.

Published according to Act of Parliament Feb. 1, 51.

The wages of cruelty. Dissection of an executed criminal.
Copperplate from the Hogarth series *The Progress of Cruelty*
(1751).

The English courts.

Debtor's prison.

The lazy apprentice, betrayed by a lady of easy virtue, is arrested with his woman accomplice in a low den. From the Hogarth series *Industry and Idleness* (1747).

The lazy apprentice is later executed at Tyburn.

John Gay's *The Beggar's Opera* (1728), the outcome of a suggestion made by Swift to write a "Newgate Pastoral" was an excellent social satire. The ballad opera was an immediate success and the play ran sixty-two nights to full houses. The principal character, Peachum, is a receiver of stolen property, who at the same time makes a living by informing against his clients. There is also an engaging highwayman, Captain Macheath, a breaker of women's hearts. Eventually the twentieth-century German writer, Bertolt Brecht, based his *Die Dreigroschenoper (The Threepenny Opera)* on it.

William Hogarth, the celebrated English painter and engraver, made social satire the subject of his pictorial work, showing an extraordinary faculty for depicting the vices and follies of his time. One of his best-known works is the twelve-plate series of engravings entitled *Industry and Idleness* (1747). As in all his work, the moral is pointed, even in names such as Beer Street and Gin Lane; the keen young apprentice becomes Lord Mayor of London, while his lazy and wicked companion ends up on the Tyburn gallows.

Most efforts in art and writing to moralize as well as to entertain were received with enthusiasm in the eighteenth century. Far from the excitement elicited by the *Newgate Calendars*, William Godwin published *Things as They Are: The Adventures of Caleb Williams* in 1794. His intention was to give a general overview of the kinds of despotism in existence at the time, "the tyranny and perfidiousness exercised by the powerful members of the community against those who are less privileged than themselves." Unlike most propagandist literature designed for a purpose, *Caleb Williams*, with its pursuit, crime, and detection, is an eminently readable book. The contrast between the poor dependent Caleb and the rich aristocrats precipitates lively action. Caleb, the self-educated son of humble parents, is appointed secretary to Squire Falkland. He becomes convinced that his employer is guilty of the murder of Tyrrel, another country gentleman. The remainder of the book is taken up with the unrelenting persecution of Caleb Williams by Falkland, in spite of the former's devoted service. In the end Caleb is imprisoned on a false charge of theft. He escapes from prison only to be tracked down by Falkland's agents. In desperation he lays a charge of murder against Falkland and although he has no concrete proof the force of his confrontation finally extracts a confession.

One of the important aspects of Godwin's work was the way in which he presented legal proceedings. By tradition these took place in public, with only the judge trained in legalities, and the jury made up of laymen from all walks of life. All arguments for and against the accused had to be formulated by the judge in such a way that the jury and the public could understand them. Visitors to the proceedings wanted to see who would furnish the most convincing proof, call upon the most reliable witnesses, press the accused the hardest—or perhaps even vindicate him. These points aroused the audience's curiosity while at the same time, by attending court, members of the public felt they were exercising their citizenship. In the case of an unexplained death, there was, and indeed still is, the need for an inquest, held before the commencement of legal proceedings. This inquest was also held in public. Everyone had the right, in fact the duty, to divulge any detail that might help discover the true cause of death. Although in many ways Godwin criticized legal procedure, he nevertheless pointed out the special character of trial by jury, with the advantages outweighing the drawbacks. One thing is certain: public admission to the courts instilled in the masses a keen interest in crime and detection. Godwin's friend, Thomas Holcroft, took up the subject of crime and punishment a few years later when he wrote in 1805 *Memoirs of Bryan Perdue*. There he pleaded passionately for criminals to be given another chance to return to society, saying: "Deal not in human blood." This demand grew louder prior to the Legal Reform in 1820.

At the turn of the nineteenth century the Pitaval case history and the crime novella continued to hold the interest of the readers, with further development in both genres. At the same time the Gothic novel remained popular alongside its close relation, the crime novel. The entire literature of crime was now about to expand on a very broad basis.

THE NINETEENTH CENTURY

Après avoir lu Poe.
Quelque chose que la critique n'a pas vu, un monde littéraire nouveau,
les signes de la littérature du XXième siècle. Le Miraculeux scientifique …
La base du roman délacée et transportée du cœur à la tête …

—Journal des Goncourts 16.7.1856

As the literature of the nineteenth century progressed from Romanticism to Realism, the two often overlapped. Romanticism thrived on the mysterious, on enigmatic twilight, and on a sense of wonder—but was not necessarily devoid of reality. Man was seen as close to nature and every aspect of humanity, even crime, provided material for the writer. The best-known outcome of this movement was the "fate-tragedy drama," in which fate, not chance, eventually decided the course of events. In his 1815 play *Der vierundzwanzigste Februar (The 24th of February)* the German writer Zacharias Werner reexplored the ancient folklore theme of "a parent unwittingly killing his child." An innkeeper robs a guest and knives him to death. He then realizes too late that he has killed his own son. The knife has played a fateful part in the history of his family. The date, the 24th of February, has always been critical for them, and the murder weapon has been the same over the generations. Fate, Werner seems to be saying, plays an important part in tragedies that mere coincidence cannot explain.

These "fate-tragedy dramas" had a short-lived success on the stage at the time, since the overloading of a plot with improbable, even outrageous, events carried with it the danger of ridicule. A good exam-

Title pages of three eighteenth-century German collections of crime stories. The illustrations are coarse, with the crime, not its solution, the focus of attention.

ple is *Die Ahnfrau (The Ancestress)* by the Austrian playwright Franz Grillparzer, which mixed "fate-tragedy drama" with a story of robbers and ghosts, and thus collapsed into absurdity.

In 1808 Heinrich von Kleist's *Der zerbrochene Krug (The Broken Jug)* was produced in Weimar and failed. A critic at the time said of it: "From the shy silence of the young heroine, the embarrassment and the nature of the injuries of the aging judiciary, it is clear that only he...could have been with her the previous night. But, heaven help us, it takes three acts and a lengthy introduction to tell a truth which is staring us in the face." The failure of the play may well have induced Kleist to shorten it and tighten up the story before it was published in book form. The final revelation of the truth is close to the Oedipus theme even though the end is not so tragic.

Kleist's 1811 tale *Der Findling (The Foundling)* is much closer to real crime fiction. Human kindness inspires Piachi, a Roman estate agent, to smuggle a boy into a city devastated by the plague, thus contra-vening the quarantine regulations. When Piachi's own son dies of the disease, he adopts the stranger in his place. This boy robs his benefactor, betrays him, and kills Piachi's wife. There is no need for investigation in this tragic tale: the reader knows everything from the beginning. Piachi kills the thankless boy, then refuses all mercy and absolution in order to meet his enemy again in hell.

The matter-of-fact way in which Kleist told this tale gained him an appointment as crime reporter on the *Berliner Abendblatt* (c. 1810). So well did he prepare his articles on murder and arson that a guard had to be placed outside the paper's offices to prevent people from storming the place. Everybody wanted Kleist's vivid and exciting reports fresh from the courts. But Kleist soon grew tired of reporting the crimes of the city's gutters and resolved to waste no further time on it. He even made fun of the police reports by including such comments as "Last Thursday, due to the negligence of two servant girls, the peas were burnt."

The Romantic Crime Novella

"Get rid of it," Hubert murmured, looking sideways and pointing his gun.
"Yes, get rid of it," Daniel sneered. "But not like that, no, not like that."

—Ernst Theodor Wilhelm Hoffmann

In the romantic novella there is a tendency to present crime in a rather heightened manner, sometimes bordering on the demoniac. This could be called "pure" crime fiction, since crime is the central theme and the exploration of human behavior takes a back seat. The main force here is fate, the effects of which are observed in the plot. The more mysterious the workings of fate, the more exciting the denouement.

The German writer, composer, and gifted eccentric, Ernst Theodor Wilhelm Hoffmann, who later changed the Wilhelm in his name to Amadeus in honor of Mozart and became E. T. A. Hoffmann, had qualified in a school of law, so that his brilliant tales, involving crime, were written with a background of professional knowledge. It is interesting to recall that Jacques Offenbach's opera, *Les Contes d'Hoffmann (Tales of Hoffmann)*, was based on this German writ-er's tales and, in fact, introduced him on the stage as a character in his favorite Berlin restaurant, Lutter's Weinstuben.

One of Hoffmann's stories, *Ignaz Denner* (1814), deals with a robber gang, an eighteenth-century theme that was still making its appearance a hundred years after its heyday. The difference is that the exciting events no longer take place in foreign countries but in the homely atmosphere of German woodlands, those same woodlands so lovingly painted by the German Romantic artists. Ignaz Denner's character is dark and gloomy, matching his surroundings: the wind howls in the pines, dogs bay, skies are heavy with threatening thunderstorms. Such an atmosphere of foreboding is very important in crime fiction, involving as it does emotion before intellect. The book also introduced for the first time the question of an

52

alibi that was to save the condemned huntsman on the eve of his execution. There was also a secondary plot that relied on a flashback. Ignaz Denner, the leader of the gang, who poses as a merchant, is in the end discovered not to be responsible for the cruel and wicked deeds of his gang. His father, Trabacchio, a quack doctor, had made a pact with the Devil and it was the Devil who caused all the evil. The unanswered question is simply: What is a crime and what is a machination of the Devil?

Hoffmann's *Das Majorat (The Entailed Estate)* deals with the old belief that eventually a murderer always returns to the scene of his crime. Once again the setting is "romantic": the family's lonely manor house, the melancholy scenery gloomy with pine trees swaying in the bitter wind and sleet. In striking contrast to this atmosphere are the boisterous high spirits of a hunting party in the mansion. What seems depressingly unaccountable, even supernatural, is a flashback that tells how the old lord of the manor met his death in the ruins of an ancient tower. The nightly apparition of his later servant Daniel intensifies the mystery and leaves the manner of the old man's death in suspense. All is enhanced by the loneliness of the scene, the semiruined manor house, the wild weather, and the darkness of the night.

"Many a time, cousin, we have talked about things that you felt rather than knew or understood." These are the opening words of the justice of the peace when he begins his investigation into how the lord of the manor met his death. He goes on: "It appears that the unfortunate man got up during the night, intending to go into his library in the next room. Still half asleep, he may, it seems, have passed the door and opened another onto the ramparts, stepping forward and falling to this death. It is an explanation, however, that does not carry conviction." A discussion follows, combining in a typical way rational thought and romantic emotion. The rational element is, of course, indispensable and shows itself even more clearly in another of his books.

Das Fräulein von Scuderi (Mademoiselle de Scudéry), published in 1818, is essentially a crime novella. The tale is set in the Paris of Louis XIV, at the time when a police force was being established for the protection of citizens. Hoffmann uses several sources as background material: Voltaire's *Siècle de Louis XIV* (1751), Pitaval's *Causes Célèbres* for the case of the Marquise de Brinvilliers, and an old Nuremberg

E. T. A. Hoffmann, lawyer, romantic poet, painter, and composer.

Chronicle (1697) that contained a report of an amorous adventure of Madeleine de Scudéry, a French writer. Scudéry's way of meeting lovers in the dark streets of Paris, many of whom were vitally concerned for their safety, made her a well-known figure. *"Un amant qui craint les voleurs, n'est point digne d'amour,"* she remarked. ("A lover, afraid of thieves, is unworthy of love.") Mademoiselle de Scudéry is the central character in Hoffmann's story in which she succeeds in clearing up a number of mysterious robberies and murders. The culprit is a goldsmith, Cardillac, who, by means of violent robbery in the dark of night, steals back precious articles he has made for clients. The motive for his deeds is not money but simply the passionate love he has for the fine things he has created. Cardillac is a criminal but at the same time an artist whose sensibilities have been warped.

It is often overlooked, in fact even denied, that Hoffmann's *Das Fräulein von Scuderi* is the forerunner of the modern detective story. The argument goes that it is not the efforts of the lady but chance that leads to the solution of the mystery, that she merely acts according to her feelings and intuition. Yet

Stills from the film *Das Fräulein von Scuderi*, with Henny Porten in the title role of Mademoiselle de Scudéry and Willy A. Kleinau as the goldsmith Cardillac (below, right).

The secret doorway.

The fanatic goldsmith.

chance *does* play a part in many later tales of detection. "Classical" detectives from Sherlock Holmes to Hercule Poirot allow themselves to be guided by intuition. In Hoffmann's tale there is a thorough inquiry into the minutest detail of the crimes. Scuderi tries to find out, for example, whether there has ever been a quarrel between the goldsmith and his assistants. Her search indeed leads her nowhere, nor is any reason found for the wicked deeds. When she asks President La Reynie of the Chambre Ardente—a historical figure—that she be allowed to speak to the accused in person, it is not just her feelings that are guiding her. This form of investigation is well known in modern crime fiction.

Hoffmann does not entirely renounce "romantic" horror, but uses it largely to highlight the mysteriousness of the case. Another historical figure makes his appearance in Desgrais, the Sergeant de Maréchaussée, who in real life arrested the notorious Marquise de Brinvilliers. He explains to the President of the Police—La Reynie—several strange experiences he has had in the Paris streets at night. He declares: "Sir, you may call me what you like—a raving lunatic or a stupid believer in the supernatural. Nevertheless I will tell you now what actually happened to me. I was standing at the wall of the garden, stock still, when suddenly several figures came rushing past me. My companions and I quickly lit our torches and groped our way along the wall. The figures had disappeared, yet in the wall there was no trace of a door or window, no opening of any kind, nothing facing us but a solid stone surface! I inspected the scene again this morning. It would seem the Devil himself is making fun of us." Encouraged by Scuderi, further investigations are made that reveal the wall to have,

in fact, a secret entrance to an underground passageway leading to the goldsmith Cardillac's house. In the end the case is resolved, but the reader is left with the feeling that little explanation has been given for the real motivations of the people involved.

Among Hoffmann's later work there is the retelling of a case from the ever-popular *Pitaval*, concerning bigamy and slander that surround a woman's marriage. By titling his work after her, *Die Marquise de la Pivardière*, Hoffmann clearly shows that, contrary to the feelings in the original Pitaval collection, his sympathy is with the unhappily persecuted woman and not with her husband.

Wilhelm Hauff, a German writer a little after Hoffmann (1826/27), wrote a novella, *Die Sängerin (The Singer)*. It is a love story, set in a landscape familiar from the paintings of the German Romantic artists, with the action taking place in an idyllic small town where an attempted murder seems quite out of place. Dubious evidence in the form of a handkerchief is produced. In the end the dagger that was intended for the singer kills the criminal. Although by this time "fate-tragedy drama" had gone out of fashion, it influenced the development of this story. The love theme proves more interesting than the slender thread of crime.

The German Romantic poet Clemens Brentano was writing on the fringes of crime fiction in his tale *Vom braven Kasperl und dem schönen Annerl (A Tale of Good Kasperl and the Beautiful Annerl)*. Once again there are the stock figures of the poor, pretty girl, in love with the chivalrous young Kasperl, seduced by the aristocrat, and driven to child murder. A common grave awaits the star-crossed lovers, and Brentano seeks the reader's sympathy for them.

Tales of Mystery and Imagination: Stories of Logical Reasoning

As the strong man exults in his physical ability in such exercises as call his muscles into action, so glories the analyst in that moral activity which disentangles.

—Edgar Allan Poe

In his work Edgar Allan Poe combines Rationalism and Romanticism. He knew and admired the English Gothic novel as well as the work of Hoffmann.

At the time he was writing, periodicals and magazines provided an outlet for short stories, a form at which Poe and many other contemporary writers

Edgar Allan Poe.

tried their hand. It is a form that lends itself to experimentation: a good example is "The Murders in the Rue Morgue," published in 1841 in *Graham's Magazine*. His publication ushered in a new literary genre: the detective story. Poe called it a story of "ratiocination," or logical reasoning. Elements of detection had occurred in Hoffmann's *Das Fräulein von Scuderi*, but they were the main ingredient in this new genre, while the description of persons and places were relegated to secondary importance, introduced only when absolutely necessary to the solution of the problems posed.

At this same time European writing was receiving stimulation from the work of another American, James Fenimore Cooper, whose tales of frontier life were enjoying great popularity on the continent. These stories laid emphasis on such seemingly mundane things as tracking down a suspect by footprints or hoofmarks. Who had ridden by and where was he going? How much time had elapsed since the rider passed? When would he have left his base camp? The author and the reader fixed their eyes on anything that might serve as evidence: flattened grass, bent branches, burnt pieces of wood.

This careful analysis of apparently unimportant details is the main feature of Poe's "The Murders in the Rue Morgue." The most important event, however, is the appearance in the story of Chevalier C. Auguste Dupin, the prototype of the later Sherlock Holmes. It is he who explains all the ramifications of the investigation to the reader. Thus the reader becomes a member of an exclusive circle—the initiated, those in the know—and feels privileged at being on the inside.

Dupin's motivation is interesting. He solves strange puzzles for the sheer love of testing his powers of reason. A few striking character elements serve to sketch in his personality. For example, he turns night into day, reading and working by candle light; so will his successor, Sherlock Holmes. As Dupin's model Poe used a true historical personage, the ex-rogue and ex-chief of the Sûreté, Eugène Vidocq. It is for this reason that the author set the tale in Paris.

Facts that appear paradoxical are the very ones that lead Dupin to the solution of a crime. He explains this over and over again in the story, maintaining that circumstances that *seem* mysterious often offer up the precise clue that leads to a puzzle's solution. First he listens carefully to everything the witnesses in the Rue Morgue have to say; for example he notes that while some assume the shouts heard were exclamations in Spanish, German, or Russian, others believe them to be the screams of an orangutan! In the end the crime proves to be less horrible than was at first believed. For Dupin the case is closed once he has found the solution. To the public and the police, however, some mystery may still remain. The selection of the word *morgue* (mortuary) in the street name—which happens to be an actual street in the St. Roche quarter in Paris—lends a touch of intrigue to the title, giving the story a tone of romantic horror.

Another long-established motif, "the locked room"—familiar in ancient folklore—was introduced into the new detective story genre by Poe. Careful investigation by Dupin reveals that the locked room in which the crime was committed does indeed possess an alternative means of entry—namely the window!

In November 1842 *Graham's Magazine* published "The Mystery of Marie Rôget," mentioning its connection with "The Murders in the Rue Morgue." The analysis, if not the final solution, is again left to Dupin. While the setting is Paris, the scene of the actual events on which the story is based was the Hudson River and Weehawken, New Jersey, just across the River. The murder itself was that of a young woman named Mary Rogers. Poe, who did not live in New York at the time, relied largely on press reports for this information. He provided no solution, but did throw suspicion on a naval officer as the possible murderer. Although Poe's hero analyzes the police reports brilliantly, the story did not prove popular with magazine readers. The reason may well be that Dupin is habituated to exceedingly long-winded monologues, without the interruptions of a third party to help hold the reader's attention. Questions a reader might have had in mind and that a Watson, for example, might have articulated, remained unasked and unanswered.

Poe's love of deduction found full satisfaction in "The Purloined Letter" (1845). Here there is no detailed investigation. Instead Dupin discovers the compromising letter of the title by studying closely the mind of the suspect. It has not been cunningly

The famed morgue of Paris at the beginning of the nineteenth century.

hidden but left—almost carelessly—in a letter rack on a desk, along with other unimportant papers, a triumph of psychology. Later crime writers frequently took up the parallel idea of hiding one particular murder away within a series of crimes.

Apart from these three well-known detective stories, Poe's "The Gold Bug" (1843) is worth mentioning. It deals with the discovery of a pirate's buried treasure, which brings to light a long forgotten crime—the murder of the accomplices of Captain Kidd. Its great interest, however, lies in the painstaking deciphering of a code that leads to the discovery of the treasure. The hunt for hidden treasure is not restricted to horror tales, and is frequently found in detective stories and crime fiction.

"Thou Art the Man" (1844) is almost a parody of the detective story. A seemingly good and honest citizen, aptly called Goodfellow, turns out to be the murderer. He tries to throw suspicion on his victim's heir by collecting false evidence against him. Intuition, not deduction, then leads an honest citizen to conduct his own investigation, in which he manages to trick the culprit into a confession. A cask of wine mysteriously bursts open and the decaying body of the victim rises to accuse Goodfellow with the ominous words: "Thou art the man." Though essentially a parody, the story contains two most important ele-

ments of detective fiction: the investigation of false leads and finally the unexpected and spectacular confrontation of the murderer by his victim.

Poe has rightly been called the first true writer of detective stories. The subject of crime is present in all his work. In "The Black Cat," for instance, the murderer gives himself away by inadvertently walling up a sinister live cat with the murdered woman; the cat keeps meowing and so draws attention to the crime. Is a macabre force at work here, or is the psychological agitation of the criminal to blame? Was Poe using the ancient motif of the ordeal, bringing the murderer face to face with his victim?

It is interesting to note that a future president of the United States—Abraham Lincoln—was fascinated by the detective story. In 1846 he wrote "The Trailer Murder," basing the story on a case from his own experience when in legal practice.

Illustration for Poe's "The Murders in the Rue Morgue" by A. Kubin for a contemporary German translation.

The New Pitaval Story
Aktenmässige Darstellung merkwürdiger Verbrechen
(Strange Crimes, Taken from Legal Files)

—Paul Johann Anselm von Feuerbach

Paul Johann Anselm von Feuerbach, a distinguished German criminal jurist, published a collection of legal cases between 1808 and 1811. His intention was to give the public interesting reading material and at the same time provide an insight into social and legal problems. Feuerbach was motivated by democratic ideas and wanted his publications to contribute something towards legal reform. Among other achievements he managed to have the death penalty for poaching abolished in Bavaria in 1806. He also campaigned against vindictive punishments and torture, maintaining that a culprit could be found and convicted by painstaking investigation and the careful interrogation of witnesses, without having to resort to the extortion of a doubtful confession. He

managed in his writing to involve his readers in such investigations; his success made his spectacular case histories very appealing. The progressive and critical reader found himself particularly interested in a collection that paid equal attention to crimes taking place among those living in abject poverty and those occurring among the privileged few.

Legal proceedings were in many instances openly interfered in by princes and their courts. In the case of Freiherr von Brettschart abuse of position, embezzlement, and other serious offenses were, instead of being punished, rewarded by the Bavarian Electoral Court with titles, honors, and even medals—among them the Maltese Cross. Only years later were the much-disputed proceedings investigated anew. Remarkable features of Feuerbach's case histories are his detailed descriptions of the locality of the crime, the physical condition of the victim, and the particular murder weapon used. Such details were important at a time when photography was not generally available, and the use of fingerprints in identification not fully developed. This meant that a complete and thorough report formed the soundest basis for further investigations. Feuerbach's case histories stemmed directly from Pitaval's case histories of the eighteenth century, but his work had the advantage of being written by one of the most noted criminal jurists in Germany. He gained wide fame for the part he played in the sad, never fully explained case of Kaspar Hauser, a foundling abandoned in Nuremberg in 1828. Feuerbach, believing him to be the abducted son of the Grand Duke of Baden, tried to help what he believed to be the unfortunate victim of an intrigue. Whether or not he carried his speculations too far nobody will ever know for sure. The mystery of the foundling remains unsolved. Two facts are as clear as they are puzzling: Feuerbach died in Frankfurt in 1833, possibly poisoned, while his protégé was stabbed to death in the same year!

Woyzeck's execution in the marketplace at Leipzig, in 1821.

In his work Feuerbach dealt mainly with cases that had actually occurred in southern Germany. In Leipzig the publisher Heinrich Brockhaus together with Julius Eduard Hitzig and Georg Wilhelm Häring, both members of Hoffmann's circle in Berlin, published between 1842 and 1863 a collection of cases titled *Der neue Pitaval (The New Pitaval)*, which greatly widened the field from which the subject matter was drawn. The title was chosen because over the years the Pitaval story had become a definite concept, describing a certain type of case history. The introduction to the second edition of the Brockhaus collection points out that spectacular cases of crime no longer belong to the country where they happen nor interest only a small group of experts, but are, perhaps sadly, common property. As interest in crime had spread across frontiers it had also spread from a few professionals to a much wider public. The first volume began with a much-discussed murder, that of August von Kotzebue, a German writer and dramatist, stabbed to death by Karl Ludwig Sand, a student from Jena. It was said that the murder was committed because Kotzebue had ridiculed the Burschenschaft, a student association dedicated to liberal ideas of German unity. The volume contained other notorious deaths like that of Johann Joachim Winckel-

Paul Johann Anselm von Feuerbach, author of *Aktenmässige Darstellung merkwürdiger Verbrechen (Strange Crimes, Taken from Legal Files)*. He was champion of reforms in the German courts.

Kaspar Hauser, the mysterious foundling.

mann, a critic and historian of Greek art, murdered in his hotel in Trieste by a traveler to whom he had shown gold coins and other curios; it included the murder of Gerhard von Kügelgen, a German painter, who became the victim of armed robbery. It was also at this time that the famous Queen's Necklace Affair from the eighteenth century became the subject of a Pitaval treatment.

These reports were taken from the files of actual proceedings and provided welcome material for progressive politicians who encouraged citizens to involve themselves in cleaning up crime. They stressed the need for reliable witnesses. As they dealt with cases that had already been solved, the authors could delve into the question of motivation, the character of the culprit, and the social background. In that way the new Pitaval story gained a psychological depth hitherto unknown. Particularly evident was the case of Gesche Margarethe Gottfried, who ruthlessly poisoned everyone whom she believed stood in the way

of provision for her old age. She was a friendly person, always willing to help others, and it took a long time for suspicion to arise against her. Yet why should so many people die in her presence? What could the motive be for the killings? Most people simply thought that the woman was dogged by ill luck and that being close to her presaged disaster.

Superstition and unreasonable fear are quite often stronger than rational thought and sober observation among the populace. This was partly due to the generally low standard of education, and it was on this social fact that the Pitaval story focused attention. Reading or listening to these criminal cases caused much lively discussion. In contrast to crime fiction, which on the whole deals with literary and aesthetic matters, the Pitaval story raised the question of crime and punishment and laid much of the blame on social evils and the deprivation that provided fertile soil for the growth of crime.

After the retirement of Hitzig and Häring, Anton Vollert, councillor to the Court of Appeal, continued the *Neue Pitaval* until 1890, by which time there were sixty volumes. Further collections of sensational and topical cases continue to be published in this series to this day. Alongside the two men of Hoffmann's circle, Jodocus D. H. Temme, a Berliner later Professor of Criminal Law in Zurich, published a collection called *Merkwürdige Prozesse aller Nationen (Strange Cases from All Nations)*. One of these dealt with Karl Friedrich Masch, a murderer who for some time terrorized Berlin and its surroundings. In the manner of the old-time robber tales, the Masch story tells of hideouts in the woods where the murderer was able to live in relative comfort under the very eyes of the Royal Prussian Police. Temme had a facility for exploiting incidental humor even in the most somber of atmospheres. He collected criminal anecdotes similar to those of Abele in the seventeenth century that dealt more with the grotesque aspects of crime than with crime itself. His fiction is of special interest in that it is a genre evolved from nonfictional case histories. The model for his 1858 tale "Hallbauerin" ("The Hallbauer Woman") was a child murder. A young girl, the daughter of a musician, is accused of murdering a child and brought to trial. Gossip, rumor, whispers—with people talking indiscriminately in order to show their self-importance: something all too common in small communities—all this contributes to the girl's misfortune. Faced in court with a hostile public, the inflexible figure of the law, and the threat of torture, she is unable to defend herself.

Illustrations for Jodocus D. H. Temme's crime novels. The artist stresses the mysterious gloom of the scene.

It is only the young artisan who has married her who protests and demands to know why he has not been asked for an alibi that would establish his presence at a certain place at a specific time, proving his wife's innocence.

But the question of this alibi counts for nothing! Torture is still a ruling factor in the proceedings. It is only in the end that the verdict turns in favor of the accused. The surprise conviction of the real murderess, indeed, does not even feature in the story. Nevertheless the court official representing the lord of the manor, and the reader who has grown acquainted with the situation in the village and the condition of officialdom, has a good idea as to the identity of the guilty—none other than a member of the aristocratic family. The politically motivated reader will fully appreciate this kind of tale.

The question of an alibi occurred again in a crime novella of 1879 entitled *Wer war der Mörder? (Who Was the Murderer?)*. A young forester has been shot in the woods. Suspicion falls on his rival for the favors of the pretty daughter of another forester. It appears, however, that he has been far away from the scene of the crime at the time it happened; thus he has an alibi. The mystery is cleared up years later when a meeting of the local court discloses fresh evidence: there is in fact a secret path through the moorland and thickets, known only to foresters,

which shortens considerably the distance between the suspect's alleged whereabouts and the place where the murder occurred. With the disclosure of the secret path, the jealous youth's alibi no longer stands up.

In crime fiction the heroine is usually faithful, charming, and sentimental, and often, too, a trifle silly. A good example of such a character occurs in *In einer Brautnacht (On a Wedding Night)*. A young lady, seeking protective company for a journey with her dowry, joins a baron and his wife in their coach. Unknown to her, both are imposters. The young woman's suspicions are aroused when the baron takes to stopping at lonely inns, looking for deep pools nearby. The author suggests that he may be hoping to find a suitable spot to dispose of a body. The story is set in the Fichtelgebirge in northeast Bavaria, where there are inns overlooked by high mountains that shelter pools of dark water in the valleys below. The baron steals away to sound out their depth with a long pole, leaving the reader to wonder what nefarious plan he is harboring. In spite of all these strange goings-on, no horrible crime is committed. To the reader's relief, at just the right moment some valiant fellows appear out of the blue and rescue the heroine. Such sudden rescues are typical of the eighteenth-

century Gothic novel, and are still popular today. Temme's intention was to provide "a good read" first, but as a liberal and democratic jurist he wished equally to guide his reader's thoughts towards legal reform—a reform that in Germany meant the introduction of trial by jury and legal proceedings that would be more open.

The counterpart to the German *Neue Pitaval* in Austria was *Die schwarze Bibliothek (The Black Library)* edited by J. Pfundheller, which included one interesting case of murder involving the popular Viennese actress Therese Krones. The fact that the editor was a literary man and not a jurist was probably the reason he added fictional changes to the tale and made a number of inaccurate statements. Some of the errors were corrected in the twentieth-century collection, *Aus dem Archiv des Grauen Hauses (From the Archives of the Gray House)*—the "Gray House" being the Lower Court of Vienna's first district.

Even if nineteenth-century criminal cases were no longer topical, collections of them remained popular well into the twentieth century, particularly with readers who wanted to study the historical background of crime and manners and customs of the past.

The Newgate Novel

Yet we intend to take a few more pages from the "Old Bailey Calendar" to bless the public with one more draught from the Stone Jug [a polite name for Newgate Prison].

—William M. Thackeray

With an ever-growing reading public the novel became the most popular literary form of the nineteenth century. Though new subjects and themes found the format of the short story to be more appropriate for artistic experimentation, the boom in the novel turned the Newgate tale into the Newgate novel. The six volumes of *Celebrated Trials, and Remarkable Cases of Criminal Jurisprudence of 1825*, compiled by George Borrow, fell somewhere between the two. His collection did not achieve the same fame as Pitaval's on the continent. The British public had long been exposed to open legal proceedings and so could watch personally the exchanges between prosecution and defense. By presenting prominent legal

cases that occurred during a specific year, Borrow kept close to the convention of the *Newgate Calendar*.

Edward Bulwer-Lytton, a politician and man of letters, wrote four novels that fall into the category of the Newgate novel. *Pelham* was the first to appear in 1828. Although mercilessly satirized by the literary establishment of the day under the leadership of William Thackeray, *Pelham* near its conclusion contains a grisly murder in an open field under stormy skies, an accused innocent, and a search through the stews of London for the real killer. Bulwer-Lytton's mastery of the criminal argot of the time gives the modern reader an intriguing insight into the mores of the day. Another Bulwer-Lytton Newgate novel was *Paul*

MURDER ROBBERY

GALLOWS HEROISM GALLUS LITERATURE BURGLARY

"The Literary Gentleman" comfortably reflects in his armchair, observing a miniature gallows and dagger on his desk. *Newgate Calendars* are piled on the floor. The scene is surrounded by dark phantoms, representing murder, robbery, break-and-enter, and all the "equipment" of the literature of crime. This caricature in *Punch* is a commentary on contemporary literary trends.

Clifford (1830), which opens with the unforgettable words—immortalized no doubt by Thackeray's attacks on the writers of these popular novels, and now serving over a hundred and fifty years later as a model of how *not* to write an opening—"It was a dark and stormy night …." The last of Bulwer-Lytton's Newgate novels, and possibly the strongest of the genre, *Eugene Aram*, was published in 1832. It is the story of a family circle with some love interest included. Aram is a clever scientist, though a criminal. A search is in progress for a former highwayman, leading to the arrest of the protagonist on the eve of his wedding. He makes a brilliant speech in his own defense, but is hanged all the same. His bride-to-be dies of grief. An investigation is launched by her brother. Eventually it turns out that Aram was indeed guilty. But it all remains within the family, although it is the brother, and not the police, who uncovers the truth.

Jack Sheppard's flight from the condemned
cell at Newgate Prison, London. From Ainsworth's
Jack Sheppard in *Bentley's Miscellany* (1839).

Sheppard's flight from Clerkenwell Prison.

The break-in, from Charles Dickens's *Oliver Twist*,
first published in *Bentley's Miscellany*. Illustration
by George Cruikshank.

Even closer to the Newgate Calendar tale and its historic "heroes" are Charles Whitehead's *The Autobiography of Jack Ketch* (1834), who was London's hangman, and W. Harrison Ainsworth's *Rookwood* (1834). The hero of the latter novel is Dick Turpin, the highwayman who was arrested for horse stealing and was hanged after making his famous ride to York on Black Bess. *Jack Sheppard* (1839), based on the life of the notorious criminal, is an Ainsworth novel known mostly for its grand illustrations by George Cruikshank, who did many of Dickens's novels.

Eventually the Newgate novel altered its character. The hero changed as the public's sympathy changed, influencing the entire construction of the genre. Towards the middle of the nineteenth century the Victorian crime novel made its appearance; this was genuine crime fiction, set in the older tradition of the family story, a kind of comedy of manners in disguise.

William Thackeray heralded the demise of the Newgate novel with a parody *Catherine* (1839–40) in *Fraser's Magazine*. His heroine, he states ironically, was chosen from the *Newgate Calendar*, "that excellent compilation for which we and other popular novelists of the day can never be sufficiently grateful." Catherine Hayes, the heroine of the story, is burnt at the stake in 1726 for inducing a lodger and her illegitimate son to murder her husband, a London

The original Scotland Yard, London.

trader. Catherine, the once innocent girl who has come to London from the country, has decided she wants to marry the man who has seduced her. He turns out to be an egotistic and stupid German ambassador with a high-sounding, but when translated, ironical, name—Maximilian von Galgenstein (Maximilian of the Gallows-Stone). At this time Thackeray was also fiercely attacking Bulwer-Lytton, their literary skirmishes fought out in the pages of *Punch*. In 1842 this magazine published a drawing called *The Literary Gentleman* by an anonymous artist. In his comfortable dressing gown, the subject sits at a table meditating; in front of him there is a pile of papers, an inkstand, and a quill pen. Next to this is a gallows, a dagger, and various other murder weapons, while on the floor stands a basketful of *Newgate Calendars*. Nebulous figures surround the hack writer, each given a significant name: Murder, Robbery, Theft, Heroism at the Gallows, and so on, obviously ridiculing the literary gentleman (Bulwer-Lytton?) working in the genre. These satirical sallies stopped abruptly, however, with the murder of Lord William Russell by his valet. He was said to have conceived the idea of the murder after reading *Jack Sheppard*. While this was an isolated, sensational case, the motive for which was never proved, the growing fear of crime, of the criminal, and especially of the thief, made it impossible to present the rogue as a fictional hero. This fear was certainly not unfounded. As early as the eighteenth century, crime had increased greatly in

Britain, particularly in the cities. The Industrial Revolution heightened social tensions, and the flow of the poor into the cities in search of work increased day by day. Hideouts for criminals were no longer confined to the city's periphery or the dock areas but were to be found close to the city's center. London, where large parts of the city were abandoned to misery and decay, provided ideal cover for criminals.

Henry Fielding, the politician and writer, was called to the bar in 1740. In 1748 he became a Justice of the Peace of Westminster and Middlesex and moved into a house in Bow Street, where he organized a private police force and succeeded in reducing the rate of crime in his district. These individuals were appointed to serve as policemen and detectives. Dressed in red frock coats, their job was to run in pursuit of thieves, an activity that earned them the name of the Bow Street Runners. They also maintained regular consulting hours, morning and evening. Despite their efforts, crime continued rampant. In 1829 the Metropolitan Police Force of London was founded and moved into a house at 4 Whitehall

Place. These policemen, dressed in blue, used the back entrance of the building, which led into Great Scotland Yard, the site of the one-time residence of the Scottish kings when visiting the English Court. Before long Londoners were calling the new institution Scotland Yard. Because the blue coats and top hats they wore were very distinctive, some policemen began wearing civilian clothes in an effort to track down criminals unnoticed. Today the detective section of the Metropolitan Police Force continues to be known as Scotland Yard.

The successful results of the Bow Street Runners and the early Scotland Yard detectives in reducing crime made these institutions into a legend—and this legend was reflected in the literature of the time. The day of the "noble robber" had come to a definite end. The everyday reader, afraid of being robbed in the street, fearful of burglaries, violence, and murder, wanted to hear of the arrest and sentencing of the evildoers. It was this preference that made the successful investigator the new center of interest in contemporary crime fiction.

The Popular Crime Story

How do you like the atmosphere of mystery and suspicion?

—Wilkie Collins

In 1827 a three-volume work titled *Scenes from the Life of a Bow Street Runner, Drawn up from his Memoranda by "Richmond"* appeared. The first part deals with Richmond's adventurous youth as a strolling player and his friendship with gypsies and highwaymen. Then Richmond and his friend reveal themselves to be Bow Street Runners, and thereafter the reader accompanies them on their investigations. As Sherlock Holmes was to do later, Richmond holds consultations with his clients in his rooms. His initial conclusions are reached by listening carefully and observing minutely every detail of his clients' behavior. He then goes out and walks around, visiting the scene of the crime, perhaps a theft or fraud or bodystripping, carrying out a thorough investigation. The book's author remained anonymous.

In 1850 Charles Dickens wrote four sketches, collectively *The Detective Police*, which introduced the concept of the detective to English literature. In his

periodical *Household Words*, he set about popularizing this character and his work by presenting him in his day-to-day round of activities. Although it may not have made for thrilling reading it was convincing in its reality, and it led top detectives from Scotland Yard to record their thanks to Dickens for his work by having tea with him in the editorial offices of *Household Words*.

Dickens was of course best known for his novels. In *Oliver Twist* (1837–38) he alluded many times to the subject of Newgate Prison. The hero is a child of unknown parentage, born in a workhouse and brought up under cruel conditions. After an unhappy apprenticeship, he runs away, reaches London, and falls into the hands of a gang of thieves run by Fagin. Fagin makes every effort to convert Oliver to a life of crime. After being temporarily rescued by a benefactor, Oliver is again kidnapped by the gang and forced to accompany Bill Sikes, a professional burglar, on one of his "jobs." Oliver receives a gunshot wound, is rescued again, and taken into a comfortable household. After a brutal murder, inspired by the gang, a hue and cry is raised: Sikes accidentally hangs himself, the rest are caught and taken to a Newgate-like prison, Fagin, their leader, is hanged.

Bleak House, published in 1852, is a very different kind of story, although the plot is closely concerned with crime, persecution, and legal proceedings. It is a lengthy work in which one of the main incidents is a murder. Chapter titles reflect events and heighten the tension: for example, "A Turn of the Screw," "Stop Him," "Closing in," "A Discovery," "The Track," "Springing a Mine," "Flight," "Pursuit," and so on. The story revolves around a traditional family circle. Once the murder is cleared up, many pages are devoted to a cozy description of family events. The crime, however, stands out as the main episode of the book, with the laying of false trails and the final conviction of the accused. There is above all the character of Inspector Bucket, thick-set and reliable, dressed in respectable dark clothes, with his lively inquisitive eyes observing everything. He is the police investigator who unravels the mysteries but he never intrudes on family secrets. The novel's framework is that of the Victorian family saga, with a strong thread of crime fiction running through it.

Family quarrels about property and inheritance usually involved criminal activities and were repeatedly a subject of crime writing in Victorian works. The crime element in *Bleak House* made it an even greater success than Dickens's previous novels. In all, he possessed literary qualities indispensable to the serious crime writer. He was able to describe his characters and the conditions in which they lived in the minutest detail, even though he may have painted them more sentimentally than realistically. His characters tended to be more eccentric than mysterious, and his letters showed the increasing interest he took in the incidence of murder. He followed most current cases, studying them critically, analyzing in particular the finer details of the evidence.

In 1851 Dickens met the writer Wilkie Collins, whom he enlisted as a collaborator on the staff of the *Household Words*. This gave Collins the opportunity to publish his own short crime stories in the magazine. They soon became fast friends. Collins was interested in the further development of crime fiction, but Dickens remained rooted in the traditions of the

Charles Dickens.

Newgate novel. Collins also used the short story to experiment with new techniques, and without any knowledge of Poe's stories produced quite independently his own tales based on logic and reason. He was also inspired by the material of the Pitaval collection.

In 1855 Collins and Dickens met in Paris. They enjoyed the life of the city, strolling around, looking at shops, finally coming across an antiquarian who had piles of battered books to sell. Among them were many dealing with crime, a real find for Collins who used some of the material later on in his own novels.

Dickens wrote *Hunted Down*, a crime novella, for the *New York Ledger* in 1859, based on a real case. In the tale a man tries to kill his two nieces to claim their insurance. He succeeds in killing one, while the other slowly dies of poison. When the insurance agent and the lover of the dead girl become suspicious, they catch the killer by laying a cunning trap

Wilkie Collins.

for him, involving disguise and entrapment. It was a fictionalized version of a case in which a London journalist, Thomas Griffin Wainwright, insured his sister-in-law for £18,000 and promptly poisoned her. He was convicted as the killer. Dickens, being more interested in the criminal's character than in the actual details of the crime, visited Wainwright in Newgate Prison to gather the material for his story.

Dickens and Collins shared a lively interest in literary matters, which led to their continued collaboration in another magazine venture called *All the Year Round*. The former's last novel, *The Mystery of Edwin Drood*, left unfinished at his death, would appear to have been conceived as a crime novel. Part of it was serialized in the new Dickens-Collins publication in 1870. Dickens dedicated the first installment to Queen Victoria, and offered to provide her with the answer to the mystery in advance. Unfortunately for

posterity, the Queen declined the offer. Dickens died before completing the novel. Many questions were left unanswered: Had Drood really been murdered? If so, where was his body? Who was his murderer? Why was the crime committed? Over the years many writers were attracted by these intriguing questions and tried to finish the story, offering a number of ingenious solutions. Each followed his own particular trail, but the mystery surrounding Drood remains unsolved to this day.

Collins's work set up just as many puzzles as Dickens's, but he provided that essentiality of crime fiction—a satisfactory solution. His short stories, first published in Dickens's magazine, later appeared in book form. "A Terribly Strange Bed" opened the collection. Here Collins was following the technique of French crime writing. Happenings similar to the Collins story had been reported by Eugène Vidocq. Vidocq reported of a lodging house in the country that was a murder inn, the old folklore tradition. In Collins's tale the fatal bed has a horrifying contraption that lets the canopy descend silently to suffocate the unsuspecting sleeper. A young Englishman, partly due to intuition and partly to restlessness caused by taking the wrong dose of a narcotic, remains awake and helps a conveniently present gendarme to arrest the felon.

In 1860 Collins resumed his connection with the Gothic novel by writing *The Woman in White*. He presents a plot of crime and detection against a familiar background of romantic horror. Reference is made early in the story to crime and the fight against it:

> If the machinery of the Law could be depended on to fathom every case of suspicion, and to conduct every process of inquiry, with moderate assistance only from the lubricating influences of oil of gold, the events which fill these pages might have claimed their share of the public attention in a Court of Justice.

The author decided at the outset that his readers should be privy to all the proceedings. The novel consists of reports by witnesses in the case. His source is Méjan's *Recueil des Causes Célèbres (A Collection of Famous Cases)*, a book Collins had picked up on that trip to Paris with Dickens. In it there was a report of the Pitaval case of the Marquise Douhalt. She was cheated out of her inheritance by a brother who arranged to have her certified as insane and committed under a false name to the Salpêtrière, the Paris Asylum. Eventually in 1787 the unhappy woman started proceedings against her brother, with only one piece of evidence in hand—a white gown. She lost the case and died in dire poverty in 1817. Collins's work was a new departure for the novel; it caused a literary sensation. The story appealed to the emotions and the intellect alike. Fashion houses named their cloaks and bonnets *Woman in White*; waltzes and quadrilles were named after her. Prime Minister Gladstone himself, it is said, abandoned a visit to the theater to read the book in peace. Thackeray, the fierce enemy of the later Newgate novel, stayed awake all night with it. *The Woman in White* gained access to the Royal Household where the Prince Consort especially admired Collins's work, recommending it to the stern Baron Stockmar.

The title did not refer to "the white lady," the ghost of an ancestress, haunting the towers of ancient castles, even though it might well conjure up such an association. This woman in white was the victim of a crime of legacy hunting, which occurred within her immediate family circle. It was not a case for Scotland Yard. In the novel, Hartright, an art teacher possessing many of Collins's own character facets, assumes the role of an amateur detective. He is motivated by personal reasons: he loves Laura Fairlie, the young heiress, and wants to save her from the nefarious scheme of the villain. But the villain marries her and embarks on a cunning plot to obtain her inheritance. Quite apart from his personal interest in the case, Hartright wants to see justice done, with Laura assuming her rightful place.

Against its background of "horror," the story therefore had valid love interest, a motif that later crime writers disapproved of. It also had that popular "family novel" must, a happy ending. Equally important was the fact that the novel began a trend of describing investigative elements in exact detail right up to the final conclusion of the case. Sir Percival Glyde, the villain of the piece, conveniently emerges not as a true gentleman but as the illegitimate son of a noble family, a fact that serves to bring to light a complicated combination of family secrets and frauds. He dies in a fire at the old village church as he is about to destroy an incriminating birth register. It all seems like an Act of God, with this final incident fitting well into the novel's gloomy theme and underlying belief in the supernatural. Walter Hartright is a man of reason. He preserves and, with the help of Laura's half-sister Marian, arrives at the logical solution, laying bare lies and intrigues.

The detailed description of scenery in the book reflects the leading characters' feelings and state of mind and prepares the reader for what is to happen. Collins's great gift for "painting in" scenery may well have been an inheritance from his father, a Royal Academician and a landscape painter. Names given to places are descriptive. Blackwater Park, the country house where Sir Percival lives with his young wife, is surrounded by somber woods; it hulks by the side of a dark silent lake, which gives the place its name, and is ironically described as "an ideal setting for a murder." Hartright, returning from his travels, reflects:

> I turned aside, and there below me in the glen
> was the lonely grey church, the porch where
> I had waited for the coming of the woman in
> white, the hills encircling the quiet burial-
> ground, the brook bubbling cold over its stony
> bed.

Apart from the hero's intuition, there is a great deal of serious investigation in the novel. The unconventional Marian takes it upon herself to eavesdrop on a conversation one night and then, scantily dressed, climbs across a roof in complete darkness. In the daytime she busies herself examining footprints in the old boathouse, all part of her effort to try to discover Sir Percival's secret.

The atmosphere of the country house of the day is strongly reflected in the Victorian crime story, exactly as is the tempo of country life. Nothing is done in haste, not even the pursuit of a criminal. Time itself, the gentry believes, will put all things right in the end. Count Fosco and his wife, two other nefarious characters involved in Sir Percival's many villainies, are trapped by fate in due course. The span of time, critical for the criminals, between the death of the Woman in White, her burial under Laura's name, and Laura's incarceration in an asylum, takes twenty-four hours, in stark contrast to the present day when one hour, or even a few minutes, can be crucial to an alibi.

There are many reasons why *The Woman in White* can be categorized as crime fiction, but critics increasingly agree that Collins's other main novel, *The Moonstone* (1868), occupies a very special place in crime-fiction history. Its structure and the technical presentation of the material make it really the first detective novel, and one of the best. As Dorothy Sayers said, "taking everything into consideration *The Moonstone* is probably the very finest detective story ever written." The book holds the reader's attention from the opening right up to the surprising denouement. From the start one knows all the facts set out in reports by the plot's protagonists. Each character gives a separate account from his own particular point of view, with some omitting and others including specific facts; thus each forms an individual judgment. The reader is thus required to be alert all the time in order not to miss a clue.

Sergeant Cuff, modeled on a genuine inspector of Scotland Yard, is sent to clear up the case. The owners of the house await with bated breath the arrival of the great man:

> A fly from the railway drove up as I reached the lodge; and out got a grizzled, elderly man, so miserably lean that he looked as if he had not got an ounce of flesh on his bones in any part of him. He was dressed all in decent black, with a white cravat round his neck. His face was as sharp as a hatchet, and the skin of it was as yellow and dry and withered as an autumn leaf. His eyes, of a steely light grey, had a very disconcerting trick, when they encountered your eyes, of looking as if they expected something more from you that you were aware of yourself. His walk was soft; his voice was melancholy; his long lanky fingers were hooked like claws. He might have been a parson, or an undertaker—or anything else you like, except what he really was.

To make this slight, nondescript man stand out, Collins gives him an idiosyncracy: a passionate love of roses. The sergeant is careful during the investigation to assure Franklin Blake, who at one point is under suspicion, that "there is a chance of laying hands on the Indians, and of recovering the Moonstone yet." Collins, in many ways an unconventional man himself, has the jewel returned in the end to its rightful place: the Temple of the Moon Goddess in India.

Apart from these familiar exotic elements, *The Moonstone* contains other features that we find common today: the country house by the sea; the party for the birthday of Rachel Verinder; many red herrings; and a detective who carefully observes events and comes to his own conclusions.

> We had walked, I should say, a couple of hundred yards towards Cobb's Hole, when Sergeant Cuff suddenly went down on his knees on the beach, to all appearances seized with a sudden frenzy for saying his prayers. "There's something to be said for your marine landscape here after all," remarked the Sergeant. "Here are a woman's footsteps, Mr. Betteredge! Let us call them Rosanna's footsteps, until we find evidence to the contrary that we can't resist."

Conversations between friends are made to sound like investigations:

> "Did you notice the time? Was it late?"
> "Not very. About twelve o'clock, I think."
> "Did you fall asleep?"
> "No. I couldn't sleep that night."
> "You were restless?" …
> "Had you any light in your room?" I asked.
> "None until I got up again, and lit my candle."
> "How long was that, after you had gone to bed?"

A psychological touch is also introduced when, trying to show his own self-importance, each character describes events from his very personal point of view. The plot structure of the novel is unusual, dealing as it does with the repeated theft of the moonstone. Again and again it changes hands, bringing bad luck to each possessor in turn, and leading to murder at the end of the story. This has the effect of concluding the book with a punishment that seems to fit the crime. The villainous cousin is unmasked as the real scoundrel and the stone is saved from destruction.

As in *The Woman in White*, although the criminals are uncovered by the investigator, final retribution is left to fate. This characteristic of Collins's writing links it to Sheridan Le Fanu's *Uncle Silas* (1864). In that work the eponymous uncle is even more heinous than his bad reputation. In his own house he murders Charke, with whom he had been involved in gambling transactions. With the help of his son, he attempts to dispose of Maud, his nineteen-year-old ward, in order to seize her inheritance. But instead of Maud, who is as foolish as she is charming, it is the sinister French governess, Madame de la Rougierre, actually their accomplice, who is inadvertently killed. Once again fate has dealt a just blow. In the end fate also catches up with Uncle Silas, who poisons himself with an overdose of opium, while his son has only just enough time to escape to Australia. The murder of Charke is also cleared up. The deed was committed in a locked room, a room, it seemed, that no one could enter. Le Fanu chose the locked-room motif, previously used by Poe, with deliberation, well aware of how effective it was. He wanted to create an increasingly sinister atmosphere, and to make events more and more puzzling. He did not explain a great deal to the reader, who is left at the end with a sense of being cheated. Actually at the first inspection of the room there is no mention of any secret entrance.

Once the criminals are suitably punished, Le Fanu gives his readers a happy ending by marrying off everyone of eligible age. The heroine gets a real lord as a reward for all the agonies she has suffered. This ending is typical of the Victorian family novel and comedy of manners, early crime fiction was very close to that genre. Le Fanu used the subject of crime in a number of his horror stories, for example in "The House by the Churchyard" (1861–62), and later Conan Doyle was to find inspiration in *Uncle Silas* for "The Firm of Girdlestone" (1889).

About this time Mary Elizabeth Braddon published *Lady Audley's Secret* (1862), the novel that was to make her famous. The lady's secret lies in her past from which she is trying to escape. She arranges to "die" by having her name inscribed on a tombstone in order to live anonymously as the wife of Sir Michael at Audley Court. George Talboy, the man she has been married to for years, remains a bothersome witness to her former secret life. She tries to drown him in a well but, left for dead, he survives. Together with a friend, Sir Michael's nephew, he calls the guilty woman to account. The uncovering of the crime once again takes place *within* the family circle.

While the purveyors of romantic horror preferred the setting of ancient churchyards, moss-covered tombstones, ruined monasteries and castles, subterranean vaults, and moonlit countryside, later writers were beginning to find that the mysterious and the sinister existed equally in the character of man himself.

Robert Louis Stevenson.

A classic example of the trend in this direction is Robert Louis Stevenson's *The Strange Case of Dr. Jekyll and Mr. Hyde* (1886). The book concerns a man's personality, split between good and evil. Even if the psychological implications are not fully explored, the atmosphere of gloom and mystery created by the author makes a strong impression on the reader. His projected novel *The Body Snatcher* was left unfinished at his death, but was completed by Sir Arthur-Thomas Quiller-Couch and published in 1895. It is a gruesome tale, based on historical fact. In the early nineteenth century, two Irish laborers, Burke and Hare, live in Edinburgh's old town where Hare runs a lodging house. An old pensioner dies in the house and the two men sell his body to a famous anatomist, Dr. Robert Knox, for the purpose of medical dissection. The ease with which they earn this money tempts them to commit a whole series of murders to

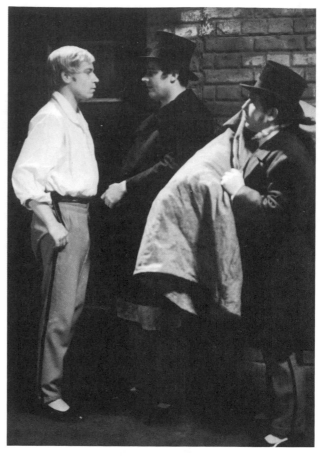

Stills from a television film of Stevenson's *Der Lei-chenschnapper (The Body Snatcher)*. Made in the German Democratic Republic (East Germany).

Frederic March as the slavering, deranged, and totally evil Mr. Hyde, with his fingers ready to throttle Miriam Hopkins as Ivy Pearson, the music hall singer, in Hollywood's classic 1932 *Dr. Jekyll and Mr. Hyde*, from the Robert Louis Stevenson novella.

Stills from a television film of Stevenson's *Der Selbstmörderclub (The Suicide Club)*. Made in the German Democratic Republic (East Germany).

procure more bodies to sell. They inveigle travelers into their lodging house, get them drunk, and suffocate them. In this way they succeed in disposing of fifteen people before suspicious neighbors alert the police. Hare turns king's evidence, and after his release vanishes into obscurity; Burke is hanged amid the curses of an angry crowd. Such is the end of the much feared "Resurrection Men"—the Burkers, as they were known in real life. With the constant demand for bodies, the Burkers took also to snatching supplies from new graves. Even now a few old watchtowers are to be found in Scottish graveyards with someone keeping guard day and night against possible intruders. As only the bodies of felons could be handed over for dissection, a situation that left Dr. Knox and his assistants short of supplies for study and teaching, this led the criminally inclined into an infamous but lucrative activity. "No questions asked" was said to have been the motto of the learned men.

In the two cycles of Stevenson short stories, *The Suicide Club* (1882) and *The Rajah's Diamond* (1882), Prince Florizel of Bohemia and his companion, using very professional and detectivelike techniques, try to penetrate the secrets of a powerful criminal, providing the reader with plenty of mysteries to think about on the way.

There are crime motifs too in *The Wrecker* (1892), which Stevenson wrote in collaboration with his stepson, Lloyd Osbourne. In the epilogue to this book the crime story is discussed: "We had long been at once attracted and repelled by that very modern form of the police novel or mystery story, which consists in beginning your yarn anywhere but at the beginning and finishing it anywhere but at the end." *The Wrecker* is in the tradition of the English adventure story with piracy, smuggling, and murder set against a backdrop of the South Pacific. *The Wrong Box* (1889), originally called *A Game of Bluff*, introduced comic elements into the crime-adventure story. The uncle of two young men has come into a fortune, which they eventually hope to inherit. When the uncle appears to have died in a railway accident, they recover the body and in a number of surreal incidents hide it in a water-barrel, then in a piano, and finally on a train. The carriage containing the valuable cargo is stolen, but their uncle has somehow survived the accident and has escaped his scheming nephews. Earlier Poe had tried to parody a crime

story but the time was then not ripe and the attempt remained an isolated effort.

Eugène François Vidocq, mentioned before, was born a baker's son in Arras, France, in 1775. As a boy he used to rob his father's till and was sent to a house of correction from where he escaped with stolen money. After a number of extraordinary adventures, he entered the army, attained the rank of corporal, and served until a wound disabled him. More adventures followed, including some disreputable love affairs, until he turned up in Paris in 1796, was arrested on a forgery charge and sentenced to eight years as a galley slave. He contrived to escape and joined a band of highwaymen who, on learning that he was a galley slave on the run, abandoned him, making him swear a solemn oath not to betray them. Vidocq took the oath and promptly delivered the whole gang into the hands of the authorities. In 1808 he offered his services to the police as a spy in the Paris underworld. At first he was received coolly but he persevered and in 1812 a Brigade de Sûreté was set up in the city with Vidocq at its head. At the beginning it consisted of only four men, but was gradually increased to twenty-eight, whose efficiency was much admired. From a gloomy house in the Petite Rue Sainte Anne the Sûreté eventually moved to the prestigious Quai des Orfèvres. As might be expected, the suspicion grew that Vidocq might well be the instigator of many of the burglaries he so cleverly detected. He left the service in 1825, started a paper mill, and then opened his own private detective office only to have this closed down by the authorities. Vidocq's *Mémoires* (1828-29), in which he detailed his misdeeds, the severe punishments he experienced, and his numerous escapes, found a wide reading public—to a great extent because of his minute descriptions of the crimes and their perpetrators he brought to justice. It was not so much his power of detection and analysis that made Vidocq a successful detective as his intimate knowledge of criminals and their methods. For example, early in his career he tracked down and caught Watrin, a notorious forger, undoubtedly helped by the fact that he himself had been sentenced for that crime. His close contact with informers, his physical strength, and the art of disguise that he practiced so perfectly—all played their part in his extraordinary success.

Although they make fascinating reading, experts do not consider the *Mémoires* entirely trustworthy.

Eugène Vidocq, former convict and later founder of the Paris Sûreté. His *Mémoires* influenced the development of crime writing.

"The Prisoners' Parade," a measure introduced by Vidocq to help policemen fix in their minds the shape, face, and manner of walking of prisoners. This was an early attempt to assist in identification of criminals.

Nevertheless many writers used the book as source material. Poe felt its influence enough to place his detective, C. Auguste Dupin, in Paris. But it was chiefly Balzac who made use of the types described by Vidocq. Vidocq himself was the model for the former galley slave Vautrin in *Père Goriot* (1835). Balzac's great *Comédie Humaine* exposes human frailties and crimes; such elements play an important part in *Une Ténébreuse Affaire (A Murky Affair)* published in *Le Commerce* in 1841.

On the continent of Europe the political and economic upheavals of 1848 and 1849 brought about a change in the form of literary output. The elegant little almanacs, destined for the few, were taken over by magazines and journals in which novels were published in serial form and were avidly read by all those who could not afford to buy books. Later the serialized novels were often published in book form. This popularizing of reading material meant that publishing was no longer restricted to fine and expensive books for the élite. There was in the air a new atmosphere of democracy, something that visibly influenced the content and presentation of contemporary writing.

Eugène Sue's *Les Mystères de Paris* (1842–43), a serial novel, was conceived merely as an entertainment to hold the reader's attention over its two thousand pages. The various installments established a feeling of rising tension so that the reader would neither cast the paper aside nor give up a subscription to the *Journal des Débats*, the influential publication in which it appeared. The *Mystères* intriguingly exposed the underworld of Paris, its gangs and their leaders, with the result that, suddenly, undiscovered crimes, hideaways, criminals in disguise, and all the rest of it became the subject of the day. But Sue's serial contained something else. The ordinary rogue was known to everybody, but not the "gentleman" variety in the aristocracy or the bourgeoisie whom Sue suddenly unmasked. Prince Rodolphe von Gerolstein, Sue's protagonist, was amateur detective, judge, and avenger at one and the same time. It was no accident that *Les Mystères*, full of adventures and with justice triumphant over villainy, was received with enthusiasm by the public. Fellow authors saw to it that every town and city soon inspired its own "mysteries." Sue's book thus had a far-reaching influence in the advancement of the crime novel.

In Dumas père's novel *Le Comte de Monte-Cristo* (1845–46) the eponymous hero is again an avenger of misdeeds. The crimes perpetrated against young Ed-

Alexandre Duma père.

Eugène Sue.

mond Dantes are known to the reader from the out-set, so that the action after Dantes's escape from the Château d'If is simply a spirited pursuit of the villains. The story takes place against the backdrop of France's Napoleonic era before the Restoration. The crime element comes to the forefront most clearly in the episode dealing with the attempted murder of Madame de Villefort, a subplot that almost becomes a separate story. Dumas later used Pitaval's case-history format when in 1839 he began to publish *Les Crimes Célèbres (Famous Crimes)*, a lesser work in his huge literary output.

In 1854 *Les Mohicans de Paris* appeared, in which, like James Fenimore Cooper's Red Indians, the amateur detectives, joined by a faithful dog and an efficient policeman, Jackal, follow a trail of clues in their investigation and coin the phrase still popular in detective literature: *"Cherchez la femme"* ("Search for the woman.")

The French master of the *roman policier*, Emile Gaboriau, had been secretary to the writer Paul Féral

and in that position had collected much literary material. Because the early members of the Brigade de Sûreté had usually pursued a career similar to that of their chief Vidocq, they were prone to unfortunate involvements in criminal occurrences. Vidocq once confronted one of his men who had just stolen a coat belonging to the wife of the Prefect of Police! Because of these embarrassing encounters, Gaboriau did not find it easy to introduce the detective Lecoq as the hero of his works.

Some of Gaboriau's novels were serialized in *Le Pays*, among them in 1866 *L'Affaire Lerouge (The Lerouge Affair* or, U. S.: *The Widow Lerouge)*. In this work a bibliophile, le Père Taboret, involves Monsieur Lecoq, a detective of the Sûreté, in an investigation of the murder of a widow. The relationship of Taboret and Lecoq is by no means a Watson/Holmes one. Taboret sets out to reconstruct the murderer's route taken from the station to her house, interrogating every witness he can find, following up the clues given by them, and then drawing his own conclusions.

A suspect is cleared when he is found to have an alibi that checks out. In the end Lecoq eliminates all suspects except an advocate, Sieur Noël Gerdy, and forces him to confess to the murder. In order to understand the motives for the crime, it is necessary for the reader to be told the history of the widow Lerouge. The novel becomes two-tiered at this point, one level concerned with the suspense of the investigation, and the other with an explication of the life-story of the widow Lerouge. The flashback segment reads like the familiar "family" novel, less suspenseful and exciting than the hunt for the murderer. Yet in its own way it lifts the mere account of a crime into a novel of substance. Publication in serial form required each installment to be of a certain length and to contain enough tension to make the reader eager for the next. The reader sees Lecoq, Taboret's protégé, develop in the course of the installments into a highly skilled detective, and looks forward to his appearance in further adventures such as *Monsieur Lecoq* (1869), in which he deals with a difficult case of entangled family secrets. *Le Crime d'Orcival*, published in 1867, came closer to pure detective fiction, with an absence of family involvements. Here the action begins in a low alehouse where two criminals have recently been shot and ends in an aristocratic setting. In the low dive, Lecoq begins his careful

investigations, crouching on the floor in an effort to trace footprints. "Now I know everything!" he exclaims. Even the vast snowy scene outside seems to him like a blank page on which are imprinted clues eventually leading to a solution of his case. Lecoq is promoted to inspector in the end. It is obvious that Gaboriau used topical events and the city features of Paris to provide authenticity not found in the early Victorian crime novel. Gaboriau even returned to the famous poison case of the Marquise de Brinvilliers to give himself a chance to sketch in the earlier period and place with consummate accuracy, although he used fictitious names to disguise the real people.

It is worth noting that most criminals in Gaboriau's books are of noble blood, albeit often illegitimate—a compromise that seemed to satisfy the smug morals of the bourgeoisie. This was particularly evident when the villain received a punishment fitting his crime, ending up on the guillotine.

The great interest shown in the serial publication of the novels of Gaboriau and Sue caused them soon to appear in book form and in translations. The circle of readers was a wide one, and those who had never cared for a mere "family" novel enjoyed Gaboriau's writing in which rational thought and the pleasure of observation and detection outweighed the usual sentimentality and pathos. Bismarck himself is said to have been among Gaboriau's many fans.

Fortune de Boisgobey followed in the tradition of Gaboriau although he did not make use of so many

A cartoon attacking the popularity of Sue's *Mystères de Paris*, especially its newly developed circle of readers. These readers were apparently prepared not just to read but actually to participate in all the excitement of the story.

Artists critical of society were attracted to the subject of murder. This lithograph of Honoré Daumier shows the brutality with which the murderer attacks his victim.

Illustrations of the reports of criminal cases and court proceedings in German popular magazines: Carrying off stolen goods from the den of a fence.

Action at the scene of the crime.

A night in Berlin's *Stadtvogtei* (city jail).

Thieves at work.

Posting a thousand marks reward. A scene in a Berlin suburb.

Arrest of a pickpocket.

melodramatic incidents. Nor did he limit his range of characters to the aristocracy. Instead he introduced merchants, dressmakers, artists, and students. In *La Vieillesse de Monsieur Lecoq (The Old Age of Monsieur Lecoq)*, published in 1878, he actually resurrected and used Gaboriau's hero! In *Le Coup de Pouce (The Finishing Touch)*, in 1875, his detective was an old priest, a forebear, as it were, of Chesterton's Father Brown. The priest, saddened by a murder in his parish, undertakes an investigation himself to prove the innocence of a member of his flock. He succeeds in demolishing a false alibi established by manipulating the hands of a church-tower clock. To his great satisfaction he unmasks the culprit—a newcomer to the village—and so saves local honor. *Cornaline, la Dompteuse (Cornaline, the Animal Tamer)*, which appeared in 1887, is an experiment with both detective and setting; the "detective" is a young reporter, and the investigation is carried out in the world of the circus.

In Germany the combination of the family novel and the crime story was not so common. The popular writer Eugenie Marlitt, the pen name of Eugenie John, was born in a small principality of Thuringia where the Princess of Schwarzburg-Sondershausen took charge of her education. Originally training for a career in the theater, she was forced by poor health to abandon her plans and turn to literature, and in that capacity she became a reader for her patroness. In 1863 she left this post to devote all her time to writing. Her romances became very popular, peopled as they were by simple, virtuous, and beautiful heroines and brave and noble heroes. But she found that this surfeit of virtue required a counterpart: a scheming criminal, perhaps of noble descent—in other words, a bigoted type. Frau Marlitt herself, like some of her heroines, was of a democratic turn of mind and took to casting her sinister characters among the upper classes, even in court circles, although naturally not in the court of her highly respected local prince and princess. Although it contains neither murder nor detective, Marlitt's 1867 novel *Das Geheimnis der alten Mamsell (The Old Maid's Secret)* contains many crimes—embezzlement, slander, legacy hunting—all occurring in the family circle. No investigation is conducted to uncover them; they are simply brought in to blacken someone's character. To begin with, Marlitt's novels were serialized in the journal *Die Gartenlaube*, a family publication, which aimed at providing "good, clean" reading matter, while at the same time giving information about important events. *Daheim* was another family magazine read in many German homes, and it too began to publish crime stories, though naturally not of the "hard-boiled" type. Discussion of criminal law reform and especially the introduction of trial by jury and open courts increased the interest of the general public in legal matter. This led to a constant demand for literature in this vein, causing editors of journals to substitute the short crime novella for the longer serialized novel. Highly sensational titles frequently belied the petit-bourgeois character of these journals.

The early novels of Laurids Kruse, a Danish writer, now seem pretty dated, but even at the time of their publication in the nineteenth century Kruse found that he had to have them published in Germany since he could not find enough readers in his homeland. These works did not contain much detection, and the reader could easily guess the outcome of the stories. Nor was the criminal even brought to trial or punishment: fate simply caught up with him in the end.

In a light but sensational form crime fiction developed in Austria too. Adolf Bäuerle, a writer of songs and light stage farces, tried his hand at it, as did Heinrich Ritter von Levitschnigg, who had read medicine and law for a while and must have gained useful insight into the subject of crime. In his own day Karl von Holtei's works were also very popular in Germany. A writer and actor, Holtei worked in a Berlin theater before becoming the director of one in Riga. It was there that he collected the background material for his novel *Der Mord in Riga (Murder in Riga)*. Although "murder" occurs in the title, it does not actually play a central part in the story. The reader is given a lengthy picture of life in Riga before the eleventh chapter, in which a tea merchant, Mushkin, is murdered. Suspicion falls on a groom who is tracked down, caught, and tortured. Only at the very last moment does an alert policeman hit upon the real culprit, the servant of a respected citizen. The use of evidence and deduction plays an important part in the tale, as well as the policeman's natural intuition.

Temme, the lawyer and writer previously mentioned, wrote a number of interesting tales. In one of them he used the familiar locked-room motif, with a robbery taking place on a moving train that does not stop between stations and from which no passengers have been seen to jump. The denouement provides a surprise twist with the prime suspect, a man in disguise, cleared as the culprit, and instead a modest young merchant's clerk identified as the embezzler of some missing money.

Authors took obvious pleasure in alluding to technological progress: murders were committed on trains, pursuits were made by rail, and telegraph lines were used for messages. Novels now introduced a crowd of examining magistrates, inspectors, and policemen, each with his own method of working.

In the short story the family theme was gradually disappearing as the subject of crime became more dominating. At the same time another theme gained in importance: adventure.

Photographing suspects for the Rogue's Gallery.

The Adventure Crime Story

*A week later I killed the miller who was on his way home with
a bagful of money. And have your colleagues
ever spotted the right trails?*

—Friedrich Gerstäcker

Naturally, adventures and adventurers do not always stay within the bounds of the law. Poe's "The Gold Bug" deals with an adventure as well as with the unraveling of a code. In Germany there was only an isolated case, but it is typical of a general development. Friedrich Gerstäcker, a writer of travel and adventure stories, wrote one tale of crime and one full-length crime novel.

In some ways Gerstäcker still clung to the familiar pattern of the family story. Family relations and traditions, marriage, and family honor played their part, but a criminal case became the center of his novel *Im Eckfenster (In the Corner Window)* (1872): the strange death of an officer that was apparently suicide.

In the course of the investigation, begun by amateurs, the death is found to be a cunning murder. The culprit, an aristocrat and deeply in debt, has committed several undetected crimes. When a young officer becomes suspicious, he forces him to fight a bloodless "duel"—a kind of early Russian roulette. The one who loses at throwing dice must commit suicide. The evildoer uses weighted dice that can only throw sixes, and the protagonist, an officer, loses. In that way the villain can dispose of his detector, with his murder appearing to be suicide and the culprit safe with an alibi. The intrigues all center around the market square of a little town, with the windows of the houses supplying observation posts for the townsfolk. Püster, the notary, gets the best view from his corner window. He is well placed to carry out the detection and to see justice done in the end.

The final confrontation with the suspect, with all parties present, takes place in the notary's office. This surprising assemblage of all the witnesses—some come even from abroad—has immediate results. A number of other crimes, including a robbery with violence for which a young artisan has suffered a term of imprisonment long ago, are cleared up. When pushed hard by the prosecution in a confrontation between the aristocrat and the innocently convicted man—with the murder weapon in full view—the real culprit is unmasked. This novel ends with a series of happy marriages, and all ends well as in so many romantic novels before and after.

The German writer Balduin Möllhausen combined the elements of adventure with crime and family interest. Among the men of America's lawless Wild West, gun battles were one way of bringing about justice; violence in a European town or village, however, was clearly a criminal act. There was no puzzle for the reader to solve, since an evildoer was usually seen committing his crime. Sometimes rogues were literally at each other's throats, as for example in a scene at a lonely lake in the 1810 novel *Fährmann am Kanadian (Ferryman on the Canadian River)*.

The German writer, Karl May, a one-time best seller of thrilling stories for the young, was a master at mixing adventure, travel, and romance. In his *Der verlorene Sohn oder der Fürst des Elends (The Prodigal Son, or the Prince of Misery)*, he tried in 1883–85 to paint a picture of the times and the manners in the way Sue did in his *Mystères* and Dumas in *Le Comte de Monte-Cristo*. In fact, the well-read author was obviously influenced by both these men. In spite of some clichés and generalizations, May offered excellent descriptions of the Erzgebirge and the poverty and misery of the workers in cottage industries there. As the son of a weaver he could speak from personal experience. The plot of the novel includes crimes of many kinds: murder, fraud, legacy hunting, breach of promise, smuggling, child substitution, robbery, break-ins, white-slave trade, commission of a sane person to an asylum, usury, the reception of stolen goods: in fact, the lot! However, the detective from the big city, who himself has been the victim of a crime, disentangles the twisted web of evil and sees to it that the criminals all get their just deserts. Fate is on the side of justice, ready to intervene at precisely the right moment.

82

"The doctor took the lamp and shone it on what appeared *(Ferryman on the Canadian River)* by B. Möllhausen.
to be a body." Illustration from *Der Fährmann am Kanadian*

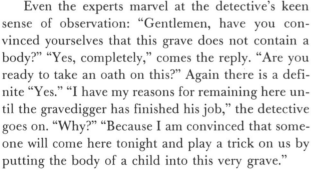

"The dog stood over him, its eyes gleaming." Illustration from *Der Fürst des Elends (The Prince of Misery)* by Karl May.

"There was a crash at the window." From the same novel.

Even the experts marvel at the detective's keen sense of observation: "Gentlemen, have you convinced yourselves that this grave does not contain a body?" "Yes, completely," comes the reply. "Are you ready to take an oath on this?" Again there is a definite "Yes." "I have my reasons for remaining here until the gravedigger has finished his job," the detective goes on. "Why?" "Because I am convinced that someone will come here tonight and play a trick on us by putting the body of a child into this very grave."

Further on in the investigation the detective proves his skill once again. Walking through the woods, he stops suddenly, startled. "What's that? There is somebody lying there." "Where?" asks the forester who is with him, trying to catch up. "Stop. Don't move!" "Why?" "There is a pistol beside him. This is murder or suicide. He is bleeding. We must not lose sight of the evidence. I can see that two men have been standing on this spot."

May's unsophisticated heroes were perhaps more globe-trotters than real investigators. Yet in his writing May relied to a great extent on various aspects of crime. *Durch die Wüste (Across the Desert)*, for example, provided the reader in 1883 with an adventurous pursuit of criminals through Africa, the Middle East, and the Balkans, a chase that deals with not one but several evildoers. In the course of the tale they are caught and punished. There is a murderer, a kidnapper, a bandit, a "false" saint, a villainous charcoal burner, and of course the head of the whole gang.

In his work May kept combining strange overseas adventures and crime in the vastness of deserts, on bare mountains, in large forests, all places of difficult access, with a homely background of towns, villages, and old country houses. He also used subterranean vaults, caves, even deserted mines. In one very exotic tale, a crafty Dr. Hilaro lures his victims into the cellars of a remote monastery in Mexico.

May's imagination and presentation of events were tailored to perfection to the taste of his public. With him the hunt for the criminal was in itself the main element of tension, although many other strands were woven into his plots. The burning questions were not: Who has done it?; How was the crime committed?; or even What was the motive? The important thing was: What effect did the deed have on the evildoer?; Did it change his attitude? It became a question concerning the criminal's personality and his environment. It is difficult to know how much the consideration of these factors reduced the reader's entertainment pleasure and how much that consideration was counterbalanced by the intellectual stimulation provided by the book. In the end it is the reader who makes the choice, with no definite division between being entertained and being stimulated into thinking.

The Realistic Crime Story

Where to? They say his body lies in the Oder.
And there we have to put him ... the sooner, the better. Today.
But I wish that bit of work was over and done with.

—Theodor Fontane

Crime was chosen by socially aware writers as a subject well suited to expose moral depravity that resulted from misery and ignorance. On the other hand offenses committed against human beings—at worst, complete physical destruction—were a sign of man's inhumanity to man. A number of writers were ready to fight such inhumanity in their writings. They laid stress on the essence of man himself in their work, rather than on exciting and mysterious plot and story elements. In Schiller's *Verbrecher aus verlorener Ehre (Lost Honor Makes a Criminal)* for example, the main theme is the motivation for the criminal deed that exposes the criminal's true character. Soon the effect of the crime on the perpetrator and on his surroundings became steadily more important in realistic writing. Thereafter nothing could ever be the same again. The effects of evil deeds became apparent everywhere, and the evildoer himself changed.

The German writer Annette von Droste-Hülshoff used this new idea as the theme of her novella *Die Judenbuche (The Jew's Beech)* in 1842. Friedrich Mergel, rightly suspected of having murdered the Jew Aaron, is not recognized by anybody when, after several years' absence, he returns to his native village. He is mistakenly assumed to be a relative of Aaron, Johannes Niemand. Friedrich has become retiring, sickly, and as unremarkable as Johannes Niemand (John Nobody). He completely lacks his former self-assurance and strength. Only at his death, when he is found hanging from a beech tree, is his true self revealed: he is the murderer. His conscience, fear, a curse, or perhaps just fate, has drawn him back to the scene of his crime. Words in Hebrew are carved on the trunk of the tree: "When you get to this spot, you will suffer the very fate you dealt me." The murderer, however, is unmasked only after he has inflicted punishment on himself. Neither he nor the villagers are able to read the Hebrew words, yet he and they all harbor a deep superstitious fear of the murder tree. The discovery of the murderer's body at the scene of the crime he committed makes the novella's ending seem like an Act of God.

The folk tradition was an ever-attractive theme to this authoress; she deliberately set the story in her native Westphalia where she knew ancient beliefs and traditions lingered from the past. As the daughter of an ancient Westphalian family, she knew and loved the people and their traditions, but she was also aware that some of her readers were more interested in the pursuit of crime than in the customs and manners of local countryfolk. That is possibly why she included a passage about a forester slain at the hands of wood thieves, an incident important to the novella's structure, because during it Friedrich is brought for the first time close to murder. She does not follow up the episode but tells her readers that the case has never been solved in spite of the interrogations of several suspected persons. As a result of

Title page for *Die Judenbuche (The Jew's Beech)* by Annette von Droste-Hülshoff. By A. Kubin.

the attention the incident drew to the scene of the crime, the wood thieves take fright and disappear. Though many a man stealing wood is caught later, there is never proof of any connection to the notorious gang suspected of having murdered the forester. Twenty years later an axe lies as a useless corpus delicti in the court archives.

In spite of the novella's somber tone, the jurisdiction wielded by the lord of the manor and the police, and the sense of justice held by the villagers, are both handled with humor. The peasants are bold enough to keep on cutting wood in the forests. On bright moonlit nights thirty or forty carts with twice as many men of all ages, from half-grown boys to the seventy-year-old village elder, ride out to the woods. The experienced elder in charge of the expedition conducts it as proudly as he takes his seat on the bench of the local court room. During his investigation the lord of the manor finds that everyone in the village knows all about the very things that are meant to be secret.

The father of Theodor Fontane, a German poet, essayist, and novelist, owned a chemist's shop in a small village in the Oderbruch, east of Berlin. In 1843, Theodor worked in his father's shop for several months. A year earlier a crime had been discovered in the village: in the garden of an inn workmen digging an excavation found a human skeleton. The inn-

keeper and his wife, a couple named Titting, fell under suspicion. Some years before, a commercial traveler had disappeared after spending the night at the inn. Rumor had it that the man was murdered and the carriage driven into the river; the innkeeper and his wife had been seen apparently removing traces of blood from the inn. Nothing definite ever came to light, and when the innkeeper got into financial difficulties, he sold the property and the two went to live in town, where he worked as a coachman.

The discovery of the skeleton, the rumors, and the inconclusive investigation were later used by Fontane as the basis of his crime novella *Unterm Birnbaum (Under the Pear Tree)* published in 1885 as a serial in the *Gartenlaube* and as a book the same year. In his fictional version Fontane based his plot on the villagers' suspicions. The innkeeper, Abel Hradschek, is guilty. His poverty causes him to murder for gain, with his wife as accomplice. He kills the traveler, robs him, and then drives his carriage down a slope into the river. The man's cap is found hanging in the bushes by the water's edge, but the man himself has disappeared, causing the court at Küstrin nearby to start an investigation.

Fontane paints an excellent picture of the period: the investigating counsel appears more interested in his mid-morning snack and glass of porter's beer than in his official business. His friend, the village pastor, is under an obligation to the suspect couple; he vouches for their impeccable character. After all, they have embraced the protestant faith some years earlier, and Frau Hradschek has even embroidered a skullcap for him! The author took the

"J'Accuse" ("I accuse") was the beginning of the open letter that Emile Zola published in the magazine *L'Aurore*. It was directed against a miscarriage of justice in the trial of Dreyfus.

Still from the film *Unterm Birnbaum (Under the Pear Tree)*, with Erik S. Klein as the innkeeper Hradschek.

Author's working sketch for *Unterm Birnbaum.* The details of the plot were so important to Theodor Fontane that he wished to have the place of the action in front of him while writing.

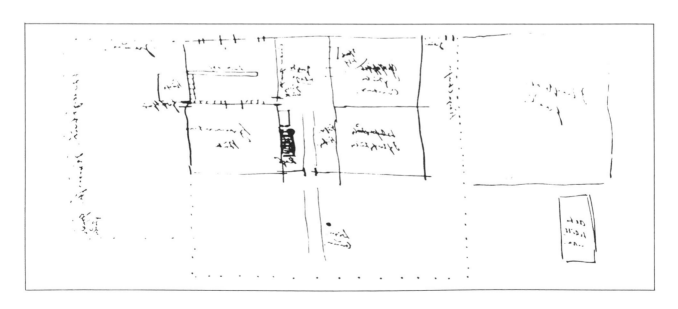

background details of his tale very seriously, to the extent that he actually made a sketch of the murder scene. While working on his manuscript he drew pictures of the inn, with the taproom, shop, kitchen, offices, stairs, bedrooms, and also the garden with its fence to the neighboring property—and, of course, the pear tree. When Hradschek is taken into custody at the suggestion of a villager, the authorities begin digging under the tree and there they find the body. The gravedigger observes: "Well, the one who lies here has been here a long time, maybe these twenty years." Over a meal the officials discuss the matter and seem about to exonerate the accused. Mother Jeschke, a witchlike personage, remains unconvinced of their innocence and uses her influence on the superstitious villagers to turn them against the murderer. Hradschek tries to get rid of the incriminating body again but is killed by a landslide the very moment he is disposing of the evidence of his crime, spade in hand. The ending is an Act of God, and it is fate, not Prussian justice, that punishes the criminal.

In an article on the occasion of Fontane's seventieth birthday the critic Paul Schlenther described this particular work as a reflection on the social evils of the period, with the robbery with violence a significant symptom.

In 1890 another German writer, Wilhelm Raabe, published in the *Deutsche Roman-Zeitung* a novel titled *Stopfkuchen*, subtitled *A Story of Murder and of the Sea*. In fact this is essentially an idyllic smalltown tale rather than a murder mystery. Heinrich Schaumann, nicknamed Stopfkuchen, a placid, thick-set little man, marries into the family of a peasant named Quakatz, who is suspected of the murder of a local cattle dealer. Stopfkuchen manages to quash this suspicion by discovering that the real murderer was the country postman. Raabe proved that just as many exciting things can happen in small "romantic" towns as in strange and exotic places.

The French crime novella thrived in a distinctly literary tradition, beginning with the prison tales of the eighteenth century and continuing to the description of the thick walls of the Château d'If in *Le Comte de Monte-Cristo* and the writings of Emile Zola and Guy de Maupassant. These men were passionately concerned with the arbitrariness and irresponsibility of the established law, with its inhumanity and two-faced morality, rather than with the simple telling of a tale. This sociological trend reached its climax in

1898 with Zola's "J'Accuse" in which, with great courage, he took up the case of the innocently convicted Captain Dreyfus. He expressed the righteous indignation of many and focused wide attention to the injustice done, eventually helping Dreyfus obtain a retrial.

Marie-Henri Beyle, who wrote under the pen name of Stendhal, adhered closely to the Pitaval format in his novella *Les Cenci*, written in 1837, in which he explored the historical sources of Shelley's tragedy of the same name. He relates the macabre legal proceedings instigated by Pope Clement VIII during the Renaissance in 1599. Count Francesco Cenci, the head of one of the richest and noblest families in Rome, after a life of wickedness and debauchery, conceives an implacable hatred for his own children. Towards one daughter, Beatrice, this animosity takes on the perverse form of an incestuous passion. After vain attempts to escape from his mad attachment, the members of his family—stepmother, daughter, and two sons—decide to take the law into their own hands. They hire assassins to murder him. Upon his death, strange rumors begin to surface, and eventually the four of them are arrested. They are tortured until they reveal the truth. They are sentenced to death, in spite of the general compassion aroused by the sad tale of the count's madness. In 1599, by direct order of the Pope, Beatrice, her stepmother, and one of her brothers are executed. As much as Stendhal was interested in characters and passions, his lengthy introduction confirms that he was equally concerned with law and justice. He focuses the reader's attention principally on Beatrice, showing her as an individual harassed not only by her father but also by the curia and by Roman justice itself.

Social problems resulting in the commission of crimes play a major part in the plots of Russian crime novellas, which often expand into full-length novels. Nikolai S. Leskov's novella *Lady Macbeth of Mtsensk District* (1865) is the story of Katerina Lvovna Ismailova, later used by the composer Dimitri Shostakovich as the basis of the libretto for his opera of the same name. It does not deal with larger than life Renaissance figures, but with the men in the street; peasants, artisans, millers, and shopkeepers. Katerina Ismailova, through her passionate love for a servant Sergeevich—an emotion that has lifted her out of the drabness of her daily life—murders her father-in-law, her husband, and her nephew to attain her objective. She becomes, ironically, the victim of her seducer. Love and jealousy are so strong in her that, after being sentenced for her crimes, she drowns herself, not with her lover, but with his new mistress. Her actions are clearly presented to the reader: she kills her father-in-law with a dish of poisonous mushrooms; she strangles and buries her husband in the cellar; she suffocates her nephew in bed. It is eventually the suspicion of the villagers that brings the crimes to light. Only then do the police confront her and obtain a confession.

In 1884–85 Anton Chekhov published *A Hunting Tragedy* as a serial in a Moscow newspaper, a form of publishing that many novelists then found attractive. Interested in Gaboriau's books and also in the work of the Russian writer, Aleksandr Andreevich Shkliarevski, Chekhov had written *The Old Court* and *Murder without Evidence*, which reached a wide public in the 1870s and made the authorities take note of his work. Some even used his help in their investigations.

In *A Hunting Tragedy*, Kamyshev, an examining judge, called by his friends "dear Lecoq," narrates the tale in the first person. Olga, a silly and egotistical woman, leaves her husband on her wedding day to bestow her favors on other and wealthier gentlemen. A short time afterwards, during a hunting expedition, she is found shot dead in the woods. Suspicion turns on three men: her husband, the estate manager, and a farm servant. In prison, awaiting trial, the servant is murdered and the manager convicted and sent to exile in Siberia. As the reader may guess, the true culprit is the judge, the person telling the story. This element of surprise was to be used lat-er by Freeman Wills Crofts, Agatha Christie, and others.

In *The Swedish Match* Chekhov parodies the ever-increasing importance given to circumstantial evidence in criminology and in crime writing. He shows how each piece of evidence can be given either an incriminating or a harmless interpretation, almost at will. In this story an estate manager and an amateur detective together consider several pieces of physical evidence that point to a retired army officer's murder—a Swedish match, a rumpled bed, empty bottles in a bedroom, and trails of blood in the shrubbery. Guards are mounted over the scene, a police officer calls a doctor and a magistrate, and all try to find the body. Then, lo and behold, the man appears alive and well, carousing in an old bathhouse with none other than the police commissioner's wife!

Another such parody is Oscar Wilde's *Lord Arthur Savile's Crime* (1891). A palmist has prophesied that Lord Arthur will commit murder. Obsessed with the burden of this prophecy he tries several times to commit the act, but each time fails as his efforts miscarry. It is only when in a rage he throws the palmist into the river and watches his large hat being borne away on the tide that he is able to find peace and happiness once more.

Both these parodies resulted from the increasing popularity of crime fiction and the flood of inferior offerings that accompanied it. Although the Wilde story is an attack more on the foppishness of the English aristocracy than on the genre itself, it does tilt at the craft, and perhaps targets the most popular writer at the time, Sir Arthur Conan Doyle, in this vein.

Conan Doyle's Detective Story

*My name is Sherlock Holmes. It is my business
to know what other people don't know.*

—Arthur Conan Doyle

Conan Doyle published *A Study in Scarlet* in 1887 and from that date on, Sherlock Holmes, the master detective, "lived" at 221B Baker Street with his friend Dr. Watson. Once the reader is introduced to Holmes, the detective, the narrator takes a back seat. Who, after all, is interested in a provincial doctor—exactly what Doyle was? Born in Edinburgh, he studied medicine there before practicing in Southsea from 1882–90. It is his detective creation who steals the limelight: Holmes, with his keen sense of observation, his lean face and hooked nose, his long legs, his deerstalker hat, his magnifying glass, and his ever-present pipe. This *personality* is what caught the reader's imagination.

Doyle had read Edgar Allan Poe's tales and the novels of Collins and Gaboriau before creating his own detective whom he allows to mock the Chevalier Dupin and Monsieur Lecoq, maintaining that not one of them can match his powers of detection. "Numerous small fry" he calls them, none of whom could handle a really big affair. Holmes was largely modeled on Dr. Joseph Bell, Doyle's Professor of Surgery at Edinburgh University, who constantly surprised his students by a snap diagnosis or an unexpected conclusion based on logical "detection."

Where earlier in the nineteenth century legal men had taken to crime writing it now became the turn of medical men. In a more effective way than Poe, Doyle provided his readers with a memorable hero and popularized the crime story. He understood the rapid progress being made in the natural sciences in the nineteenth century and featured the scientific approach in his story telling. In his view, close observation to factual details was the only sound basis for arriving at sensible conclusions! This modern attitude appealed to a public longing for a change from the somewhat wearied find-de-siècle atmosphere that permeated the writing of the time. The "master" himself believed that when all other possibilities were exhausted the most *unlikely* possibility might be the explanation. At times Doyle pushed his detective close to the brink of irrational thought, only to bring him back to reason by the process of careful deduction.

> Nor were there any human footmarks.
> "Holmes," I cried, "this is impossible!"
> "Admirable!" he said. "A most illuminating remark. It is impossible as I state it, and therefore I must in some respect have stated it wrong. Yet you saw it for yourself. Can you suggest any fallacy?"
> "He could not have fractured his skull in a fall?"
> "In a morass, Watson?"
> "I am at my wits' end."

The reader was flattered that he too was required to use his intelligence. In that way he stood between Holmes and Watson and was given a definite part to

Arthur Conan Doyle.

play in the detection. As the plot progressed, he could search for the solution on his own. Naturally he was not as clever or knowledgeable as Holmes and the denouement always took him by surprise. Tension, maintained to the end, allowed the reader to remain happy in the knowledge that he was at least as intelligent as the good Dr. Watson, if not more so. In this fashion Doyle turned a mere monologue into a lively dialogue.

Although Holmes became an almost mystical figure, his author never lost sight of reality. As mentioned before, Holmes had a "real" address where a hansom cab would call at the door and take him through London's streets, generally in thick fog, barely penetrated by the pale light of the gas lamps. The two bachelors were looked after by a housekeeper who kept their house in order and received their visitors. She too became a real person, at times annoyed by the muddle in which they tended to live, or by the smoking of a faulty chimney.

Dr. Joseph Bell, professor of surgery at Edinburgh University, Conan Doyle's teacher and the model for Sherlock Holmes.

In contrast to his literary ancestors, in particular Poe's Dupin, Holmes did not limit his detective work to the armchair variety. It was full of action as he roamed through London, going into pubs, disguising himself at times like Vidocq, and spending whole nights following up clues. He might perhaps get lost in lonely places, yet he usually managed to arrive at the scene of the crime before the police.

A Study in Scarlet was not a great success nor was his second Holmes novel, *The Sign of Four*, published in *Lippincot's Magazine* in 1890. The latter was a short work, appearing in one issue. Doyle then tended to concentrate more and more on the short story, which had always been a reliable vehicle for introducing a new subject or a fresh point of view. Edgar Allan Poe, perhaps one of its finest practitioners, had firmly established the short story early in the century. Another American, Ambrose Bierce, continued the tradition in the late nineteenth century, although without Poe's sense of wild fantasy combined with sharp logic and reason. By then the reading public had increased considerably and at the same time had changed. While a middle-class reader could take his time and comfortably digest a thick volume or the complicated plot of a serial, the common man, particularly the industrial worker, newly come to reading, had less leisure and less money to buy thick books. It was he who welcomed the short story or novella. He could read it in two or three nights. Detailed descriptions of scenery, or characters, and of their emotions were no longer wanted or were used only when absolutely essential to the plot. Writing had to lift the reader for a moment out of the daily monotony of life. In fiction there were, to be sure, exotic countries, puzzles to solve, and daring adventures—all these were acceptable fare—but at the same time the average reader wanted to be on familiar ground where he could feel at home.

The popularity of crime writing, as indeed the popularity of science fiction, which saw its beginning at this time in the work of Jules Verne (and was tackled by Doyle himself in *The Lost World* in 1912) was not restricted to any one stratum of society: industrial workers, cooks, housewives, scientists, even bishops, enjoyed whodunits. Certainly this type of work provided problems for the intellect, though these were often hidden beneath seemingly more dramatic matters. Holmes and Watson made friends with many and varied readers and gained admirers all over the world.

Looking at this literary tradition objectively, one notes that the role of the police and the men of Scotland Yard was going through a sea change. Their investigations, which had formerly solved all fictional crimes, often appeared less successful than those of Holmes and Watson. This attitude differed from that of Dickens and Collins; perhaps the slight hostility noticeable might well have been due to the poor performance of the law in the case of Jack the Ripper, one that was never solved.

From 1890 onwards the newly founded *Strand Magazine*, rapidly growing in popularity, published a dozen detective stories one after the other under the title of *The Adventures of Sherlock Holmes*. This collection soon appeared in book form. Through them Conan Doyle achieved sudden fame, a fame for which perhaps he had not even wished. His real literary ambition was to become a writer of historical novels. Again and again he tried them, and even left some attempts unfinished at his death. His mother, however, encouraged her son to stick to what he could do best—namely the Sherlock Holmes stories—and their financial success certainly was an inducement to the smalltown doctor in need of money. At first he only received thirty-five pounds for a story, but later he got a thousand pounds for a dozen Holmes adventures.

Enthusiastically the public joined the master detective on his nightly expeditions, investigating the dark mysteries he had been hired to solve. Book in hand, the reader vividly experienced all these adventures in the comfort of his armchair. The point of departure was always the familiar flat in Baker Street. Whenever the famous man was sitting in front of his fire, bored or perhaps even a little depressed, some new client would arrive, agitated, maybe even desperate, clothes in disarray. Once calmed, the new arrival would tell of mysterious and frightening happenings and in a nonchalant manner Holmes would take on the investigation. This nonchalance became his hallmark and he would, for example, casually remark that his last client had been a Scandinavian king or that quite recently he had tried to be of service to the Pope. Of one thing the reader could be sure: a cab would arrive in time to take the detective and his faithful companion, Watson, through the streets of London, with the journey ending at an empty house or perhaps at Waterloo Station. Only then did the real adventure begin, far away from the Baker Street flat with its comforting atmosphere of smoke from the master's pipe.

The reader familiar with tough modern crime fiction may marvel at the relatively innocent happenings of the Sherlock Holmes tales. There is fraud, theft, blackmail, desire for revenge, unexplained epidemics, manipulation of horses, cheating at cards, and so on, but murder takes a back seat. Readers were full of admiration for their hero who, though not a legal man, had only one ambition—to see justice done. As an author, however, Doyle did privately harbor murderous thoughts. He felt that over the years the person of Holmes had kept him from achieving his true aim to become a successful writer of historical novels. There was only one thing to do: kill off his creation. He started out by getting rid of Watson by marrying him off. When Doyle found that his stories still needed a narrator, he persuaded Mrs. Watson to allow her husband to join once again in his friend's adventures, now well wrapped naturally in a nice woollen scarf.

Then in 1893, in "The Final Problem," Sherlock Holmes and his most dangerous opponent, Professor Moriarty, fell into the gorge at Reichenbach Falls in Switzerland, engaged in a death struggle. All that remained of the famous detective was an alpenstock and an obituary written by an afflicted Watson. But Doyle had made one grave mistake; he had sinned against the code of the detective story by committing violence against his hero. Readers resented losing their knight in shining armor, the dragon slayer of the nineteenth century, the fighter against evil and injustice. They mourned the death of their idol. In the meantime, as writers of crime stories multiplied, Fergus W. Hume (pseudonym of Ferguson Wright Hume) in *The Mystery of the Hansom Cab* (1886) set his plot against the background of Holmes's London, but a hansom cab, without Holmes in it, held little attraction. The public wanted Holmes back.

In real life there existed a master detective, one Allan Pinkerton, born in Glasgow and emigrated to Chicago in 1842. There he organized a famous detective agency that developed eventually into an almost

The first meeting of Sherlock Holmes and Dr. Watson in the laboratory. From a book illustration.

private army of mercenaries. Their most famous exploit was the putting down of the "Molly Maguires," an Irish secret society that had terrorized the coal regions of Pennsylvania. The name was adopted from another Irish gang that had committed many serious crimes while its members were disguised as women.

Pinkerton's National Detective Agency, to give it its full title, advertised the fact that "they never sleep," with a wide-open eye as its trademark. Pinkerton was a careful observer, always alert, searching out the facts methodically and carefully planning each step in an investigation. At the beginning of his career he succeeded in discovering a burnt-out campfire that led on to the capture of an infamous gang. The poor state of the police in America at the time played a major part in the development of the Pinkerton's Agency. Many policemen were inefficient and others corrupt. Attacks on trains and stagecoaches had increased to an alarming degree, and guns were used not only in the unsettled West but in city streets where bands of gangsters terrorized whole districts. Even the system of coroners, imported from England, had fallen into disrepute. For practical reasons a local undertaker was often made coroner, and might find himself chairman at an inquest connected say with a sudden, possibly suspicious, death, for which he had no special training. In order not to jeopardize his own livelihood or incur the anger of the deceased's relatives, he might sense it wise to leave well alone and to forgo intense investigation. It was not surprising then that people soon came to look for protection outside officialdom. By the second half of the century Allan Pinkerton had been able to turn his smallish business into a flourishing family firm. President Lincoln was saved by him from an attempt on his life, with the result that he became extremely popular, almost in fact a national hero. In the eighteen volumes of his memoirs Pinkerton set down his most important and interesting cases. He was an excellent promoter, giving his publications arresting titles like *The Expressman and the Detective* (1874) and *The Bank Robbers and the Detective* (1883), with the detective the chief actor in each piece. The books may have been written by Pinkerton as head of the firm, or they may have been ghost-written, since he had few literary ambitions.

One could say the same for the reporters who recorded sensational court proceedings and of the writers of the later "dime novels," cheap paperbacks that appealed to a wide reading public. In 1886 John Russell Coryell introduced into these slim booklets a detective, Nick Carter, in *The Old Detective's Pupil*. While this tale had a certain claim to be literature there followed many others, by a variety of authors, that were unashamedly hack work. In them a super-detective was chased through endless pages from adventure to adventure. Each time he would fall into some trap from which he barely escaped but would subsequently track the criminals down successfully, using false beards, wigs, and other tools of the detective trade. He became an idol, "a regular killer." Though it existed on the fringes of literature, the dime novel enjoyed enormous popularity and was translated into other languages and frequently imitated.

An American writer of repute, Mark Twain, the pen name for Samuel Langhorne Clemens, took up the subject of crime in his novels *Tom Sawyer* (1876) and *Huckleberry Finn* (1884). *Tom Sawyer, Detective*, a novella published in 1896, is possibly the first detective story written for children. In it Tom appears for the defense in a murder case against Tom's Uncle Silas, proves his innocence, exposes the real murderer, and at the same time unmasks false witnesses and traces two stolen diamonds. Tom and his devoted helpmeet, Huck Finn, earn much praise although Tom modestly explains to a surprised judge and public in court that all he has done is to look at the facts and draw his own conclusions. It is merely a piece of detective work in which he has carefully watched the unconscious gestures the murderer makes at the trial, thus revealing his true identity rather than the one he has assumed.

Twain later turned to the subject of fingerprints at a time when the use of such evidence was not yet officially established. Only in 1901 did Scotland Yard start a special department of dactyloscopy and abandon the Bertillon system used worldwide at that time to identify criminals by complicated body measurements. By then Twain had used the subject of fingerprints twice, in *Life on the Mississippi* (1883) and *The Tragedy of Pudd'nhead Wilson* (1894). In 1892 Sir Francis Galton had published *Finger Prints*, the first book on the subject. Twain got a copy from his London publisher. He later said that Galton changed the whole plot of *Pudd'nhead Wilson*, in which he had planned to use footprints as a means of nailing the murderer. Twain's story goes as follows:

A lawyer, David "Pudd'nhead" Wilson, settles in an idyllic small town on the Mississippi, collecting fingerprints as a hobby. A baby who is only one-thirty-second black is maliciously substituted for a white baby, the only son in the town's best family. When eventually the ne'er-do-well (surrogate) heir kills his uncle and guardian, an innocent suspect is tried, with Wilson appearing for the defense. He not only unmasks the real murderer, but also helps the true heir to obtain his birthright—all through the proof in the fingerprint file he has kept since coming to the town. The novel's conclusion is laden with typical Twain irony. The true heir, brought up servile and cringing, is illiterate as well, and unable to take his proper place in society; he sinks back into slavery with the people he knows best. Besides, the estate has been so badly managed it is in debt to creditors. The governor of the state grants the murderer a pardon,

New Scotland Yard, London, finished in 1892.

and sells him as a slave to help pay off the estate's debts—proving that a working slave is worth more to society than an imprisoned murderer! Even though critical undertones pervade Twain's writing, he is first and foremost a humorist, and his "crime" stories often show signs of the near-grotesque.

Anna Katharine Green, daughter of a famous American defense lawyer, was a different kind of writer. She had read Gaboriau's novels and decided to write one herself, in his style. The title, *The Leavenworth Case*, with the subtitle *A Lawyer's Story*, shows that in 1878 something new was happening. The writer had succeeded in separating the case itself from the family story involved, and in that way created a pure detective story.

A rich bachelor is found murdered in his library—a very popular location in crime fiction—and an investigation is set in motion. After long interrogations concerning suspicious facts, with one man's statement balanced against another's, the city detec-

Murder in the cemetery, from Mark Twain's *Tom Sawyer*.

tive, Ebenezer Gryce, appears. A sketch of the scene of the murder is included in the text. As the investigation goes on, suspicion falls on the victim's nieces, but in the end it is revealed that the crime has been committed by the victim's secretary, a figure to become familiar in time as a convenient fictional killer. With the interrogation of the victim's servants and relatives the household *does* form a background to the crime, but the progression of the story line differs greatly from that of the traditional family story. Mrs. Green's American upbringing precluded her from using the typically aristocratic characters so important in Gaboriau's writing.

With her first novel a success, Mrs. Green continued to write and published another forty. As a novelty she introduced a woman detective, Violet Strange, but she was not well received. Another character, Miss Amelia Butterworth, an old maid of good family and uncertain age, proved much more likable. She is an ardent investigator with a solid knowledge of the trivia of everyday life. She knows about hats and hat pins, keeps an eye on strange visitors, and her thoughts to herself. Because she verges on the comic, Amelia is not the stuff real heroines are made of.

No detective in the novels of the times was a true match for the great Sherlock Holmes—drowned, alas, at Reichenbach Falls. Readers demanded his return. Doyle had to give in. In 1902 Holmes appeared again in a sensational case—*The Hound of the Baskervilles*—related by Watson in the role of executor. Doyle had heard the old legend of a ghost hound from a friend, and decided to turn it into a detective story. In the novel the tension is maintained by interrogation, quick question and answers, and a series of exciting adventures. Even with all the success Sherlock Holmes had brought him, Doyle never forgot the primary rule of writing—"Tell a good story." Here he did so handsomely.

The possible existence of a "ghost" hound presents a challenge to the worldly, rational detective. Quite simply he *has* to take on the case in which gigantic footprints have been found next to a baronet's dead body. Given the scope of a full-length novel, Doyle was able to contrive any number of false trails, something impossible to do in the short story.

Dr. Watson sets off with a young heir, Sir Henry Baskerville, to start the investigations at Baskerville Hall in Devonshire, while Holmes supposedly stays

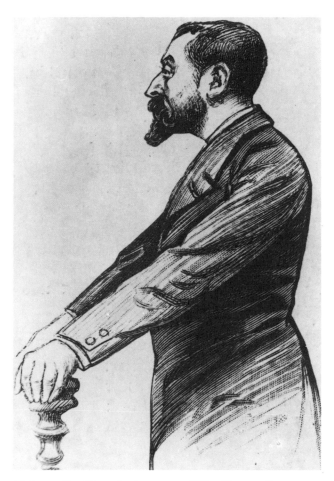

Alphonse Bertillon, the inventor of "Bertillonage," a system of identification founded on body measurements. Developed at the Paris Sûreté, it was used in many countries before the development of fingerprinting.

on in Baker Street to receive his friend's report. The Hall is a gloomy place, its whole front draped in ivy with only a patch clipped bare to reveal a window or a crest of arms. Faint lights shine from one or two windows; thin smoke rises from a high chimney. The surrounding moors are gloomy and dangerous: one step off the path and a man or beast can disappear forever. Against this threatening background the baying of a hound is heard. On the moor appear both an escaped convict and, later, a mysterious stranger. And so the stage is set.

The stranger however turns out to be none other than the master detective himself, who is secretly working in the neighborhood. In a highly dramatic scene, and to the astonishment of Watson and the reader alike, he reveals the identity of the baronet's

Sherlock Holmes's study at 221B Baker Street.

murderer. Holding up a candle to the portrait of a Baskerville ancestor said to have lived under a curse, he covers the wide-brimmed hat and the curls, showing a startling likeness to the killer. The criminal is an evil descendant of the man in the portrait, determined to kill all who stand between him and the inheritance. This discovery is made well before the final chapter; the reader then delightedly joins in the hunt for the villain and for the ghost hound that has been his accomplice. In a last-minute attack, the hound is shot while the murderer perishes trying to escape across the moors.

This novel was reprinted over and over again and was several times made into films. Without doubt it is the best of Doyle's four detective novels, skillfully combining rational and emotional elements. The reader finds himself involved from the very beginning in the strange question of the ownership of the

walking stick left behind at Baker Street; he feels a chill tingle in the spine when the baying of the hound echoes across the dark moorlands. One small offense against fair play occurs when Doyle fails to tell the reader that Holmes has in fact observed that the warning letter is scented with a certain perfume. But it is only a minor defect in a superior work.

In 1914 Doyle wrote his fourth Sherlock Holmes novel. It was published first in *The Strand Magazine*, consisting of two novellas joined together. The structure of the novel is reminiscent of Gaboriau's *L'Affaire Lerouge*, with one concerning present events, and the other past occurrences that have led to the present complication. One of the stories tells about a murder in a country house, and the other follows the crimes of a gang in industrial America. Inspiration for the latter may possibly have come from a detective Doyle met on a journey to the United States. Or he may have got the idea from *The Molly Maguires and the Detective*, a book published by Allan Pinkerton in 1877. Pinkerton's detectives in real life were often used as strikebreakers, and the author's personal biases were bound to color his tale. In the trade unions criminals were always found and rooted out, as in Pinkerton's story about the Molly Maguires.

The *Casebook of Sherlock Holmes* appeared in 1927. In it the master detective, as always with magnifying glass in hand, carried out his investigations in the role of physicist, chemist, and ballistics expert—in fact whatever was required. This was a time when Scotland Yard had begun to call in experts from learned university faculties to help with investigations. No reader's attention could be maintained by piles of experts' certificates alone, nor could adventures be confined to the four walls of a laboratory or in sometimes contradictory and carefully expressed professional opinions. Instead the lucid and precise statements of Holmes created a vivid atmosphere of mystery and intrigue. Doyle saw to it, however, that Holmes never appeared before a court: his statements are made to clients and friends, or perhaps a puzzled police officer.

The success of the Holmes stories is reflected in the many translations and imitations that were made, some pretty poor and none really fitting into the cate-

Stills from *The Hound of the Baskervilles*.

At the edge of the moor.

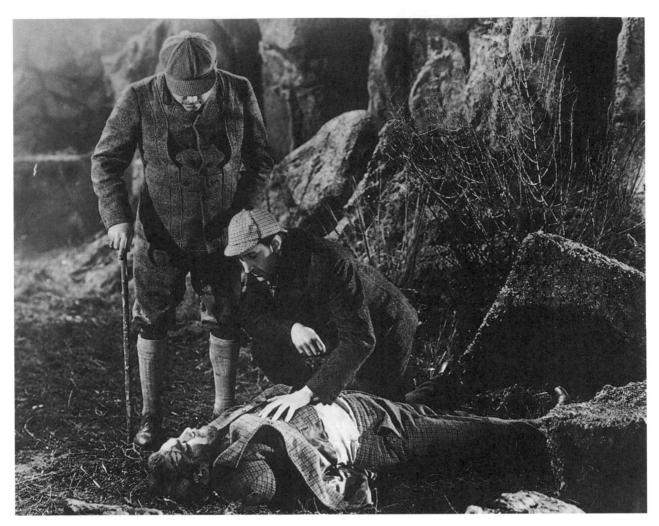

Nigel Bruce as Dr. Watson and Basil Rathbone as Sherlock Holmes stumble across a murder victim on Grimpen Moor. Can it be the body of Sir Henry Baskerville?

gory of literature. At the coronation of Edward VII, Conan Doyle was knighted. The honor was bestowed on him for a nonfiction book he wrote on the Boer War. Many maintained that it was Sherlock Holmes who really earned it for him. It was perhaps a lucky coincidence that *The Hound of the Baskervilles* appeared at that time, fascinating the public then as it does to this very day. Among the many congratulations Doyle received for this honor was one for Sherlock Holmes!

In due course Britain and the English-speaking countries of the world were to experience the greatest boom in crime fiction in history. Yet on the continent, in Germany for example, critics paid little or no attention to the genre, except to attack the earlier

Gothic novel and to complain that realism was being carried too far in descriptions of crime and criminals. Yet an interested segment of the reading public was to grow rapidly, ranging through all strata of society. Reading had established itself as a popular pastime with books and magazines providing entertainment, information, and instruction.

After the Pitaval case history in the seventeenth century, and the crime novella in the eighteenth, such writing was to inject a new realism into literature. The growth of science and scientific thought in general of course played an important part in this development. It widened the scope of the content, increased the number of publications and the size of the editions, and provided impetus to continue the growth of crime fiction through the early years of the twentieth century.

Some traditional features remained. The emotional element was, and still is, an important factor in

Holmes unmasks the murderer, pointing to a family portrait to identify him.

all writing. Some authors continue to use Sue's *Mystères* as their model, ignoring clues and concentrating on action; but to write in the style of the Holmes stories was to prove more profitable. Sherlock Holmes seemed immortal. On January 8, 1954, the BBC broadcast a special program on the master's hundredth birthday. All the guests wished him health and prosperity. It appeared that, now retired, the old gentleman was enjoying a quiet contented life at his country house in Sussex.

THE TWENTIETH CENTURY

*There is an intellectual pleasure in solving the mystery a crime novel poses
to the detective and the reader alike.*

—Bertolt Brecht

By the beginning of the twentieth century the crime novel had become an established favorite with the reading public. Critical attention was paid to it, even prompting, among others, the German writer Bertolt Brecht to write an essay extolling its virtues.

In fact, the crime story ideally met one of man's needs in a scientific age. It encouraged empirical observation and the formation of conclusions that required decisions and judgments. Over and above this intellectual exercise, it provided suspense and a sense of adventure that made the reader escape for a while the drabness of everyday life and its anxieties. Up to the time of World War I, light reading followed in general nineteenth-century traditions. The war proved a watershed, with a great number of books

published containing "war adventures." With the advent of two new media—radio and film—the novel also changed. However, these media did not supplant the printed word, but rather made crime fiction even more popular. Film relied heavily on crime to supply exciting raw material. The opportunity to have a novel turned into a film influenced many authors both in their choice of subject and in their treatment of it. Many enjoyed instant success.

Radio, film, and later television all became increasingly more closely associated with the genre of crime literature. Wherever crime fiction found a place in literary tradition, an eager public demanded new titles all the time, much of the work being directly influenced by Conan Doyle.

The Crime Novel after the Turn of the Century

To begin with my suspicion was merely an abstract concept.

—Gaston Leroux

In France Gaston Leroux was working in the tradition of Gaboriau. With his first and most interesting work in 1908, *Le Mystère de la Chambre Jaune (The Mystery of the Yellow Room)*, he consciously harked back to Poe with the old "locked room" motif. In contrast to Gaboriau, Leroux did not introduce aristocratic characters; like Gaboriau nevertheless he did keep to the well-tried remote setting, in this case an ancient castle. A young detective, Rouletabille, is a reporter modeled on the author, a journalist on *Le Matin*. At night ghostly noises are heard and mysterious animals howl, while in the day a cat roams around the place. Then, out of the mysterious "yellow

room" staggers Miss Stangerson, a young American scientist, with serious head injuries inflicted by an unknown assailant or assailants. Her desperate cries are very real, not at all connected with ghosts. She uses the room, situated in an old pavilion, as her bedroom. There are no clues or explanations as to how anyone got in or out of the room, since the windows are shuttered, the door under observation, and no secret exit can be found. The local police call in help from Paris and in this way Leroux confronts his young reporter with a puzzling case and with the presence of a famous inspector from the Sûreté. Rouletabille does not even consider the possibility of ghosts or the influence of the Devil or the supernatural: he applies reason in making his deductions. Eventually, in front of the full court, the reporter-hero provides the solution to the mysterious crime. The attempted murder of Miss Stangerson took place *before* the windows were secured. The intruder is exposed as the famous Paris detective, who in fact has a criminal record. There is also a story of love and abduction. The whole plot is pretty close to a penny dreadful. Nonetheless the reader enjoys this mix and at the end the author skillfully draws attention to his next book, *Le Parfum de la Dame en Noir (The Perfume of the Lady in Black)* (1909). Novels with Rouletabille as the protagonist continued to appear up to 1916 each one with considerable success.

Leroux's *Le Fantôme de l'Opéra (The Phantom of the Opera)* (1910) is a different kind of tale. Accidents and deaths in the Paris opera house are thought to be caused by a ghost. The actors and the public live in a state of alarm and the supernatural seems to have taken charge completely with scenes set in gloomy cemeteries midst heaps of bones. Some brave men, however, decide to search out the ghost, down in the basement vaults of the opera house, where they eventually corner him. The ghost turns out to be an outcast, seeking to revenge himself on mankind in general. He understands how the mechanism of the stage works and knows intimately the labyrinth below the opera house, how to lock and unlock doors, and so on. He is not the intrinsically evil man of the traditional crime story, and at the end it is decided, instead of handing him over to the police, to leave him to die somewhere in the subterranean corridors where his body is only found years later during excavation work. The novel opens with this gruesome discovery and continues as a factual report. This old but ever new formula of mixing crime and horror again proved very successful. Nevertheless, there was no place in it for the logic and reason of the amiable Rouletabille.

This shadowy enigma, the almost supernatural element of the criminal who is never caught, whose face is not seen nor identity known, who might in fact be the most unlikely person, was to be used again and again in novels. In 1909 Marcel Allain, at first in collaboration with Pierre Souvestre, created the character of Fantômas who appeared in thirty-two novels and, together with the clever Inspector Juve became a great favorite. Pursuits, disguises, and

Cover design for Gaston Leroux's *The Phantom of the Opera*.

escapes made for exciting and turbulent action: it is in fact the raw material of films but unfortunately, despite sustained tension and an agreeable tingling in the spine, the reader is denied the scene of satisfying denouement.

The English crime novel has a firmly established tradition that is, of course, to be seen clearly in the work of Conan Doyle. Richard Marsh, one of Doyle's contemporaries, tried to introduce an element of the extrasensory, but without great success. In *The Beetle* (1897) the murder investigation concludes with an unexplained death due to "exhaustion." The author ends with a quote: "There are more things in heaven and earth, Horatio, than are dreamt in your philosophy!"

The Lodger (1913), by Marie Belloc Lowndes, was originally planned as a short story, and contains its

Children at court: "That's something I couldn't say aloud."

Tragicomic elements of crime were discovered and represented by the Berlin artist, Heinrich Zille, who combined social criticism with a sense of humor.

"What about a new murder in the papers?"

The Berlin *Stadtvogtei* (city jail) facing a boat on the river
Spree, in a setting of trees, seems almost romantic.

The Berlin crime squad is easily recognized by their melon-
shaped hats.

From a police report: "The prostitute had been
hanging for several days, cause unknown."
Text is a comment on the social evils and injuries
ot the period.

Artists who took up the subject of crime were more concerned with its inhumanly cruel aspects than its gruesome ones. Examples: pen drawing by René Beehs; woodcut by Félix Vallotton.

own fair share of horror. The cruel murders of Jack the Ripper, who was never caught, provide the subject matter. The author sets her story in late Victorian London and offers a solution to the mysterious events. A friendly, elderly man takes lodgings with a couple, the Buntings. Although he is generous with money and sits quietly for hours in the drawing room reading the Bible, Mrs. Bunting is frightened of him. He has a habit of going out for a walk around midnight and always on the nights when Jack the Ripper claims another victim.

During a visit to Madame Tussaud's made by Mrs. Bunting and her lodger, they learn by chance that the police are now on the trail of the murderer and that he is in fact the escaped inmate of an asylum. The lodger immediately disappears and is never seen again. Mrs. Bunting and the reader are in no doubt that he is in fact the Ripper himself. This knowledge, it must be said, is founded only on misgivings and conjecture, but Mrs. Belloc Lowndes manages to convey the atmosphere of menace to perfection, in a way that even made an impression on Ernest Hemingway.

E. C. Bentley tried another solution: in contrast to Sherlock Holmes, the "superdetective," he uses as his investigator a very ordinary individual who manages to be wrong not once but several times. In *Trent's Last Case* (1913) a painter, Philip Trent, agrees with a London newspaper to investigate the murder of an American financier. The murder has taken place in an English country house, with a small circle of suspects. Trent believes he has collected enough circumstantial evidence against the financier's secretary when a thought occurs to him: the victim committed suicide, but made it look like murder, since he was jealous of the secretary and wanted to incriminate him. But just as this solution comes to be accepted, Trent discovers that the victim was killed by one of his relatives in self-defense! The title of the book alludes to the poor detective, who feels defeated and never again wants to take on a case. Nevertheless the author puts him to work in later novels.

As we have seen, Anna K. Green established the detective story in America, inspired not by Poe's tales but by the novels of Gaboriau. She was followed by Mary Roberts Rinehart who, to pay off a considerable number of debts, began writing mystery books. Her first novel, *The Circular Staircase* (1908), was her greatest success. Like Anna K. Green she introduced a woman detective, Miss Letitia Carberry, aided by a nurse, Miss Hilda Adams, known as "Miss Pinkerton." As they were amateur detectives, the two ladies could never be entrusted to take charge of an investigation nor could actually be sent to the scene of a crime in later adventures. This meant that Rinehart had to have them present by chance when a murder occurred so they could be caught up in the subsequent events. Even if they were on the spot to protect the victim or to help avoid disaster, there had to be a lapse on their part at the vital moment or the murder would not take place; then there would be no crime and no plot. Thus the two young women were made to look rather silly in fact. Far from being literary heroines, they always allowed themselves to be deluded by the criminal and seemed to fall into every trap possible. In spite of all their misadventures, their often threatening position, their misfortune and fear, however, they survived, saved at the end to marry their sweethearts. The Rinehart heroines are really the descendants of the heroines of the nineteenth-century Gothic novel. As Mary Roberts Rinehart lived in the United States, she was not much influenced by World War I, and continued publishing best sellers long after she had paid off her debts.

Boredom Leads to Crime: The Gentleman Criminal

"And also," said Arsène Lupin, "I held an incredible trump card in my hands, a card fashioned by myself: everybody expected me to run away."

—Maurice Leblanc

Against the advice of his brother-in-law, Conan Doyle, who said: "You must not make a criminal a hero," Ernest William Hornung created the character of A. J. Raffles, a somewhat worthless, disreputable person. From 1899 onwards Raffles became the hero of a number of short stories and one novel, *Mr. Justice Raffles* (1909). He stands for justice from the point of view of the man in the street, fleecing upstarts and swindlers and lawbreakers the police are unable to catch. He is really a descendant of the noble robber although his life-style does not match his noble ambitions. He dresses with elegance, frequents exclusive clubs, and behaves altogether like a man of society in a somewhat fin-de-siècle manner. Bored by life, he decides the only romantic and exciting career is that of a criminal. He steals for the sheer excitement of it and in his own way clings to a principle, popular in his day: *l'art pour l'art*. In the Raffles stories the middle-class desire for security, seen by many as totally boring, is amusingly and playfully attacked.

In France Maurice Leblanc also created a Raffles-like figure, adding a touch of Parisian charm. In 1907 he established the gentleman rogue, Arsène Lupin. His aim is not just taking from the rich, he wants equally to ridicule the police. Through skillful disguise he manages to become head of the Sûreté for several years and to assist in clearing up some of the misdeeds of Arsène Lupin himself. This particular plot gambit is clearly based on the exploits of Vidocq, but is treated here in an almost farcical manner. When Leblanc makes his hero steal things from securely guarded buildings and allows him to escape from his pursuers, he uses a touch of psychology even though the disguises, tricks, and escapes through trapdoors seem a little naive and old-fashioned today. There is certainly constant action: break-ins, escapes, and for extra excitement the theft of a watch from the examining magistrate during an interrogation.

The Lone Wolf (1914), by the American writer Louis J. Vance, is in the same vein. The hero, however, is not a gentleman, just a rogue who turns to law and order and becomes the main figure in a number of novels. Although certain episodes, particularly the pursuits are exciting, they are not really convincing and *The Lone Wolf* does not compare with Raffles and Lupin.

With the feeling of security fading in Europe, the spy novel made its appearance just before World War I. There are undoubtedly certain similarities in the crime and spy novels. Both deal with crimes that many be discovered or even prevented, but the field

107

Jacket design for E. W. Hornung's *Mr. Justice Raffles.*

of action in the spy novel is more restricted even though there may be many changes of scene. The motivation for the crime of spying is clear and does not need to be discovered: the spy acts on the orders of a foreign power. He is thus not an individual evildoer but has quite special qualities. No longer is the life of an aunt in danger from someone who wants to inherit; instead the life of whole nations is now at stake. The spy novel—even more than the novel of crime—does take into account historical reality, but in spite of its use of many of the elements of the mystery novel, it is not always considered a part of the game by the purist.

The first novel of this kind is *The Riddle of the Sands* by Erskine Childers, which, as early as 1903, pointed to a possible conflict between Britain and Germany. At times the themes of crime and espio-

nage overlap, as in the novels of William Le Queux, who was a correspondent on a London newspaper.

Another and quite different development is the Western. Owen Wister's *The Virginian* (1902) was at the time of its publication a historical novel, a retrospective glance at the conquest and opening up of the American West. The writing hews close to the adventure tale with its descriptions of lonely gorges, the burning of farms, villainous deeds, cattle rustling, and pursuits across the prairies. There is usually a sheriff, standing for law and order, on the trail of the "baddies." He may carry a Colt pistol in his belt and a star of office on his chest. Spurs and boots make him look the tough guy he is meant to be, while his intellectual powers take very much second place. Nevertheless, he may be called upon in some cases to isolate and identify a thief or killer, and in this sense he becomes a true cousin to the amateur detective hero in crime fiction.

G. K. Chesterton: Practice and Theory

*The first and essential value of the detective story lies in this,
that it is the earliest and only form of popular literature in which
is expressed some sense of the poetry of modern life.*

—Gilbert Keith Chesterton

There were, quite naturally, many who opposed the growing popularity of crime fiction. In Germany Dr. Ernst Schultze attacked all cheap horror stories in *Die Schundliteratur (Trash Writing)* (1909). He maintained that such writing was responsible for a dangerous overstimulation of the reader, leading to crime and general moral decline. His wrath was directed particularly at Wanda von Brannburg, a woman detective, a big-bosomed lady with a sharp penetrating eye. Schultze was probably justified in fighting against a style of writing that was much later to be glamourized as "sex and crime." His fight was not directed against crime fiction per se; while he praised Poe and Doyle, he took a firm stand against abuses and commercialization. Voices at the time predicted the imminent eclipse of all writing on the subject of crime, although, as it happened, its Golden Age was just about to begin. Its defense, however, was taken up by many eminent writers, first and foremost G. K. Chesterton, author of the Father Brown stories. In these books the hero is a Roman Catholic priest who proves to be highly successful at solving crimes by intuitive methods. In his essay, "The Defense of Detective Stories" (1901), he claims that it is an important branch of popular writing. In contrast to the Gothic novel, which dealt in country people, Chesterton's characters were city dwellers. In an atmosphere of adventure and mystery his detective moved through London at the hour when the city's lights began to shine like the eyes of a cat in the darkness. He loved to describe the atmosphere of the city whose poetic possibilities he recognized; equally important to him was the moral of the story. He succeeded in mastering both aspects. Detectives were the agents of social justice, with the police knights in shining armor. In contrast, crime was something that disturbed world order, generating chaos, and creating criminals. To remedy this situation he created his own very special detective, not a knight in armor but a modest, benevolent priest, Father Brown, whom he

modeled on a Father O'Connor who had worked in a deprived district of London where he heard confession from many a poor wretched criminal.

The Innocence of Father Brown appeared in 1911; four further volumes were to follow. Altogether Chesterton wrote fifty Father Brown stories. Like Conan Doyle, he favored the short story, a story in which he

Gilbert Keith Chesterton.

reported a case and supplied the solution. Father Brown, wearing his wide-brimmed, dark hat, framing his head like a halo, captures the reader at once by his humanity and simplicity of heart. His intellectual powers are not immediately obvious although it soon becomes clear that Father Brown's reasoning is as good as Holmes's. In fact he was tailored to be the counterpart of the famous man. When Father Brown is asked at the end of a case how he has recognized the murderer in his cunning disguise, he says that the mere confusion over church problems gave the man away. He obviously was not what he pretended to be. It is true that in the discovery of this special crime Father Brown had professional advantages, but in most other cases his creator gave him keen powers of observation and deductive ability, the reader himself was involved, spotting important evidence. Even though reason certainly played an important part, Chesterton did not make his characters stereotypic pawns in a game of chess. Father Brown maintained that there were no labels for either good or bad social types or professions. As a member of the clergy, he was single-minded in fighting superstition, which anyhow did not appeal to his rational mind. He believed that superstition existed particularly in the countryside and so Father Brown visited remote villages and ruined manor houses in order to fight curses that had been laid on whole families. Quite often Chesterton used the properties of the horror story. He once had the murderer creep up secret staircases to the resounding chimes of an ancient clock. When he used the detective story as a vehicle for preaching, he offended against the rules of the game. This is particularly so in his late work when he dealt with scarcely credible matters that were contrary to logic. Definite rules for the detective story had not yet been established; readers were not overcritical of Father Brown's solutions.

More and more crime fiction, particularly the detective story, now began to differ from earlier work because its practitioners took into account developments in science—especially in forensic medicine. In

Germany Hans Gross had published a book for examining judges in 1893 in which he set out a great number of cases from criminal history. From this German authors learnt how to equip their criminals with technical tricks or rare poisons and provide their detectives with up-to-date methods of catching cunning evildoers. In time the scientist himself appeared as detective. Richard Austin Freeman in *The Red Thumb Mark* (1907) introduced Mr. Thorndyke, a forensic scientist and able investigator of crime, especially murder. Freeman was a medical man himself and he portrayed his detective accurately and in a professional manner. All scientific detail was not necessarily interesting to the reader. In a collection of short stories, *The Singing Bone* (1912), Freeman laid all the evidence before the reader, so that together with the detective he could come to his own conclusions and bask in his cleverness. In this collection, Freeman invented the "inverted story," which means that he exposed crime and criminal at the very beginning and supplied the necessary narrative suspense by allowing the reader to follow the detective's investigations step by step to the final moment when the culprit was caught.

Sensational cases dealt with at the Old Bailey helped popularize the scientist and the detective, and influenced all writing generally. In 1910 proceedings were started against Dr. Crippen, a London physician, who had poisoned his wife and hidden her body under the floor of the cellar of his house at 39 Hilldrop Crescent. He then fled the country for Canada on the steamer *Montrose* with his young mistress. With the help of the newly developed wireless telegraphy, Crippen was traced and arrested on his arrival in Quebec. Pathologist Bernard Spilsbury was given the task of identifying the corpse and providing proof of murder.

Now, scientists stood next in importance to the men from Scotland Yard, particularly in the sensational reports from the court, although the importance of science was less evident in the film made from the case. It was a story fit for Pitaval.

The Golden Age

Anyone who hopes that in time it may be possible to abolish war should give serious thought to the problem of satisfying harmlessly the instincts that we have inherited from long generations of savages. For my part I find a sufficient outlet in detective stories.

—Bertrand Russell

The twenties and thirties of our century were to become the Golden Age of crime fiction, particularly so in Great Britain and the United States. The period is closely linked with the names of A. Berkeley Cox, Dorothy L. Sayers, Agatha Christie, Ronald Knox, A. E. W. Mason, Joseph S. Fletcher, and Freeman Wills Crofts, while Chesterton and Richard Austin Freeman still held their keenly loyal readers. Edgar Wallace is excluded from this particular group, although he was generally accepted as a fascinating teller of tales. Not all Wallace's work, however, found equal favor, since devotees of the pure detective story did not like the author's work and some rejected him completely. Certainly, his stories are very different.

Edgar Wallace

And then she heard something drop with a heavy crash to the floor and looked. The shingle was still sliding down like sand in an hour-glass but now something big and heavy thudded to the ground. The gold, the gold: screamed Harvey.

—Edgar Wallace

Detection, the main ingredient of the true detective story, plays a minor part in Wallace's work, although it is important in the tales concerning Mr. John G. Reeder, a man who works in the office of the public prosecutor. Balancing an old-fashioned pair of steel-rimmed spectacles on his nose, he wears a bowler hat and carries a rolled umbrella. This serious, somewhat strange fellow solves the most mysterious cases by rational thinking and a certain amount of intuition. The series began with the short story titled "The Mind of Mr. J. G. Reeder" (1925). Wallace gained a large and devoted circle of readers, including King George V, for his novels that are a mixture of adventure and love story, harking back to the Victorian family novel. As noted, the detective interest is slight, and this is the more surprising at a time when purveyors of the pure, now almost classical detective story, were trying to eliminate all love interest in an effort to cut out emotion in favor of reason. Wallace's heroines, however, are nubile, harassed maidens; the detective's part is usually taken by the men from Scotland Yard. In fact, Scotland Yard played a major part in the novels, familiarizing the institution to the extent that the reader soon grew to know the men intimately as John, Jim, or Dick. In the end Wallace himself became an institution, so much that flags were flown at half-mast when the *Berengaria*, with his body on board, steamed into Southampton from the United States where he had died in Hollywood.

In the stories of Wallace, the man from the Yard reveals his identity only at the very last moment. He then perhaps wins the hand of the innocent maiden whom he has saved at the eleventh hour and—according to the rules of the family novel—she is discovered to be the heiress to a large fortune. At times this heroine is made to appear a little silly; but of course she is not Wallace's original creation, but a true descendant of the harried heroines of the Gothic novel. Of course there would have been no plot, no tension, nor sympathy had the good girl stayed sensi-

Stills from *Der Zinker (The Forger)*, *Die toten Augen von London (The Dark Eyes of London)*, and *Die Gruft mit dem Rätselschloss (The Secret House)*.

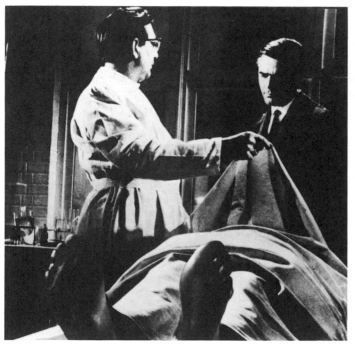

112

Edgar Wallace.

bly in her cozy home, telephone in hand, instead of rushing off to a lonely cemetery at the witching hour of midnight. A situation had to be created for near-catastrophe. The author understood to perfection how to construct his melodramatic backgrounds: ancient castles with secret passages, dismal warehouses on the Thames, dubious clubs, and disreputable hotels. Wallace fabricated a complicated and sometimes not very credible plot in order to get his characters into dangerous situations. He wrote his novels quickly, one after the other, not caring very much about language or style. With no literary ambitions, all he was really anxious to do was to earn enough money to support his expensive life-style. He exploited the market with great skill but his "made to measure" crime stories lacked the personal element of, for instance, Dorothy Sayers or Agatha Christie. Critics were quick to point out that Wallace abandoned motifs, left questions unanswered, and intro-

duced characters about whom he then forgot in the course of the action. To the uncritical reader these flaws were immaterial. One scarcely noticed the omissions in the quick-moving action that was the hallmark of Wallace's writing rather than logic and sound composition. His material suited the silent cinema to perfection. The pure detective story, built on deduction, reflection, interrogation, and analysis of witness's statements, reports and findings of experts, is not easy to convey on the screen. At the time of the silent cinema, quick action was essential—exactly what Wallace provided. Films of action continued to be in great demand, and his books were filmed again and again. An early novel, *The Four Just Men* (1905) was not a great success on publication and became nearly a disaster as a result of heavy publicity expenses. It might have turned out differently if there had been a flourishing film industry at the time of the book's appearance. As it was, he became greatly involved in the world of the cinema later and it is fitting that he should have died in Hollywood while working on a new film.

114

The Two Ladies of Crime:
Agatha Christie and Dorothy L. Sayers

One does not, you know, employ merely muscles. ...
It is enough for me to sit back in my chair and think.

—Agatha Christie

After 1920 appeared a new group of authors who saw the detective story as a puzzle, a puzzle to be solved by author, detective, and reader together. There were, of course, differences in concept and style. Freeman Wills Crofts was sober and matter-of-fact, Agatha Christie had a quiet sense of humor, while Dorothy L. Sayers was influenced by literary ambition. Yet the group had enough in common to band together in 1932 as the London Detection Club. The members of the club made their own rules and swore by Erik, a skull, to adhere to them, although in actual fact they did not treat them very seriously, frequently ignoring them. A novel that revealed such sins, for example, was *The Red House* (1922) by A. A. Millne. A contributor to *Punch* and the author of such children's classics as *When We Were Very Young* (1924) and *Winnie-the-Pooh* (1926), Milne also tried his hand at the detective novel. He related quite consciously to Conan Doyle, giving his detective a Watson and using Holmesian methods: when he once posed a question as to where to find the safest place to hide something, the answer was where nobody could see it or, better still, in a place that had been searched already. He made law and order triumph, although his plots were not always credible.

Twenty-two years later Raymond Chandler in his essay, "The Simple Art of Murder," pointed out other discrepancies in Milne's work, yet he agreed that his method of telling a tale succeeded in covering up these doubtful points at least for the reader who still thought along traditional lines.

The novels of A. E. W. Mason, too, used the sort of unlikely facts and overworked motifs that were later forbidden in the rules of the Detection Club: an unknown Indian arrow poison, a subterranean passage—without even the castle that usually goes with

Klaus Kinsky in the film *Der Zinker*, from a novel by Edgar Wallace.

it—and gangs of criminals and secret societies. In Mason's works the Yard detective was assisted by Monsieur Hanaud, a man from the Sûreté.

Freeman Wills Crofts was a railway engineer until he wrote his first novel, *The Cask* (1920), during a lengthy illness. It was an immediate success and Crofts turned to full-time writing, using his previous professional experience to create complicated alibis with the help of railway timetables and his detailed knowledge of the movements of trains. One of the alibis, for example, cracked by his slow and methodical Inspector Joseph French, was based on the fact that the murderer had secretly installed an outboard motor to his row boat, thereby increasing its speed. In *Death on the Way* (U.S.: *Double Death*) (1932) the reader follows a young engineer during a working day. He is with him on his way to work, at the building site of a new railway line, in the office, and on tours of inspection. Only once, in the evening, does he lose sight of the man—and of course that is the very moment when he murders a colleague who suspects him of embezzling money! The engineer, to build his alibi, is able to manipulate the times of the trains carrying material to the building site; he does this so cleverly that nobody, including the reader, spots the flaw in the alibi. As the ambitious young man remains the hero throughout the story, always in view of the reader, he appears beyond suspicion. At the end there is a wild chase in the night through a park, starting with the murderer chasing a girl who has managed to identify him and alert the police who then in turn join in the pursuit of the pursuer!

The trick of having the main character always in the reader's view and so appearing to be obviously innocent was to be used later by Agatha Christie in *The Murder of Roger Ackroyd* (1926). Christie's first book was *The Mysterious Affair at Styles* (1920). Then Agatha Mary Clarissa Miller, she was serving in a hospital infirmary during World War I when she de-

Agatha Christie.

cided to write a detective story in the Sherlock Holmes tradition. Her knowledge of hospital pharmacy routine inspired her to introduce murder by poison. The detective she created to solve her mystery was also influenced by her surroundings. Belgian refugees lived in a camp nearby and from her observation of them the character of Hercule Poirot, the private detective who relied on his "grey cells," slowly emerged. Robert Barr (1850–1912) had used a similar figure in his Eugène Valmont, also slightly comic with his broken English. At first a Captain Hastings was introduced as Poirot's faithful Watson, but the author soon got rid of him by marrying him off. Agatha—now Mrs. Christie—had Poirot solve some very complicated cases over the next few years. When eventually it came to *Curtain* (1975) he must have reached a ripe old age but the years do not seem to count with superdetectives who never knew the bounds of time and space.

Poirot was created for the reader who identified with an individual detective. Instead of a high-powered investigator, Mrs. Christie presented a man who enjoyed the comfort of his own armchair, drinking hot chocolate and being vain enough to wear too narrow shoes and being annoyed that they pinched him.

She allowed him a few buffoonish characteristics, but essentially he was not very different from an ordinary man. Later, in creating her other detective, Miss Marple, she again used the pattern of an ordinary, familiar person. This lady was to alternate with the small Belgian gentleman in most of her works. Knitting in hand, she was always ready to enjoy a cup of tea no matter what the situation. She was the quintessential English village spinster.

The Mysterious Affair at Styles is based on one of the most important principles in English Law, that nobody can be charged with the same crime twice. However, there are many false trails to be cleared up in the end. In 1926 *The Murder of Roger Ackroyd* became a best seller. Dr. Sheppard, a village doctor, tells the story in the first person; he takes the place of Dr. Watson although, in fact, *he* is the murderer. He keeps a diary in which he notes many details of the case, including the way he left the room where Roger Ackroyd was found murdered a few hours later. The doctor has murdered his patient in his last ten minutes with him and has carefully prepared an alibi. In the final denouement it is revealed that "the little that remained to be done" before the investigation began was the hiding of a dictaphone in the doctor's bag. Not all readers picked up such skillfully inserted clues. Some were indignant about what they felt was the author's lack of fair play while others applauded, maintaining that she had not unfairly concealed anything. Those who complained had allowed themselves to be too easily diverted instead of paying close attention. In any case the book made Agatha Christie famous. She had received inspiration for the unusual structure of the story, which broke all the conventions, from two parties, as she was to tell later in her autobiography. The basic idea came from Lord Mountbatten, who himself claimed this to be so. Earlier on Mrs. Christie's brother-in-law, James Watts, had said that some day he would like to see a Doctor Watson commit the actual murder; the author kept this point in mind.

Agatha Christie continued her happy experimentation in further novels, creating variations of the locked-room motif. One crime was committed in an airplane, another on a lonely island, and yet another in a snowbound train. Technicalities such as how the criminal got to the scene of his crime were not deeply considered. It was more important to work out which one, among a group of people isolated together, was the culprit. Monsieur Poirot in the course of detection relied, as has been said, on his "grey cells": he preferred, although he was by no means entirely an armchair detective, to leave such minor tasks as the measurement of footprints or the search for cigarette ends and matches to others.

When called in to investigate he arrived quickly on the spot, attaché case in hand, trusted colleague by his side. In several novels the author gave him the slightly eccentric Mrs. Ariadne Oliver as helpmate. She was a crime writer, sometimes simply coiffed, sometimes with the addition of a few false curls, always with some apples in her bag. Her ardor for the hunt made her ready to trail suspects almost to the point of her own physical exhaustion. In fact, Mrs. Oliver is a caricature of Mrs. Christie herself. Like Monsieur Poirot, she does not point to the obvi-

ous suspect but is always on the lookout for somebody whose character and motivation make him or her the likely villain. Poirot is always ready to compliment her on her achievements, gallantly acknowledging his indebtedness to her. All good ideas, he maintains, come from her.

If the early surroundings of a pharmacy had inspired Agatha Christie with ideas of murder by poison, she was later, surprisingly enough, inspired by children's jingles and games. These might become the recurring motif of a detective story or be brought in to supply models for the characters in the tale. *Ten Little Niggers* (1939) (U.S.: *And Then There Were None* [1940]; *Ten Little Indians* [1965]) is perhaps the best-known example. Nine people die, one after the other, and the perpetrator of the last murder is never brought to justice. The important character in this assorted company on a lonely island is a judge who delivers the final verdict and becomes his own executioner. In this tale, too, Mrs. Christie tries to find neat

Jacket designs for *The Pale Horse* and *At Bertram's Hotel*, both by Agatha Christie.

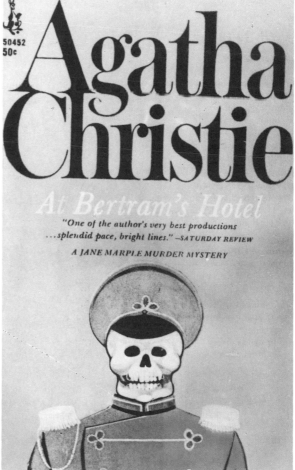

solutions. Like most crime writers, she avoids putting the noose round the criminal's neck herself. She is content for Hercule Poirot to trace the culprit and hand him over to the police. To her the subsequent proceedings are of little interest. The criminal may well meet with an accident: fate or even suicide may provide the final answer. A charming evildoer may be allowed to evade justice altogether by escaping to a far-off country. The main thing is that the culprit must disappear and law and order be reestablished. It is this that provides a satisfying solution for the average reader not only in Britain but worldwide.

A main ingredient of all these novels is a carefully constructed alibi, although once, in *The Sittaford Mystery* (U.S.: *The Murder at Hazelmoor*) (1931), the author made a mistake. The murderer, an old major, provides himself with an alibi by skiing instead of

simply walking. However, there is a discrepancy here: the speed desired by Mrs. Christie could have been reached only on an Alpine ski run and not on a road in Britain.

The detective who demolishes a skillfully built alibi is, intellectually at least, superior to the criminal. But he must never be an athletic figure. Poirot is a case in point and so is—after 1930—Miss Jane Marple. Agatha Christie modeled this amiable and energetic elderly lady on her own grandmother. Miss Marple is always ready to use her wealth of experience, for she realizes that there is not a crime or wicked deed in the world that does not remind her of something that has happened in St. Mary Mead, the small village where she has spent all her life. She succeeds by exercising intuition, sympathy, and observation to penetrate many an intrigue. *The Murder at the Vicarage* (1930) is well suited to the village atmosphere that Miss Marple knows is by no means one of peace and quiet. At the end of the story the author

Still from *Murder on the Orient Express*, with Albert Finnay as Hercule Poirot.

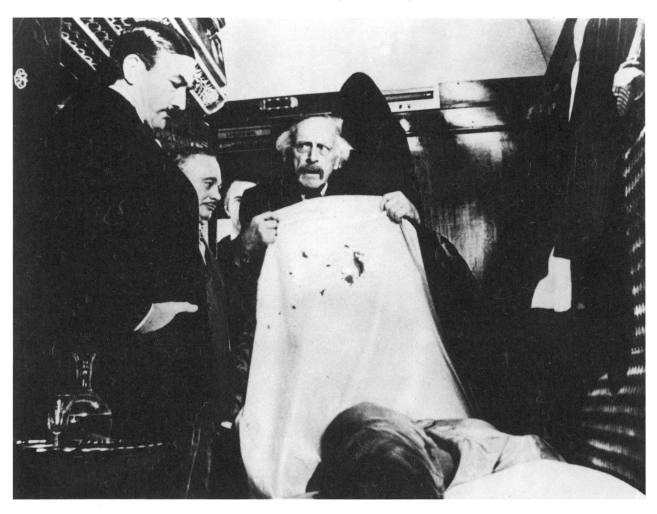

Stills from *Witness for the Prosecution* with Marlene Dietrich in the title role and Charles Laughton as prosecutor.

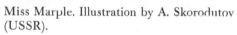
Miss Marple. Illustration by A. Skorodutov (USSR).

Dorothy L. Sayers.

gathers together all the suspects involved in the murder of the old colonel, who are then questioned by Miss Marple. After careful consideration she quietly names the murderer and once more emerges triumphantly from an investigation.

In spite of quiet rural settings, the reader can be certain that wherever Miss Marple turns up, murder waits just around the corner. This, of course, is not real life but a skillfully arranged game. The increasing use of psychology by Agatha Christie becomes noticeable in the character of Miss Marple even more so than in that of her predecessor, Poirot. In advance of her time Agatha Christie paved the way for the psychological thriller, while other representatives of the Golden Age mystery grew more and more reticent. After a divorce from Colonel Christie, she married Max Mallowan, later to become Sir Max Mallowan, a well-known archeologist whom she met during a visit to Baghdad. He was then assisting Sir Leonard Woolley, in charge of the joint British Museum and Museum of the University of Pennsylvania Expedition to Ur of the Chaldees. Through him she became

acquainted with the Middle East where she spent some time on digging sites. There she found a new setting for the crime story, for which she abandoned the traditional background of London, country houses, and villages. The Middle East, its age-old sites, its tourist attractions, and the mystery surrounding archeological finds seemed excellent material to combine with an unexpected murder in an unusual atmosphere. But how to get Poirot there?

In *Appointment with Death* (1938) Poirot is, quite simply, a tourist. A campsite forms the background for *Murder in Mesopotamia* (1936). *Death Comes at the End* (U.S.: 1944; U.K.: 1945), set in ancient Egypt, is an experiment inspired by a friend of the author, the Egyptologist, Professor S. R. K. Granville. Even though there are no obvious anachronisms, the point of this story—that the world holds no secrets—is doubtful when applied to the year 2000 B.C. In addition, it seems strange for an Egyptian grandmother to be taking a part usually played by Miss Marple. Actually, the journey back in time is not very convincing.

Early in her career Christie followed Conan Doyle's pattern in writing short stories as well as novels. Some of these stories were collected according to their themes—for example, *The Thirteen Problems* (1932) (U.S.: *The Tuesday Club Murders* [1933]).

The second "Lady of Crime," Dorothy L. Sayers, worked in the genre for a few years only. In contrast to Mrs. Christie, who stressed the mechanics of technique, Dorothy Sayers, an Oxford graduate, stressed literary qualities. It is for this reason, no doubt, that she made her detective, Lord Peter Wimsey, a bibliophile and a connoisseur. His urbaneness and savoir faire are almost farcical, and so is the devoted attention of his valet, Bunter, who almost takes the part of a Watson. With Sayers the search for clues takes second place to the description of scenery and social life. *The Nine Tailors* (1934) and *Gaudy Night* (1935) prove the point. The English countryside forms an essential part of *The Nine Tailors*. Waterways with ancient locks, remote villages, and fine old churches are reminiscent of the author's early years in the fen country. Rough weather forces a snowbound Lord Peter to accept the hospitality of the vicar of Fenchurch St. Paul, and Wimsey and his valet get to know the place and the people and something of the traditional ritual of bell ringing. Strange things happen in the long winter nights. An unknown body is found in a newly dug grave; an old story of a stolen necklace makes the rounds again; a scoundrel involved in the theft dies under mysterious circumstances. The puzzles are all solved by Lord Peter when after the great thaw he returns to the village. The criminal, hiding in the bell loft, is killed, the ring of the *Nine Tailors* providing a final Act of God. This particular crime novel—not recognizable as such by the title—clearly shows the author's wish to write on a high literary plane. While one of Agatha Christie's murders had taken place in a vicarage, that at Fenchurch St. Paul simply becomes the scenic background for talk on church ritual, art, and rare prints. And, to a certain extent, these discussions and the description of scenery and local history almost overwhelm the crime plot.

Gaudy Night is a work typical of an Oxford graduate who would be well acquainted with the details of

minor academic feuds that might just be bitter enough to end with the destruction of manuscripts and the driving of young women students to the verge of suicide. The culprit of the story is a young woman who, not understanding Oxford life, grows to hate it. The reason for her attitude lies in the past. She is not brought to trial by representatives of the colleges, by Lord Peter, nor by the crime writer, Harriet Vane (the alter ego of Dorothy Sayers). In the story all guilt seems problematical.

As by unwritten law amateur detectives always seem to attract murder, so Lord Peter is forced even on his honeymoon, when at last he has wooed and won Harriet Vane, to clear up a new murder. *Busman's Honeymoon* (1937), relating this event, began as a play, written in collaboration with a close Oxford friend. Produced in the West End in 1936, it was then novelized by its author; play and book both appeared in print in 1937. Clearly feeling that she had almost left crime fiction behind, Dorothy Sayers let

The cab drives quickly to the post office. From A. Groner's *Warum sie das Licht verlöschten (That's Why They Switched Off the Light)*.

her readers suspect this in the book's apt subtitle: *A Love Story with Detective Interruptions.*

Her first detective tale, however, *Whose Body?* (1923), was certainly a full-blooded murder story. Others followed, among them *The Unpleasantness at the Bellona Club* (1928) and *Murder Must Advertise* (1933). In the latter, Sayers used her own experience in an advertising agency to lend credibility to the writing.

In the author's short stories there is little description of background and atmosphere. The macabre element prevails as, for example, when a woman's body is silver-coated and then appears as a Roman couch, or a motorcyclist loses his suitcase containing a bleeding head, or a ghost coach drives along a village street. In the story of the leopard lady the idea of "murder by order" is brought in, a theme Agatha Christie later expanded on in *The Pale Horse* (1961). The uncle and guardian of a young heir gives a personal check to a "society for the transport of surplus persons" and, returning from a journey, learns that his nephew, a highly gifted child, has poisoned himself while playing with deadly nightshade berries.

Illustration by Walter Trier for Erich Kästner's *Emil and the Detectives.*

The verdict is accidental death by solanine poisoning, no questions are asked, nor is justice done. The author's short stories introduced Montague Egg, a new detective and a complete change from Lord Peter. He is a traveling salesman, dealing in wine, who has an astonishing gift for observation and an ability to deduce truths.

Fascinated by the theoretical possibilities of crime fiction, Dorothy Sayers offers many variations of murder: poisoned teeth fillings, a cat with poisonous claws, poisoned gum on stamps, and even poisoned shaving brushes and mattresses. Lethal "weapons" include a dagger made of ice, rats infected with the plague, lice with typhoid, henbane, and boiling lead. The list is imaginative and at the same time reassuring, since the reader seems certain that such extravagant murder weapons would be conjured up by writers only, never used by everyday criminals. It is interesting to note, however, that a weapon, frequently referred to in police reports as "a blunt instrument," is also a favorite in fiction.

In her introduction to *Great Short Stories of Detection, Mystery, and Horror* (1928, 1931, 1934) Dorothy Sayers dealt with the crime story and gave Sheridan Le Fanu an astonishing revaluation. In time she turned to other forms of literature, abandoning crime writing altogether. For a writer to turn from crime writing to what is considered "more serious" literature is more common in English-speaking countries than on the continent. In Germany such fiction has always been considered a second-class form. Thus, the lack of local crime material makes translations from the English, though at times poor, very popular—ever since the days of Sherlock Holmes.

In Britain a writer with many and varied literary interests was Monsignor Ronald A. Knox, who began a new translation of the Bible in 1939. Yet he wrote six detective novels, beginning with *The Viaduct Murder* (1925), and essays on crime fiction. He laid down ten rules for the crime writer, which were to ensure fair play for the reader. He thought that secret passageways and fortuitous accidents should disappear altogether from the genre.

In spite of the low repute of the mystery in Vienna, two writers actually did produce crime fiction of their own. They both began writing in the late nineteenth century and stayed popular well into the twentieth. Auguste Groner, an elementary schoolteacher, wrote a number of novels between 1900 and

1912, of which several were translated into English. The other was Erich Ebenstein, disguised under the pen name of Annie Hruschka. He worked largely with the elements of the nineteenth-century family novel: missing heirs, doppelgängers, family secrets, intrigues, and strange happenings in ancient castles. Wicked plans and foul deeds were foiled by upright and noble characters. In the declining days of the Hapsburg Empire there were many great families with their own traditions and castles; these made Ebenstein's novel seem fascinatingly real.

In 1929 the German writer Erich Kästner created the first detective story for German children in *Emil and the Detectives*, which became a world success. In it Kästner tells how shy Emil from the provinces, with the help of some Berlin children, recovers money stolen from him. At the same time he succeeds in arresting a bank robber.

Golden Age authors varied considerably in their styles. Some stuck to the classic detective story while others—like Edgar Wallace—used the Gothic novel as a backdrop.

Joseph S. Fletcher overlapped the two eras. Though his greatest popularity came in the 1920s, his works belong essentially to an earlier period. His plots were played out against lonely stretches of moors and sea coasts, and his characters included foreigners and pirates. In *Ravensdene Court* (1922) the hero and heroine are searching for hidden treasure among crumbling walls, derelict buildings, and gravestones overgrown with moss. Perhaps Fletcher's finest achievement was *The Middle Temple Murder* (1919), which found favor in high places; for example, it delighted President Wilson. Although many sophisticated readers regarded Fletcher's plots as oversimplified, his characters—particularly the strict, puritanical farmers—exerted influence on Melville D. Post's *Uncle Abner* stories and on American crime writing in general.

G. D. H. and M. Cole, a husband-and-wife team, wrote some forty crime stories together as a relaxation from their professional work and to make a little extra money. They were both economists and university lecturers. In these stories the reader is witness to many interrogations, some repetitious, in which important facts are not always disclosed—violation of the rules of the Detection Club.

H. C. Bailey with his detective Reginald Fortune—his first collection of short stories was titled

Cover design for Alfred Hitchcock's short-story collection entitled *Grave Business*.

Call Mr. Fortune (1920)—is considered a master of the "clever" plot. Bailey created a second hero, the dilettante lawyer Joshua Clunk, who worked with Scotland Yard and at the same time was known to the underworld for his brilliant defense in court. Clunk is the ancestor of the type of detective featured in the later private-eye story. Clunk's *Shrouded Death* (1950) is a good example of one of Bailey's "clever" plots.

John Rhode, under the pen name of Major Cecil J. Street, had his detective, Professor Priestley, consulted regularly by Scotland Yard to consider in great scientific detail each case presented to him. Priestley succeeds in solving all problems in the end. The author never allows a love story to be mixed with his tales of crime. Anthony Berkeley Cox, a journalist and writer of humorous tales, frequently had the cul-

Alfred Hitchcock with his family embarking at Southampton from the United States.

prit in his crime fiction convicted on psychological grounds. In *The Poisoned Chocolates Case* (1929), written under the pseudonym of Anthony Berkeley, poison apparently meant for an old gentleman in fact kills a wealthy married woman; however, once the characters are examined critically, it becomes questionable whether the mistake was mere chance. Psychology and "the inverted story"—with the murderer identified from the beginning—are combined in the novels that Cox wrote under a second pen name of Frances Iles. In *Malice Aforethought* which appeared in 1931 the first sentence states that Dr. Bickleigh has decided to kill his wife, although it takes a few weeks before he embarks on what he calls this "serious enterprise." His wife Julia is portrayed as a thoroughly unpleasant person, and her death gives rise to more rumors than the doctor has expected. He has all along been having little flirtations, one of which seemed rather serious. In the end Dr. Bickleigh is hanged not for the murder of his wife, his "malice aforethought," but for the death of the husband of one of his many amours.

Before the Fact (1932) deals with Johnny, a good-looking but unscrupulous young man, who kills his father-in-law, his friend, and 'his wife—and escapes punishment. The faithful wife, knowing her husband has served her a poisoned cup, writes a letter in which she makes her death appear as suicide; it is at this point that the reader's feelings are turned against this distortion of justice and the wife's silly infatuation. The theme of ironical retribution recurs in crime plots. In Max Murray's *The Voice of the Corpse* (1947) a major is accused of the murder of a wicked, gossipy old maid. He neither can nor will provide himself with an alibi, since through it he would incriminate himself for the murder of his wife. Compared to Frances Iles's vivid psychological presentation, Murray's writing is colorless—in spite of his use of horror, cemeteries, and strange forebodings.

Apart from the well-known authors of the Golden Age who introduced new subjects and new ideas to develop the detective story, many lesser ones helped make crime fiction, particularly in English, a favorite with readers.

There was an increasing tendency among writers to overexpose circumstantial evidence and the deductions made from it—something that could make the modern plot sketchy in contrast to its Victorian counterpart. With secondary romantic plots scarce, there was constant danger that action could become static and the story lose tension, even though the author continually tried to heighten it. Plans of buildings, sketches of rooms, all kinds of schedules and timetables were now increasingly included in the pages of the genre in an attempt to supply straightforward yet actually circumstantial evidence. The idea was that the reader should have the pleasure of arriving at his own conclusions in an attempt to solve quite complicated cases. The new structure was a failure, since it considered one question only: *Who* is the culprit? In an effort to provide clues to the question, some authors and publishers included in the books small envelopes containing actual objects that were pieces of evidence: used railway tickets; cigarette ends; even a photograph of a mutilated body. Readers were not impressed, preferring a skillfully constructed tale to a game with clues.

The steady rise in popularity of the cinema became an immediate threat to the classic puzzle detective story whose reflections, conversations, and interrogations, as has been pointed out, do not lend themselves to cinematics. In contrast, the action-packed romantic tale, full of chases across rooftops and through subterranean vaults, makes for ideal visual material.

The stage, however, offers excellent possibilities for the classic mystery, since the action can be limited to a small number of people. An example is Agatha Christie's *The Mousetrap*, an enormous success on the London stage, now in its thirty-fifth year. It is adapted from her short story "Three Blind Mice."

With certain changes and adaptations, often to the author's displeasure, some classic detective stories were made into films. A producer-director who made his name in this special genre was Alfred Hitchcock, a master of the suspense thriller. He was also editor of a number of anthologies of crime stories.

Side by side with mystery and horror went the crime story's advance into the realm of scientific thought, something that was particularly obvious in the work of John Dickson Carr.

The Rational and the Irrational

I said: "Who's that?" and "What do you want?" and then I could have bitten my tongue off for speaking at all. It turned round. It seemed to have no head. That was the worst; it seemed to have no head.

—Carter Dickson

John Dickson Carr, born in Pennsylvania, settled in London and there began writing in the tradition of the English detective story. Dr. Gideon Fell, one of his master detectives, was modeled on G. K. Chesterton. Carr's speciality became the "locked room" motif. In *The Hollow Man* (1935) Carr made Dr. Fell analyze a locked-room problem and present seven different answers. Examples: The suspected murder turns out to be a sudden natural death; the room is actually firmly locked. Or the dead person has been driven to suicide. The most interesting possibility is that the murder has occurred only after the police have entered the room.

Carr expressed his admiration for Edgar Allan Poe in *Dark of the Moon* (1967), hinting at pirates, their treasures, and Poe's popular "The Gold Bug," but this spooky artificiality does not make up for a scanty plot. The author was more successful when he returned to the Victorian scene. *Scandal at High Chimneys: A Victorian Melodrama* appeared in 1959. More and more authors, incidentally, now used pen names, unwilling either to become known as crime writers or not wishing to be accused of turning out too many books. This often meant that anything outside thei normal work was published pseudonymously and by adopting a new name a writer could change his style completely and even get rid of his master detective who might be turning into a bore in the long run.

In 1913 Carolyn Wells, a little known American writer, composed a guide to the writing of crime fiction under the title, *The Technique of the Mystery Story*. More influential, however, was the work of the art critic and writer Willard Huntington Wright who wrote detective novels in the twenties and thirties under the pen name S. S. Van Dine. He also produced theoretical studies on the subject and, most important, a list of do's and don'ts for crime writers, stricter even than that of Monsignor Knox. To take a few interesting examples: The reader and the detective must be given equal opportunities for solving a mystery. All clues must be presented clearly. There must be no romance; the task in hand is to bring a criminal to justice and not two lovers to the altar. The detective or official involved in an investigation must never turn out to be the culprit. The culprit must be discovered through logical conclusions and not by chance or by unmotivated confession. Secret societies, camorras, mafias, and the like have no place in the detective story. A detective novel must not have long descriptive passages, nor dwell on incidental matters with oversubtle analyses of character, nor go to great efforts to create "atmosphere." Crimes must be committed for personal reasons. International plots and the politics of war must be avoided. A murder story must remain "comfortable," reflecting the reader's everyday experiences and supplying him with an outlet for his wishes, dreams, and emotions.

The list itself was of no great help to authors but the rules did draw attention to the gamelike character of all crime writing. Their strictness left the writer no scope, hence they were bound to be broken, even by Wright himself. His master detective was the snobbish Philo Vance who, like his creator, adopted an elitist attitude. Wright even used footnotes, appealing to his reader's erudition and love of pretense.

Mignon G. Eberhart, the U. S. writer, modeled her novels on the classic English detective story. The American scene, however, made her task difficult; ordinary houses are very different from the castles and stately homes of Britain and the remote villages and picturesque inns with their small and snobbish cliques. A central figure in Eberhart's novels is Susan Dare, a sensitive writer who sets out to solve criminal cases and to find the answers to extraordinary mysteries. One, for example, is to clear up a murder committed beside a strange stone statue from Easter Island. Such picturesque, romantic plots and settings were hardly realistic depictions of crime in the United States.

Frances Noyes Hart used a country-house setting in *Hide in the Dark* (1929). Earlier, in 1927, he had published *The Bellamy Trial* as a serial in the *Saturday Evening Post*. This dealt with the solving of a real case while the actual legal proceedings were in progress. The novel had a good public reception. The background influenced later writers, in particular, Erle Stanley Gardner.

Crimes committed in America's large cities, gun battles in the streets with police involved, had not yet become the raw material for contemporary writing. Only hesitatingly did authors abandon the country mansions that for so long had been the traditional setting for tales of crime. Rex Stout, however, decided to place his master detective, the portly, beer-drinking Nero Wolfe, in a brownstone house in New York's West 35th Street. His cases mostly concerned old-established families—a traditional theme—yet not unconnected with reality. Wolfe, not given to moving about much, has an assistant, Archie Goodwin, who makes the inquiries and takes on the Watsonian role of narrator for the reader. The books are written in the first person from Goodwin's point of

view. This makes it easy for the reader to identify with the ever-eager Archie and participate in his investigations. From time to time facts are relayed to the portly detective who then draws his sometimes surprising conclusions. Of course Wolfe and Goodwin are Holmes and Watson, with Wolfe serving as the intellectual half of Holmes and Goodwin as the physical half of Holmes and all of Watson. Looked at from another point of view, Wolfe serves as the armchair amateur of the classic (puzzle) detective novel, and Goodwin as the mobile investigator of the contemporary "private eye" novel discussed in a later section. The combination is a successful marriage of the soft-boiled intellectual puzzler with the hard-boiled action-detective novel.

Ellery Queen, the son of a police inspector, also lived in New York. He was in fact two cousins, Frederic Dannay and Manfred B. Lee, who used their hero's name as a pen name. Their success lay in giving their cases a sense of being true, realistic stories, with the action taking place not in the slums, but in skyscrapers and elegant old houses that for generations had been owned by the same family. Ellery Queen, a snob like his predecessor Philo Vance, solves the most complicated cases, most of which do not really belong in the atmosphere of a giant city. Ellery's father, old Inspector Queen, is always there to order the arrest of the criminal once he has been unmasked. With the growth of Ellery Queen's popularity, Dannay and Lee published collections of crime stories under the pen name Ellery Queen and since 1941 *Ellery Queen's Mystery Magazine*.

The status that crime fiction had slowly but steadily achieved in the United States was firmly established when President Franklin D. Roosevelt himself conceived an idea for a detective novel. He left the writing to several authors, each supplying one chapter, and gave it the intriguing title *The President's Mystery Story* (1935).

For a considerable time the figure of the mysterious, treacherous oriental had a place in American and British crime fiction. Edgar Wallace used the figure so often as antagonist or villain that the Detection Club protested. He became a hero, however, beginning with *The House without a Key* (1925), in which Earl Derr Biggers decided to introduce an oriental detective. He called him Charlie Chan. Chan was a police inspector in Honolulu, Hawaii, clever but never sly. When his American and British colleagues are around, he keeps to the background. In order to give his Honolulu detective a fair chance in the field, Biggers's plots grew more colorful. In *Charlie Chan Carries on* (1930), murder strikes a party on a world tour. After all the members of the group, including the murderer, have become suspect, Chan manages to corner the culprit and make him confess. The culprit has actually given himself away by a slip of the tongue; though the reader may well have noticed this, he has not necessarily guessed its ingenious implications, nor the conclusion.

Sometimes plots were set in holiday paradises or even desert regions, far from the milling city crowds. The basic patterns of the traditional detective story were now well known and could easily be brought up to date and adapted to suit a rapidly changing world. New and diverting backgrounds were introduced. In

Jacket designs for novels by John Dickson Carr and Ellery Queen.

Murder in a Blue Moon (1948) the Australian writer Margot Neville took her readers to a land of picturesque villas and beaches with gardens full of flowering hibiscus and viburnum. This was not what the reader really expected Australia to be. Arthur W. Upfield provided an Australia of wide, empty spaces, farms, flocks of sheep, kangaroos, and aborigines. He also added robust plots. As the black sheep of an English family, this author had been dispatched to Australia where he had worked on a sheep farm, as a laborer, prospector, and trapper before becoming a successful writer. He had the ability to combine elements of travel and adventure along with a solid story line. His detective inspector, Napoleon Bonaparte of the Queensland Police, was modeled on an aboriginal friend; Bony not only knew all about detection, but had equally a good understanding of the local population, their behavior, their background, and their traditions. Bony could gain the confidence of the aborigines and, with their help, lay hands on

the culprit. Nature and scenery were important features in these stories.

Slowly but surely the Golden Age was coming to an end. The scope had become smaller, with too many novels milking a good idea dry. Also, World War II had a harmful effect in some parts of the world. In Hitler's Germany all writing in English was banned. Fascist Italy forbade the sale of books by Edgar Wallace and Agatha Christie. On the other hand spy stories began to flourish, and in the forties many experienced crime writers included aspects of the spy in their work. In *N or M?* (1941), for example, Agatha Christie tells how a small circle of guests at a boarding house becomes involved in the uncovering of a spy ring. While in the pure detective story a couple of murderers are unmasked, here it is a couple of traitors. The Beresfords—known more popularly as Tommy and Tuppence—and who do all the detective work, are the heros of the tale. Christie had used them in a novel set just after World War I, and in *N or M?* naturally they were older—and married—the author's concession to reality.

The Modern Pitaval Story

In front of the house Herr Mrázek called the first cab that came along and with Frau Vlková drove direct to the police headquarters, at public expense.

—Jiři Marek

In the twentieth century the Pitaval case history retained the popularity it had enjoyed for some two

Jiři Marek

hundred years. Contrary to the often unreal elements related in crime fiction, the case history always had the advantage of dealing with true events.

In his *Prager Pitaval (Pitaval of Prague)* (1931) Egon Erwin Kisch looked back to historic crime cases that in some ways seemed to have foreshadowed the collapse of the Hapsburg Empire. Kisch was less concerned with the discovery and punishment of crime than with the explication of political and social themes. He advanced new and provocative judgments when, for example, he presented certain types of criminals as "noble robbers" of folklore, even though they died in prison.

Jiři Marek also published several volumes of case histories between 1968 and 1979. From the very beginning Marek made it clear he was dealing with the times under Kaiser Franz Joseph as well as Republican days. He talked about smart ministerial councillors who did not believe in modern forensic techniques and would rather solve cases on the spot instead of in the laboratory. One councillor in particular, a certain Knotek, distrusted fingerprints to the end of his days, relying—not without success—on a natural flair for picking up clues and intuiting their meaning.

These very qualities led him and the reader into exciting adventures along narrow, eerie lanes in Prague's old town as well as into blocks of modern of-

Jacket design for *Panoptikum alter Kriminalfälle (A Collection of Old Criminal Cases)* by J. Marek.

Illustration for Marek's *Panoptikum der Altstadt Prag (Rouges' Gallery of Old Prague)*.

fice buildings. Horror that had been an element in crime stories since the days of Ann Radcliffe and Sheridan Le Fanu was now at times interwoven with humor, a humor based on the understanding of human weaknesses. Marek found his case histories in everyday life, usually gleaning them from old newspaper files.

The reader who had had his fill of master detectives must have felt some sympathy for the hardpressed men of the Prague Crime Squad when at times they did not succeed immediately in clearing up a case. In the end their success might depend on small things: the barking of a dog, the meanness of a sleeping-car passenger who had made himself suspect by haggling over forty *centesimi*, or even the discovery of a red petticoat. In fact, solving crimes *was* a game of mere chance.

Macabre subjects such as murder, robbery, and arson were now relieved by comic details, disproving the belief that humor and crime could not coexist. Marek shared his sense of the grotesque with his compatriot Karel Čapek, though satire played a greater part than crime in Čapek's work.

The continued tradition of the Pitaval case history in German-speaking countries was taken up after World War II in the Federal Republic of Germany (West Germany). Two writers, Gerhart H. Mostar and Robert A. Stemmle, presented a mixture of historical and contemporary cases. Side by side were the case histories of sixteenth-century Rebecka Lamp and little Lucie Berlin murdered in the Kaiser's Germany. Other crimes belonged to the immediate past, for example, that of Dr. Petiot who in occupied Paris systematically robbed and killed peo-

Frank Arnau, after receiving an Honorary Degree at Humboldt University in Berlin.

Among others he reported on the proceedings against a gun-happy estate owner named von Kähne, accused before the Potsdam Assizes of having shot an apprentice. The trial ended with an acquittal, yet the acquittal, accompanied by loud protests, seemed to Kaul symptomatic of the confused social setup of the period. It was not the verdict—a foregone conclusion—in which he was really interested, but the *way* the proceedings were conducted. The weight of his criticism, however, and the implied censure of the judiciary and of society as a whole interfered with the telling of the story; his aim to entertain the reader intelligently became secondary to his desire to analyze contemporary politics and the conduct of the law.

A Swiss, Frank Arnau, became well known through his political activities. In particular he dealt with sensational criminal cases that were politically important: for example, the murders at Serajevo, trade in illegal drugs, art forgeries, and kidnapping. He also analyzed cases widely discussed in the newspapers, and exposed gross mistakes in the investigations as well as in the verdicts. In reaching one verdict, the court cited three totally different days on which a particular crime was said to have been committed! Along with his record of the proceedings and the verdict Arnau presented his own ideas as to the real culprit. In addition, he wrote twenty crime novels that dealt with contemporary conditions. These were translated into a dozen languages, the sales reaching a staggering million copies.

Edgar M. Lustgarten's famous collection of case histories collectively titled *Prisoner at the Bar* criticized the British system of justice in an entirely different way. *Verdict in Dispute*, the first, appeared in 1949. *Defender's Triumph* followed in 1951. In it, the one-time lawyer reported a number of spectacular cases that had been tried in the British courts during the last sixty years. The extraordinary thing was that in every case the guilt of the accused was practically certain, yet an acquittal was obtained through the sheer skill of the defense. Lustgarten began with the proceedings against Adelaide Bartlett, accused of the murder of her husband, a London trader. The defense used brilliant technique in interrogating the prosecutor's witnesses. Unlike their counterparts in fiction, these defense lawyers did not solve the case before the courts, pointing to the true culprit, but let the jury discover so many discrepancies and uncertainties in the prosecution's case and in statements of

ple who had come to him for help and protection. In the introduction to his tales Mostar described his work as being in the long tradition of Voltaire, Rousseau, and Montesquieu.

Three authors in the German Democratic Republic (East Germany) styled their work in the Pitaval tradition. Günter Prodöhl, a crime reporter, published a collection of contemporary cases, casting his net as wide as the Boston strangler. Hans Pfeiffer carried on the Pitaval tradition by publishing *Mordfälle, dem Neuen Pitaval nacherzählt (Murder Cases Retold from the New Pitaval)* (1962); Friedrich Karl Kaul, a lawyer, collected cases representative of the Kaiser's Germany and the Weimar Republic in *Pitaval der Weimarer Republik (Pitaval of the Weimar Republic)* (1965). His *Ein Pitaval (A Pitaval)* (1966) dealt with twenty cases between 1894 and 1964.

its witnesses that they finally had to return a "not guilty" verdict. This was a triumph for the defense attorneys, for their insight into human behavior, and for their rhetoric. The question that might be asked by the addicts of crime fiction—"What then is the real truth?"—was never answered. The facts were rarely as simple as presented by the prosecution, a point always stressed by the defense. In these cases from real life the reader was left with the problem of a crime unsolved, in contrast to cases in crime fiction when usually the author provides a neatly constructed solution.

The collection *Famous Trials* (1964) presented spectacular and at the same time problematic murder cases. *True Murders* (1976), edited by Mary Hottinger, was another collection of case histories, including some reports by Lustgarten. The editor provides tension and psychological interest in her search for motivation of the crimes.

In America the Pitaval story took a welcome turn from the usual plodding "fact crime" treatment of criminous detail piled on detail in chronological fashion until the traditional denouement of capture and punishment. The new departure combined psychological insight, narrative suspense, and sociological comment, forming a kind of psycho-sociological study of crime.

The breakthrough came in 1955 with Lucy Freeman's *Before I Kill More*, an in-depth probing of the inner workings of a real-life Chicago serial killer's character and personality. Freeman, a journalist, interviewed the killer, his foster parents, his friends, and his teachers who had known him as he grew up. Familiar with psychoanalysis, she subjected the killer to her own "analysis." The book was a best seller, demonstrating the public's interest in the new approach.

This "psychological Pitaval" type of study reached its apogee in 1966 with the publication of *In Cold Blood*, by Truman Capote, a major literary figure, in his similar study of a pair of maverick psychopaths who massacred an entire middle-class family in Kansas.

In each work, the author traced the killers, the crimes, the pursuit, and the punishment of the perpetrators. The literary effect achieved was not unlike that accomplished by Dashiell Hammett and Raymond Chandler working in the fictional area.

The Private Eye Story

He marched to the desk and took the Colt. He held it down at his side and went to the door. He put his left hand to the knob and twisted it and opened the door a foot and leaned into the opening, holding the gun tight against his thigh.

—Raymond Chandler

In America realistic crime fiction began with the "private eye" story. The "eye" in "private eye," incidentally, is a punning homonym on the capital "i" in the descriptive term "P. I." for "private investigator"—the use of the "eye" clearly connecting the term P. I. to the symbol of Allan Pinkerton's "never sleeping" detective agency. At first sight the "realism" in this type of story seems to consist mainly in the fact that large quantities of whiskey are consumed and that the detective and supporting characters constantly engage in fisticuffs. There is no doubt that in the typical country house in Middlesex life progressed in a more elegant manner, but things had changed with the turn of the century, and what was right in a stately home in Britain was out of place in a large American city. Mrs. Eberhart had tried to make the transition with some success, yet her work did not represent true home-grown crime fiction, nor did it indicate clearly how the change could be achieved. There were certainly many interesting attempts in the United States from the nineteenth century onwards that foreshadowed a new form—for example, Ambrose Bierce's bitter little tales, and later the sophisticated, sparse, and deliberately unsentimental prose of Ernest Hemingway. Melville D. Post's *Uncle Abner* stories were pure crime fiction, although they might have been simply the "tales of a grandfather" had they been written between 1840 and 1860. But Uncle Abner was no grandfather. Strictly puritanical, modeled on the Old Testament patriarchs, he dispensed stern justice among the settlers of the Appalachian mountains. He was a larger-than-life figure who might equally have been the hero of a Western. The background was right; but did these mountains, fields, and farms really serve as milieu for an American detective story? Of course not. It was the authors of the private-eye story that can claim with justification to have established a true and realistic background for the American crime story. However, their writing was not only set in the big city; their characters, too, were different. The detectives, and even the police officers, worked hard, received little recognition, and were often poorly paid. In the classic English detective story police and detective looked for the murderer within a small circle of suspects. In the writing of Dashiell Hammett, Raymond Chandler, and Erle Stanley Gardner the police and detective looked for the murderer all over the city; it was their combined task to search him out and find him wherever he might be.

If the pure European crime story resembled a fencing duel, the American version resembled bare-knuckle fight in the dark without protective clothing. It was everybody against everybody else. The detective story, as established by Conan Doyle and the Victorian writers, reflected the life-style and sentiments of the British middle and upper classes. The Empire was at the zenith of its power, firmly established. All natural sciences, it seemed, were about to unlock the last riddles of the universe, a universe that had lost all its mystery.

The detective of classic crime fiction observed the world in a bird's-eye view: everything was clear from the start. Small details might irritate him for a moment, but the roles were all clearly cast: the villains were on one side, the detective on the other. The victims were puppets on whom the latter could display his brilliant skill. Nobody need feel sympathy for them.

In the United States, especially after the late twenties, the picture was entirely different. The world was upside down, turned topsy-turvy on Black Friday with the heralding of the Great Depression. The

sciences, particularly physics, were changing fast. "Relatively" became the fashionable catchword, with the Einstein theory comprehended by most of the population.

The private-eye story did not recognize the black-and-white world of good and evil. The detective and his clients might be as implicated in crime as the pursued, with nobody automatically clean. Often the former knew less about what was going on than the latter, since the clients did not necessarily wish to let the detective know *every* intimate detail as there was usually *something* to hide. In contrast to classic crime fiction, the detective did not stand outside and apart from the others. Certainly nobody saw him as a father figure, a guardian angel, or a confessor in whom one could unreservedly confide. The American detective was subject and object at one and the same time. It was as though he were given a role in an improvisation and told to make up his lines as he went along.

To solve a case the detective was required to disentangle complicated relationships among many characters. The traditional question "Who killed the rich old man?" was unheard. The major ingredient of the classic story—to find the motivation and opportunity for a crime—required detailed analytical work of the type employed by Sherlock Holmes or Hercule Poirot. The private-eye story bothered little with this nor was the detective given to much reflection. It was generally conceded that the easiest cases to solve were those in which the criminal had tried to be smart. In these tales the detective was a man of action, paid to carry out his client's commission. Complications might force him into action; for example, he might suddenly come upon a body, placed there by his opponents to get him into trouble with the police, or merely to frighten him. It was important for the detective to find out with whom he was dealing. The quest for the culprit was thus a quest for the characteristics that would identify him as one. The classic detective story took place in a firmly established circle of characters, some perhaps stereotyped. Generally the culprit was the one whom the reader did not believe capable of murder—a respected businessman, or a harmless country postman. This element of surprise, the unexpected carried to an extreme, caused many characters to appear unreal. Only when the "harmless" person was found to be the culprit would the reader remember that he had some unpleasant feature—a strange fixed stare, per-

Illustration for a short story by Dashiell Hammett in *Black Mask* magazine (1924).

haps. In other words, the culprit's character was blackened—but always in retrospect.

Dashiell Hammett and Raymond Chandler did most to develop a particular style in American crime fiction. Almost alone, they founded the tradition. Hammett came from a poor family, and before he was fourteen years old he had held a number of jobs, ending up eventually as one of Allan Pinkerton's de-tectives. Soon he began writing short stories about crime, and in a decidedly American idiom. These sto-ries were published in the early twenties in a maga-zine named *Black Mask*. Since the turn of the century cheap magazines had largely taken over from the familiar serial publications popular in France and England. Their editors, particularly Joseph T. Shaw of *Black Mask*, gave encouragement to new authors in an effort to keep readers up to date on crime and ad-venture. Hammett's stories were new—almost shock-ingly so—both in technique and in style.

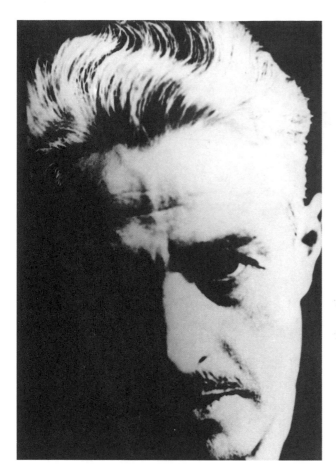

Dashiell Hammett.

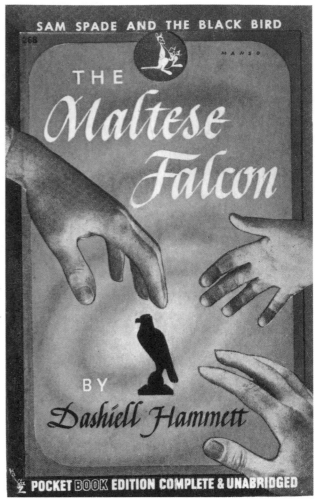

Cover design for Dashiell Hammett's *The Maltese Falcon*.

The novels that made Hammett famous were published between 1929 and 1934. After that he wrote very little. *Red Harvest* (1929) ends with a bloodbath, even though the detective, in pursuit of justice, manages to stay alive. Hammett's next book was *The Dain Curse* (1929), and his last *The Thin Man* (1934). *The Maltese Falcon* (1930) is perhaps his best and most famous work. In it the detective, Sam Spade, becomes involved in clearing up the murder of his partner, Miles Archer. Archer was killed, shot from the front, while trailing a gangster. Although Archer is not portrayed as terribly intelligent, he is not a man stupid enough to allow himself to be lured into a cul-de-sac by a known killer. Therefore he, without doubt, could only have gone there with a person he trusted, a person who might have been his client, for example. Bridgid O'Shaugnessy has in fact planned the murder to force her friend and protector to leave town. He is the man Archer is trailing, and

Archer's death is designed to make the town too hot for him to stay.

The "falcon" of the title is a jewel-encrusted artifact of great value. Its theft is carried out by a group of people who subsequently fall out. Greed is the key to all these characters, each wanting the bird for himself, carefully watching the others, and waiting to seize the first opportunity to double-cross the rest. Spade realizes he cannot trust anybody, least of all Bridgid, now his client. Behind her façade of schoolgirl innocence she is cold and ruthless. Spade is aware that she is only using him in order to get the falcon for herself. When she tires of him, or fears that he knows too much, she will simply dispose of him. When Spade is certain that she shot Archer, he becomes a potential danger she must eliminate.

Only a person like Bridgid could kill a complete stranger without a truly compelling motive: and there lies the close relation between deed and evildoer.

The similarities in style and subject between Hammett and Chandler, as well as their differences, can be shown best by comparing two of their novels. Chandler's *The Little Sister* (1949) could almost have been conceived as a counterpart to *The Maltese Falcon*. Although they are very different, they have one thing in common: a cold-blooded murderess.

In contrast to Hammett, Chandler came from a well-to-do family. He went to an English public school and to a business college in Paris, became a journalist, returned to the United States, and eventually became the director of several oil companies. Out of work in the Great Depression, he began writing crime stories and novels for a living. His best-known novel was *The Big Sleep* (1939), made into a film with Humphrey Bogart as Philip Marlowe, the same actor who played Sam Spade in *The Maltese Falcon*.

Chandler once made a statement to the effect that he "supposed his education had not done him much harm." This remark could not possibly have been uttered by Dorothy Sayers, who was very proud of her Oxford days. She made this clear in the creation of her hero, Lord Peter Wimsey, himself an old Etonian and an Oxford man, and a success wherever he went. Marlowe is different. He does not know how to turn his profession of detective into the successful earning of real money. No one could ever imagine him as an academic. Both Spade and Marlowe are men who rely for their survival first and foremost on their common sense and practical experience.

Nobody could be more ordinary than little Orfamy Quest, the "little sister," a small-town girl, working as a receptionist to Dr. Zugsmith, a dentist. Tidy, correct, and unremarkable, she is a bigoted young woman, convinced of the complete correctness of her notions, her morals, and her view of life. Smoking, for example, is something dirty to her, which she feels the law should forbid. Because of her views, Orfamy's paralyzed father must suck on an empty pipe, and do it only outside on the verandah. Orfamy's brother is a professional blackmailer. When he refuses to share his loot with his mother and his sister, Orfamy travels to the big city in search of a detective. There she finds Philip Marlowe. She bargains about expenses to the last penny, unwilling to spend money, not taking into consideration the fact that Marlowe may have to risk his life to carry out her wishes. All she wants is for Marlowe to find her brother Orrin, hiding somewhere in the city from a dangerous gangster whom he has blackmailed. When Orrin eventually refuses to share his ill-gotten gains, Orfamy betrays him for a thousand dollars—with a completely clear conscience. She is, in fact, convinced that she is in the right. Only when Marlowe confronts her with the fact of her betrayal does she seem momentarily uncomfortable. Orfamy is a monster, who never acknowledges it to herself; Bridgid O'Shaugnessy plays the innocent, *knowing* she is a monster. Orfamy considers herself blameless; it was not she who murdered her brother, but the gangster who fired the shot. Spade hands Bridgid over to the police; Marlowe resigns himself to Orrin's death. Orfamy goes scot free.

Murder committed in this sort of setting is realistic; it is, if anything, commonplace, unlike murder by exotic poisons. Orfamy and her kind of murderer are much more horrifying than classic detective killers because they are *real*.

Women play an important part in Chandler's later novels. In *The Big Sleep* a young girl sends men to their deaths, while in *The High Window* (1942), a wicked old woman destroys the heroine in a way that appears both ruthless and naive. Chandler's plots are complicated and sometimes not entirely plausible, yet characters, episodes, observation, and language are true to life. This turn towards realism brought with it increased social criticism, most noticeably in *The Long Goodbye* (1953), in which the search for a friend involves Marlowe in the investigation of police work, medical care, and old people's homes. The judgments and moral verdicts on the evils of his day are Chandler's own.

It seems worthwhile casting a glance at the role of brutality in the typical private-eye story. Big-city life in reality was tough, and was presented as such in U.S. crime fiction. A murder is a murder; it is and remains a horrible crime. In the P. I. novel, crime is not escapism, a flight from reality. In his essay, "The Simple Art of Murder" (1950), Chandler distanced himself from classic English crime writing in which, he maintained, villains, made of papier mâché, were unmasked by detectives of incredibly aristocratic stupidity. Chandler takes his place in a development alongside Hammett and Hemingway, writers who present an unpleasant world in a realistic fashion. They write about the world in which they live. Hammett portrays people who murder for logical reasons,

Still from *The Maltese Falcon* with Humphrey Bogart as Sam Spade threatened by Peter Lorre as Joel Cairo.

not simply to produce a body for a novel's beginning. In committing murders these people use everyday means, not handmade duelling pistols, South-American poisons, or tropical fish. They are real people and Hammett makes them talk and think in the language they use every day. Chandler describes the readers of the classic detective story as excited old aunts—male, female, or even neuter—and of any age. They like their murder cases magnolia-scented, never wishing to be reminded of the truth—namely that murder is something quite awful.

By 1954 Chandler softened his harsh verdict on classic crime fiction. In an essay he admitted some literary value to novels and tales that had succeeded in creating character and atmosphere well enough to last for several decades.

Because Hammett and Chandler experienced and presented hard and dangerous conditions in their stories, they were driven to adopt a hard style of writing. Inhumanity and cruelty being crimes, both authors took this as a starting point for their world view. Tough statements were made in tough style. This kind of writing goes well beyond the limits of entertainment, that, by and large, had been the function of crime fiction. Yet Hammett's and Chandler's books are not read by the intelligentsia alone; they do entertain, if on a higher level. In condemning cruelty and inhumanity, they represent an important strand of American literary realism.

Although Erle Stanley Gardner, a lawyer, began writing about the same time that Hammett and Chandler did, and also appeared in *Black Mask*, he eventually abandoned the persona of the detective for a protagonist more suitable to his talents—the lawyer. After several years of writing short stories for the pulp magazines, he made a comprehensive analysis of hundreds of currently popular detective novels, synthesized his findings into a formula, and began writing a series of "detective" novels featuring a lawyer-hero as private-eye surrogate.

Using himself as a model, he sketched in the character of his protagonist Perry Mason, basing the efficient Della Street on his own secretary. In effect, his crime novels *began* where those of Hammett and Chandler *ended*: in the courtroom.

Mason never pretends to be a detective, nor does he do any routine detective work; he leaves those chores to Paul Drake. Nevertheless he tries to help his clients by the skilled use of legal procedure, often

Jacket design for Raymond Chandler's *The High Window*.

twisting the law for his own purposes. Mason theorizes that it is stupid to tell the simple truth when that truth is hard to believe and cannot usually be verified anyway. To clear an innocent person and see justice done, Mason believes a lawyer can frequently "bend the law."

And bend the law Perry Mason continually does. The real fun in reading a Gardner detective novel is in watching Mason rearrange clues and spread misinformation, and in following the convoluted machinations of Gardner's story line. Gardner knows how to spin out a yarn and keep the reader turning one page after another, even though the "plot" behind the façade of "mystery" may strike the reader as somewhat thin in the end.

In contrast to the "mean streets" characters that people a Hammett or Chandler novel, Mason's clients

In Raymond Chandler's only original screenplay, the
moody, intense, and darkly somber *The Blue Dahlia* (1946),
returning servicemen Alan Ladd as ex-Navy flier Johnny
Morrison and William Bendix as Buzz Wanchek dine with
Doris Dowling as Ladd's wife Hel Morrison—shortly
before the unfaithful Dowling is murdered, throwing suspicion for the killing on Ladd.

and citizens are solid middle-class types. Business executives, housewives, ordinary laborers, professional men and women—these are the usual dra-
matis personae of a typical Mason story, people
easily recognizable to the reader.

From a standpoint of sales figures and popularity,
Gardner's "detective" was much more successful than
either of the prototypical private eyes developed by
Hammett and Chandler. Like the works of Hammett
and Chandler, Gardner's too were made into motion
pictures and later a television series; in fact, Perry
Mason on television was one of the most successful
of all P. I. enterprises.

In contrast to the more or less humane attitude of
these three writers working in the 1920s and 1930s,
other authors in the private-detective genre soon be-

gan portraying violence and crime for its own sake;
they succeeded in making a great deal of money out
of what looked like the exploitation of sordid story situations. Some of them were indeed extremely successful and outsold authors who stuck more closely to
the established traditions of the mystery genre. By far
the most successful of the blood-and-guts subgenre
was Mickey Spillane, who at one point even outsold
the Bible.

Spillane's astonishing success when he burst onto
the literary scene in 1947 was a direct result of
changes that had occurred in the American psyche
after the conclusion of World War II. Men who had
hitherto stayed close to home and lived unadventur-
ous lives had been exposed to the brutality of war
and its full horrors, and had seen the vastness of the
world and the sordid reality of conditions elsewhere.

The psychological mindset of the returning GI
was one of pragmatism and practicality; if the World
War II soldier could destroy a tremendous evil
threatening the world, why could he not wipe out local evil that seemed to exist everywhere without challenge? "Do something about it!" became the underly-

ing psychological consideration of the ex-soldier, restless and impatient with a world that didn't seem to be functioning at all well on the home front.

Spillane's writing introduced a vigilantism that was in direct contrast to Gardner's restrained courtroom demeanor. Gardner's restraints against the use of fists and guns, observed to keep well within the letter of the law, were cast off by Spillane. If Mason worked within the system to right wrongs, Mike Hammer, Spillane's protagonist, worked outside the system. The sales figures tell the story in dramatic fashion. Gardner's last book to sell over one million copies appeared in 1958. Spillane's first, *I, the Jury* (1947), sold six million copies! In all, a typical Spillane title sold over a million and a half *more* than Gardner's biggest seller.

The title of his first book—*I, the Jury*—says it all. Mike Hammer is always "I," the epicenter of the universe. "I" do this and that; "I" right wrongs. Hammer's creed is individualistic: it's Hammer against the world. The world of Hammer is a world almost exclusively composed of crime and violence—with a bit of steamy sex thrown in. If Hammett's stories end when the detective turns the murderer over to the police, and Gardner's when the trial is over with the killer unmasked in court, Spillane's continue until judgment is made (by the detective) and justice executed (also by the detective). Yet the tradition is not new; it is rooted in the works of Eugène Sue with the action of the hero—the aristocratic Prince Rodolphe von Gerolstein, undercover in the stews of Paris—acting as detective, judge, *and* executioner in *The Mysteries of Paris*.

But there is a difference. Hammer is not an aristocrat with a free run of the world. He is a private citizen, living democratically amidst lawlessness and violence. There is almost a semblance of existentialism in Spillane's world view. The codes men live by have become outmoded, possibly destroyed by the outrages perpetrated in World War II; Hammer is forced to make up the rules as he goes along. Evil is judged evil because of its effects on the individual; what works in a practical sense for the protagonist is right and good.

The standard plot device in a Spillane novel is an attempt by Hammer to avenge the death of someone close to him—a friend, a G.I. buddy. The standard plot twist is the discovery that the woman Hammer has temporarily "fallen in love with" is the killer.

Typically he dispatches her at the end of the work, with a minimum of wordage and a maximum of blood and gore.

Spillane's world is far removed from the middle-class scene recognized by the average city dweller. In *his* cosmopolitan milieu, all cops are greedy and corrupt, all criminals surly and crass, all women sex objects and little else. Yet in his dealings with his secretary Velda, Hammer is as circumspect sexually as Perry Mason is with Della Street. Spillane picked and chose from the established clichés of the genre and out of them created his own manner of writing.

Although his output was thin—six novels in his peak years of production in the 1950s—his readership was astonishingly extensive. After *I, the Jury* came *My Gun is Quick* (1950), *Vengeance Is Mine!* (1950), *The Big Kill* (1951), *One Lonely Night* (1951), and *Kiss Me, Deadly* (1952). These titles all sold in the multimillions.

Spillane's influence was widespread, not only on the public, but on the American publishing world as

Stacy Keach in a typical feisty attitude as Mickey Spillane's famed Mike Hammer in CBS-TV's *Mickey Spillane's Mike Hammer* (1984), and later *The New Mike Hammer* (1986).

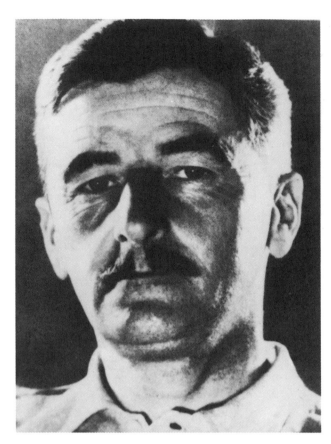

William Faulkner.

well. Imitators of Spillane sprang up overnight, with hundreds of writers grinding out copy in the style of the "master." A few of these lasted a year or two. Most of them are long forgotten.

But Spillane is not forgotten, even though his output diminished and his sales figures simmered down after those postwar years of the 1950s. In no way did Spillane offer any social criticism through his depiction of good guys and bad. If anything, his criticism was of a different nature—a cry for individual effort to root out evil. Yet most critics to this day feel that Spillane was a glorifier of stark brutality, of sex, and of crime, appealing to the lowest instincts of the reader in his depictions of violence and bloodshed. Julian Symons has called Mike Hammer a "monster."

If to Hammett and Chandler social criticism was an important part of their work, and if to Spillane it was unimportant and minimal, Chester Himes's novels in the 1960s combined social criticism with race problems in the United States. The author, himself an Afro-American had little popularity in his own country, and it was only when he went to live in France that he achieved literary success. *A Rage in Harlem* (1964) received the *Grand Prix de littérature policière.* Hammett and Chandler were at home in the sophisticated milieu of large cities, while Himes restricted himself to the black ghettos. With some irony he called his novels Harlem Domestic Detective Stories. It was his intention to point up the senseless cruelty and misery of life in the slums. In an effort to make things seem real, Himes turned to melodrama. In *Blind Man with a Pistol* (1970) rats are actually shot. The author created a macabre atmosphere of horror, presenting a picture of a dangerous and wicked world. In his writing emotion outweighs clear thinking—which is, after all, the life's blood of crime writing.

In any discussion of American crime fiction the great novelist, William Faulkner, must be mentioned. His work covers the entire human condition, and it is therefore natural that he should include the aberrations and crimes of mankind. The special attraction and tension Faulkner creates in his novels stems largely not from asking "Who did it?" but from posing the question "How did it happen?" His knowledge of everyday matters and his joy in describing them down to the smallest detail are his most powerful gifts. Whether he is reflecting on a fisherman's boat and all its paraphernalia or describing how people in the South prefer their whiskey with sugar, which they put into the glass to dissolve in water before actually pouring out the spirit, he creates a tense atmosphere and maintains it by the logical succession of events that eventually lead to an inevitable solution. Faulkner's work has a special place in American literature, since it is all set in the deep South, a background he uses most evocatively. American crime fiction has generally preferred an urban setting, scenes that Chandler especially managed to describe lovingly. Faulkner, on the other hand, portrays with equal love the wide-open countryside with its fields of cotton and corn. His perception of his fellow man is clearly shown in his detective stories, most convincingly in "Knight's Gambit" (1944). Gavin Stevens and the sheriff try to unravel a murder case. "Is it your contention, Gavin, that there is a connection between Mr. Holland's will and Judge Dukingfield's murder?" "Yes," the country attorney said, "And I'm going to contend more than that."

The character of Uncle Gavin, striving for justice, seems to be modeled on the Uncle Abner stories. But Faulkner polished the rather rough Abner figure and improved it. When Uncle Gavin sits in front of a chessboard comparing his moves to those of the criminal, Faulkner has moved very close to the classic detective story, which, in its best examples, is very like a chess problem. In stressing the psychological element he opened up American crime fiction to a wider horizon.

Ross Macdonald, the true successor to Hammett and Chandler, worked in almost the same vein as his models. His detective, Lew Archer—note the name "Archer," borrowed from Sam Spade's murdered partner in *The Maltese Falcon*—is an ex-cop who has left the police force to get away from the constant menace of corruption. In the early novels, from 1949 onward, Archer still uses revolvers and fists, but later acts in a less hard-boiled manner and grows quieter and more reflective.

His clients' cases typically begin as family affairs but the subsequent investigations lay bare intricate networks of avarice formed by lust for power, by jeal-

ousy, and by greed, all of which lead eventually to murder. Gangsters, even whole families, all belong to the same complex, degenerate world.

The crimes in Macdonald's novels are committed frequently in the wealthier parts of Southern California, in white-washed villas, surrounded by palm trees, with the rich wicked and the police corrupt. Again and again somebody is in need of protection and difficult as it may be, Lew Archer simply has to survive to help uncover the morass of complicated motives lying beneath the integument of the laid-back and permissive society.

Almost in a Freudian sense, the identification of the ills in society is enough to start the client on the road to recovery. Archer can keep himself aloof from the relationships of the people he encounters in the same way a psychiatrist distances himself in a personal way; his duty is simply to unmask the evil and let it show in all its hideousness. Rehabilitation is up to the patient.

Sam Spade, Philip Marlowe, Mike Hammer, and Lew Archer are only a handful of the scores of names that carried the private-eye tradition—and the surrogate private eye (reporter, photographer, attorney, and so on)—from its inception in the 1920s up to the present. In the twenties there was Carroll John Daly's Race Williams, a precursor to Dashiell Hammett's Continental Op. As Hammett and Chandler

Paul Newman as private eye Harper in a tight spot in the movie *Harper* (1966), based on Ross Macdonald's novel *The Moving Target* (1949). The name "Harper" is an invention for legal purposes; the role Newman plays is actually that of Lew Archer, the P. I. of the novel.

Julie Smith.

Sara Paretsky.

Jane Langton.

Linda Barnes.

perfected their craft, there was Raoul Whitfield's Jo Gar, Frederick Nebel's Tough Dick Donohue, George Harmon Coxe's "Flashgun" Casey, John K. Butler's Steve Midnight, Norbert Davis's Max Latin, Robert Leslie Bellem's Dan Turner, Jonathan Latimer's William Crane, Cleve F. Adams's Rex McBride, and Brett Halliday's very popular Mike Shayne. After the war, there was Howard Browne's Paul Pine, Wade Miller's Max Thursday, Harold Q. Masur's Scott Jordan, Bruce Cassiday's Johnny Blood, Bart Spicer's Carney Wilde, Michael Avallone's Ed Noon, Richard S. Prather's best-selling Shell Scott, Thomas B. Dewey's Mac, William Campbell Gault's Brock Callahan, Michael Collins's Dan Fortune, Robert L. Fish's José da Silva, Baynard Kendrick's Captain Duncan Maclain, Bill Pronzini's nameless protagonist, Michael Z. Lewin's Albert Samson, Joseph Hansen's Dave Brandstetter, Arthur Lyons's Jacob Asch, Lawrence Block's Matt Scudder, Joe L. Hensley's Donald Kobak, and Stephen Greenleaf's John Marshall Tanner—along with dozens more, including a 1980s crop of female private eyes and surrogates, handled in the classic hard-boiled tradition: Sara Paretsky's V. I. Warshawski, Sue Grafton's Kinsey Millhone, Lillian O'Donnell's Mici Anhalt, Liza Cody's Anna Lee, Marcia Muller's Sharon McCone, Julie Smith's Rebecca Schwartz, and Shannon OCork's T. T. Baldwin.

Of best-selling private eyes, only John D. MacDonald's Travis McGee made it a habit of appearing on the hardcover best-seller lists in the sixties, seventies, and eighties.

Starting out in the pulps, like many of those already mentioned, but moving eventually into the slick magazines, MacDonald—who was an engineer by training and inclination—eventually pioneered a series featuring the irrepressible Travis McGee, an individualist who owns a houseboat off the Florida coast, and who takes on a case only if it happens to suit his own private moral and social code.

MacDonald had finished writing the first books in the series late in 1963. The first, *The Deep Blue Good-By*, was to be published simultaneously with the second, *Nightmare in Pink*. The main character was named Dallas McGee—a felicitous combination of the Western genre and the detective genre, cousins springing from the same American literary roots. In late November President John F. Kennedy was assassinated in Dallas; the decision was immediately made to delay the publication of the McGee books and to expunge the name Dallas so as not to arouse unpleasant memories in the minds of readers.

Joe L. Hensley.

Bill Pronzini.

Jacket design for John D. MacDonald's *Cinnamon Skin*.

Lawrence Block.

Stephen Greenleaf.

When a friend suggested MacDonald name his hero after an Air Force Base—like Travis in California—Dallas McGee became Travis McGee. No matter, even without Dallas McGee, the series was a hit from the beginning.

All the titles feature a color, a marketing gimmick that makes a McGee novel instantly recognizable on the racks, the titles moving rapidly from Blue to Pink to Orange to Amber to Yellow to Gray to Indigo to Lavender and so on. But McGee is more than a private investigator who solves clients' problems. He is a mouthpiece for the author, espousing his attitudes about contemporary issues of a sociopolitical nature.

Thus McGee is an arbiter of sociological and political realities in the world around him. Not only is he unhappy about the decline of quality in America, but he eschews the corruption and venality in business, in government, and in life generally. He assaults those who despoil the environment in particularly evocative prose. He is essentially a detective-philosopher-teacher, not just a man of action with a gun. In spite of McGee's enlightened sociological outlook, MacDonald has been accused of antifeminism by those who feel that Travis McGee's macho attitude is demeaning to women.

Although there is a great deal of action in the McGee stories, they are not overtly violent or offensively bloody. The evil men are sometimes not basically evil at all, but mixtures of good and bad. It is the "good" guys who are sometimes more evil than the bad, which is MacDonald's way of showing the reader that the world itself is not all black and white—but an inscrutable mixture of shades and tones.

McGee is fundamentally an alien, an outsider, a maverick against "progress" and conformity. Use of the Western term "maverick" is deliberate, since the Western motif is quite evident. McGee is the "masked stranger" who rides into town, kills off the villains terrorizing the community, and then rides off again into the sunset. MacDonald says that McGee "whips my dead horses." Travis McGee is a fantasy creature, who involves the reader because of his amorous escapes, his fights, his triumphs, and above all because of his sense of adventure and bravado.

Despite MacDonald's obvious success in America, there are critics who consider him an overrated writer. The sales figures and the size of his worshipful following seem answer enough to that charge.

As can be seen by now, the hard-core, harsh, tough exterior of the early private investigators—the Sam Spades, the Philip Marlowes—over the years has become mellowed into a more soft-boiled shell. When Spade and Marlowe talked, or listened, the dialogue was one-syllable, curt, blatant. With the years, the P. I. has become less and less curt and stiff-lipped and more and more sophisticated.

Almost half a century of fictional private eyes lies between Spade and Spenser, yet both are carved in the same image and both walk to the same beat. Yet Spenser is careful to correct the unwary's spelling of his name, reminding that it is spelled with an "s" just

Robert B. Parker.

Robert Urich, center, as Spenser, Barbara Stock as Susan Silverman, and Avery Brooks as Hawk, in a tense moment on a Boston street in the ABC-TV series *Spenser: for Hire* (1985), based on a novel of Robert B. Parker.

145

like Edmund Spenser. Would *Black Mask* have allowed a private detective to talk about Edmund Spenser? Would Hammett have let Spade quote "Musée des Beaux Arts," a W. H. Auden poem, on viewing a young girl's dead body, as Robert B. Parker, Spenser's creator, does?

The Hammett and Chandler plots and the Robert B. Parker plots are similar, of course. It is the *treatment* that is different. Spenser himself, paradoxically, is the same as Spade and Marlowe and Archer—yet *different*. His very persona presents a curious composite of conflicted elements.

An ex-heavyweight boxer, the man is six feet one, weighs 195 pounds, and can benchpress 250 pounds ten times. Yet he is a consummate amateur sculptor, and cooks so well his gourmet meals are the talk of intellectual Boston. And, of course, his reading and cultural interests are wide-ranging and prodigious.

The plot of the first Spenser novel, *The Godwulf Manuscript* (1973), involves a $100,000 rare-book manuscript that is being held for ransom. But then two murders occur, and it is around their resolution that the plot revolves. In *God Save the Child* (1974), his second, the plot involves a kidnapping, and later a killing. Blackmail, embezzlement, armed robbery, and even terrorism eventually swarm in on Spenser, but he survives, in classic private-eye style.

Yet the tone *is* different. Instead of Spenser pulling a McGee and railing out at society or the world in general, Parker assigns Spenser's girlfriend, Susan Silverman, the role of counselor and analyzer of character subtleties. And Parker assigns Spenser's attitudes about human rights to Hawk, a black on the other side of the law. Yet somehow, even with the disparity of their positions in society, Hawk and Spenser usually see things eye to eye.

Not only is the tone of the writing different, but the dialogue is completely "today"—clever, witty, compelling. The characters are vivid, interesting, and skillfully handled. Hammett taught mystery writers to pare down their diction to a terse, vital style. Chandler taught them to hone their metaphors, depict the world through humorous word pictures. Ross Macdonald taught them to keep the action moving.

Parker learned a great deal from his masters. And the result is a thoroughly readable and diverting exercise in private-eye country. The hatred is there, the violence is there, the diverting characters are there, the suspense and the fear are there. It is all done in a

literary way that is pleasing and stylistically acceptable.

There have now been almost a dozen novels, each one growing a bit more independent from the early style of Hammett, Chandler, Spillane, and the two Macdonalds. There are still some signs of Marlowe, Archer, Spade, and others, but Spenser is becoming his own man.

Parker has remained faithful to the precepts of the game and keeps to the conventions of the genre—rules laid down by the men he has aspired to follow. He is—along with Spenser, his protagonist—the legitimate heir to the Hammett-Chandler-Macdonald tradition.

But times have changed in many ways since the early 1900s. The mores have altered considerably; the demarcation between right and wrong is blurred. Traditional morality has been all but abandoned for practical considerations. Whatever works is okay; the existentialism that began surfacing during the time of Spillane in the postwar 1950s has in the 1980s become almost a way of life.

Spenser *feels* his way between the rocks and cliffs of right and wrong. Tightrope walking was not necessary for Spade or Marlowe. The way was clear then, the code of knight errantry was secure and in place. Spenser *senses* the way to act; in fact, note how close his name "Spenser" resembles the key word "senser." It is his sensibility and his ability to establish simpatico with others that makes him a 1980s hero.

Fighter he may be, good with his fists, better with a gun. Fearless and brave he may be, able to wade into a fight with all odds against him. But it is the *direction* he takes and the way he treats clients, enemies, and associates that so clearly delineates his character lines.

Adrift on a sea without a compass, Spenser is a composite of the rest of us, trying desperately to find the way to go amidst all manner of dangers and perils. What is right? What is wrong? What is good? What is evil? There are no pat answers anymore. People, Spenser *feels*, are more important than statutes. Therefore, when it comes to judging a person, Spenser uses his own value system, evolved painstakingly through the years by trial and error in reading the signals sent out by society.

Like his creator Parker, Spenser is essentially a teacher with lessons to be dealt to those he comes in contact with. Forget that Susan Silverman is the counselor; Spenser has an urge to reform. In *The Judas Goat* (1978), when he finally catches one of the terrorists who is bombing innocent citizens in London, Spenser decides to let the young woman go because he feels she is redeemable. Hawk almost goes berserk, calling Spenser a fool and, worse than that, a naive, an innocent.

One critic believes Spenser and Hawk to be both sides of one coin, with Hawk's set of values those of the earlier Spade and Marlowe, and Spenser's the makeshift values of today's everyman.

Again, when Spenser in *Promised Land* (1976) finds a runaway wife who has been helping out a pair of bank-robbing political activists, his instinct is to shield her and give counsel.

It is interesting to contrast this compassionate attitude—obviously an attitude that reflects the American public's ever-changing tastes—with the already mentioned attitude expressed many years before by Sam Spade after he has unmasked Bridgid O'Shaughnessy as the murderer of Miles Archer and listened to her plea to run away with her:

"Well, if I send you over I'll be sorry as hell," he says in that voice eternalized onscreen by Humphrey Bogart. "I'll have some rotten nights—but that'll pass."

Or, even earlier, as he tells a killer:

"What difference does it make which killing we can prove first-degree murder on? They can only hang you once." Followed by that patented "pleasant" smile of Spade's, the punch line: "And they will."

Dürrenmatt and Requiem for the Crime Novel

One would not be unjustified in believing that when drawing the Hedgehog Giant, Gritli Moser drew the portrait of her murderer.

—Friedrich Dürrenmatt

World War II had brought mankind in a horrifying way face to face with crimes, with hunger, fear, terror, and with the death of millions of people. Guilt and atonement are not essentially themes of fiction, but war novels did take them up and reports from concentration camps and stories of life in the occupied countries revealed an even greater reality.

The Swiss writer, Friedrich Dürrenmatt, was interested in the question of guilt and atonement and he utilized the concept in the crime novel format. *Der Verdacht (Suspicion)* (1952) describes the life of a concentration camp doctor who, managing to conceal his past, becomes the respected director of a Zurich clinic. In order to expose the criminal doctor, Commissar Bärlach risks putting himself into a dangerous position. The detective work of the police is touched on only marginally by the author. His interest is in the psychological development of the main character. He often allows quite irrational elements to intrude into the down-to-earth surroundings of the clinic. In *Der Richter und sein Henker (The Judge and His Hangman)* (1951) Commissar Bärlach can only tackle his opponent, a rogue and international tycoon, by means of fraud and a bit of "dirty work." In the end a policeman, himself a murderer, shoots down the villain. The "triumph" of justice thus becomes questionable. Dürrenmatt is best known, apart from his plays, for *Versprechen (Promise)* (1958). He wrote the script for the film, which deals with a number of sex murders of little girls. Inspector Matthäi succeeds during his investigations in sketching a kind of psychological identity of the criminal; he also baits a trap with a little red-skirted girl who plays by the roadside. With this bait he catches the criminal. Later, however, Dürrenmatt himself changed the script into a novella, which he called *Requiem auf den Kriminalroman (Requiem for the Crime Novel)*. It is quite usual for fate to provide important witnesses, often decisive proof, in the mystery story, but in this case Dürrenmatt decided to let chance *impede* the solution. The detective's calculation is right. The red-skirted girl plays in the woods near the road. Matthäi watches everything from a nearby garage. Yet no criminal is caught in the trap. On the way to the scene—to the deed that is

Friedrich Dürrenmatt.

never committed—the sexually excited murderer meets with an accident. Matthäi perseveres, waiting and waiting. In time he becomes a tragic figure, driven to drink through his sense of failure; ironically the little red-skirted girl grows up to be a disreputable slut. Dürrenmatt's message is that in the real world there are chance factors that may interfere in the logical course of a crime plot. Fate decides the punishment, while the reader remains unsatisfied, left with a bitter feeling of injustice. The hero has sacrificed himself for truth and justice, but this very sacrifice goes unrecognized, understood by nobody. This unhappy ending tends to alienate even the serious reader.

As has been pointed out, the desire for entertainment remained strong during World War II and particularly in the years to follow. Some continental countries translated mysteries by English and American writers, since there was little native material available. Inevitably much writing of small value either in content or presentation was published to fill in the gap of the war years.

In some cases, usually for economic reasons, manuscripts became shorter so that often novels were closer to the short-story length, with resultant changes in structure and in plot. The plots had to be simple with little description of scenery and background. Thus the novel underwent much tightening up since the loose-ranging Victorian days; now there was only a minimum of detail: attention perhaps drawn to a sofa on which somebody was to be murdered, or to the importance of a bunch of wax flowers standing on a small ornamental table. To create credible characters on fewer pages meant introducing less people—in fact only the most important ones. The culprit and the victim could then both be given full attention. Some stories were reduced to these two, interacting together. The time for stereotype figures, cut to a pattern, was past. Dorothy Sayers had given her fictional crime writer these selfsame problems to solve. A. Berkeley Cox, mentioned before as a Golden Age author, maintained that the days of the old crime puzzle, pure and simple, had gone, and that the future lay with "puzzle of character rather than a puzzle of time, place, motive, and opportunity."

These changes had by no means brought about the demise of crime fiction. There was during this period much demand for entertainment at all levels in the years after World War II, and continental countries, including the East European states, all produced and translated a great deal of material. The detective story, now international, had successfully adapted itself to the changing world. The media welcomed it, encouraged by the public's desire for a type of entertainment that appealed both to the intellect and to the emotions.

In this rapidly changing situation, three writers in particular should be mentioned: writers who continued to write in the literary tradition of the 1930s classic mystery, maintained the quality of the English comedy of manners in its conception, and added their own individual flourishes to the established formula. They are Michael Innes in Britain, and Amanda Cross and Emma Lathen in America.

Although it was Cecil Day-Lewis in England—elected Poet Laureate in 1968—who brought real distinction and literary quality to the mystery genre with his detective novels written under the pseudonym of Nicholas Blake, he soon lost interest in producing them year after year. It fell to another literary figure, J. I. M. Stewart, a don at Oxford, to spin out what must be the longest and most consistently entertaining line of erudite mystery novels to bridge the time span from the absolute peak of the Golden Age in 1935 through World War II and to the present mid-1980s—what might be called the "Gilded Age" of the mystery, or a kind of "Golden Age Redivivus."

Innes's output—Innes is the "I." of J. I. M. Stewart—is almost incontrovertibly intellectual, with story lines that involve spectacularly convoluted plots and long, intriguing segments of conversation woven through their pages. From the very beginning, with the publication of *Death at the President's Lodging* in 1935, and the almost immediate reprise in *Hamlet, Revenge!* in 1936, the Innes canon has consisted mostly of urbane, intellectualized, "donnish" works. "President" in the first title, incidentally, refers to a university president and not the President of the United States, causing the book to be retitled in America—rather lamely!—*Seven Suspects*.

Featuring Inspector John Appleby, later Sir John Appleby, the main body of Innes's work involves plots that are somewhat unconventional, although they tend to sacrifice the ingenuity of the best of Ellery Queen or S. S. Van Dine to accommodate the irrepressible jocularity of the court jester that cohabits with the writer in the Innes body. *Hamlet, Revenge!*, for example, involves a complex murder plot with the solution wrapped up in layer upon layer of detailed scholarship regarding the proper and improper manner of producing Shakespeare's plays.

His work can generally be broken down into four basic types of mystery subgenres: the classic puzzle mystery, the "university" mystery, the art-world mystery, and the espionage-adventure mystery of flight and pursuit.

At his best, Innes is an exciting, amusing, and literary writer, providing page-turning episodes that propel the reader through alarmingly extensive morasses of conversation and explication, through sometimes contrived and hard-to-believe developments, but always eventually to satisfactory denouements.

In his "art world" mysteries, Innes is adept at producing sleight-of-hand forgeries—even forgeries *of* forgeries—to keep the ball rolling. His art information is valid and esoteric, and his knowledge of treasures and antiques extensive, providing a gold mine of trivia for the reader as the various characters romp through the plot turns.

In spite of Innes's university background and his first-hand knowledge of college life as a don himself, he rarely uses his settings or his characters to exploit social problems or to espouse political causes. Essentially conservative, he presents both leftists and rightists as potential fanatics, and rarely takes side with either, but rather distances himself from what he seems to feel are intrusions in the general format of the mystery.

Resembling Innes in the ability to evoke the university milieu, Amanda Cross in the United States writes her stories of mystery and murder usually in a setting of an American university campus. A professor of English herself, Cross—whose real name is Carolyn Heilbrun—tunes her stories and characters at a much more realistic pitch than Innes, with the result that her delineation of the university scene is more perceptive, studied, and credible than his.

Michael Innes.

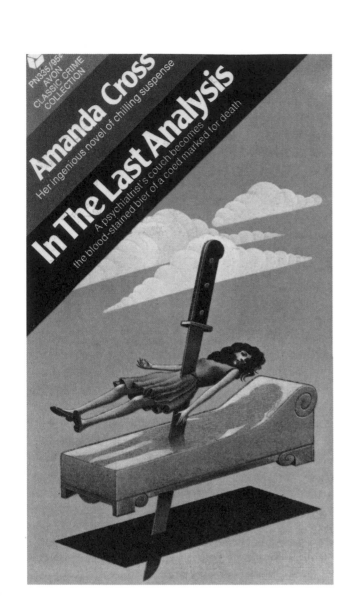

Cover design for Amanda Cross's *In the Last Analysis*.

Cross is literarily a direct descendant of Dorothy L. Sayers rather than Agatha Christie, if one accepts the similarity between "Amanda" and "Agatha" as being deliberate. Like Sayers, Cross is a true scholar and feminist, and a writer interested mostly in the classic mystery rooted firmly in the English comedy of manners.

Her detective creation Kate Fansler *is* Amanda Cross *is* Carolyn Heilbrun, and in the Cross stories she involves herself not only in the particular details of the mystery plot, but becomes emotionally swept up in the crises of the times as well—student revolts in the sixties, the human rights struggle, the women's liberation movement, and so on. From a literary

standpoint, Fansler is a combination of two of the author's favorite literary models—Lord Peter Wimsey and Harriet Vane.

In the Last Analysis, Fansler's debut, appeared in 1964 and is a novel that focuses almost exclusively on the puzzle behind the crime featured. Cross almost studiously follows the elements laid down by the Detection Club in constructing the novel, having present not only a member of the law-and-order establishment in the guise of a prosecuting attorney, but a legman—a male cousin distantly related—to search out clues and observe suspects. The plot itself is classic: it involves disguise, deception, and even murder with a knife. It is in the dialogue and the style of writing that Cross excels.

The puzzle in *Death in a Tenured Position* (1981) is structured around the consequences of the suppression of women by men, especially in the higher echelons of the university hierarchy. Is the death of Janet Mandelbaum suicide—or murder? Has she come to believe that she was hired simply as a visible female to fulfill a university's desire to gender-balance its staff? Or has someone become so jealous of her position that she has become a murder victim? A complication in the presence of the man who is Janet's former husband *and* Kate Fansler's former lover provides a bit of diversion from the academic jousting.

Cross adroitly guides the reader along as she traces the attitudes and beliefs of Kate Fansler from her early feelings about women's liberation (slightly negative and standoffish) to the final stance (almost entirely opposed to the man-oriented university structure).

Even though the traditional puzzle of the classic mystery is present to a degree in all the works of this complex author, the unearthing of clues and the ratiocination involved in deducing truths from them is not the be-all and end-all of her work. If anything, Cross tends to minimize the plot to maximize character interaction, character development, and the presentation of a social environment in terms of her own vision of life.

She also carefully distances herself from violence and the realities of death. In most instances she uses the Greek drama's technique of letting all the murderous action take place offstage—in many cases even *before* the action commences. Thus the details of a murder are only discussed second- or third-hand

and are rarely seen firsthand by the protagonist or reader.

Because Kate Fansler is an English professor, Cross lets her *act* like one; she quotes from literary works—classic and modern. In fact, Kate Fansler even remarks herself that she quotes too much. The bulk of Cross's dialogue is couched in the balanced and rolling style of Samuel Johnson, Oscar Wilde, and, especially, Jane Austen.

In the actual writing of her prose she is much closer to the comedy of manners than the Golden Age of the mystery novel. Think about it: it is indeed no small feat to write a comedy of manners in the style of Jane Austen—and espouse and elucidate at the same time the cause of modern feminism! And Cross does just this.

The works of Emma Lathen are not couched in the prose typical of the English comedy of manners, but they do, nevertheless, deal in a highly literate manner with matters centered in a milieu not much explored in detective fiction: Wall Street, and the world of high finance.

Lathen herself is a collaboration of two individuals—Mary J. LATsis and Martha HENnisart; Emma is a composite of the M in Mary and the M in Martha—one an agricultural economist and the other a lawyer.

The financial background works, and the amateur sleuth Lathen writes about is the vice president of a large bank in Manhattan. John Putnam Thatcher himself is a cool, mature, intellectual, unflappable male, as cold-blooded as any stereotype of a banker, but with some eccentricity inbuilt to allow him occasionally to kick up his heels in an unconventional and engaging manner.

Each Lathen murder case involves a different aspect of the business world—the oil business, the fast-food industry, the pharmaceutical business, the food-processing business, and so on. Through Thatcher's all-knowing eyes, the reader gets a glimpse of the fascinating inside workings of a special type of business venture, with the clues bobbing up every so often to keep the puzzle addicts on the hook.

Lathen is a true clone of Sayers and Christie, with the ability to create likable characters and invent easy-to-read dialogue. Given the public's interest in business ventures, along with "inside stuff" on high finance here and there, the author continues to attract a growing audience of interested readers.

Beginning with the first appearance in *Banking on Death* (1961), Lathen's output continued with *A Place for Murder* (1963), *Accounting for Murder* (1964), and on through *Murder against the Grain* (1966), through *Murder to Go* (1969), *Double, Double, Oil and Trouble* (1978), and on through *Green Grow the Dollars* (1982).

Unlike Amanda Cross's books, and *like* Michael Innes's, Lathen's tend to report the international mores of business as they exist rather than to criticize them. The society that Thatcher inhabits is fundamentally a sound one, even though there are evidences of governmental and personal corruption in the plots that surface with obligatory regularity.

Yet the characters in the novels are people of good sense with an understanding of human behavior and a healthy respect for money. In fact, it is this respect for money and the profits of business that balance out the forces of evil, anarchy, and instability, and inspires Thatcher and his associates to uncover the crimes and bring order once again into the disorder. Peace and quiet, the leitmotif seems to say, is profitable.

Thatcher displays a latent detachment to the world and an ironic, civilized attitude toward his contemporaries that projects to the reader the illusion of a secure world. Contemporary, vivid, and similar to a story read in a daily newspaper, a Lathen crime story is evidence that the classic detective novel, with its link to the Golden Age of the mystery, is alive and well today in the slightly modernized garb of the classic and irrepressible comedy of manners.

The Psychological Thriller

*He seemed only a voice and a spirit now, the spirit of evil,
all he despised, Guy thought, Bruno represented.*

—Patricia Highsmith

Representatives of the traditional detective story, among them Berkeley Cox, had brought to their work strong psychological traits, and what counted now was not the fingerprint, not a gap in the alibi or a careless word, but the actual mentality of the criminal. Margery Allingham, too, who wrote her novels mostly in conjunction with her husband, the editor of *The Tatler*, had tried since the thirties to build her novels on the basis of psychology. This she combined with a touch of irony. The actual plot tended to be overshadowed by sometimes tedious dialogue in which the protagonists all revealed their true character.

Agatha Christie had introduced in Monsieur Poirot and Miss Marple two people unsuited to dangerous pursuits—certainly to hand-to-hand encounters. More and more she relied in her later novels on the use of psychology, subordinating the whole structure of the novel to this concept. She preferred to take cases from the past, using strange happenings of years earlier. New clues were found only in the fate of the characters and in psychological aspects of the case. In the introductory chapters to *Five Little Pigs* (U.S.: *Murder in Retrospect*) (1942) she explains that although the tangible clues are no longer there, the case can well be examined without them. After speaking to people who witnessed the events, the detective needs only reflection. The role of intuition is emphasized in *By the Prickling of My Thumbs* (1968) when a child's seemingly unfounded fear is discussed. "Was it your poor child? She had been frightened then, frightened. She was frightened now. She was as yet not quite sure what she was frightened of, but the same fear was there. Looking at that benignant face, that kindly smile." As it turns out, it is the smile of a murderess. The foreboding of disaster and crime is the chief characteristic of *Nemesis* (1971), in which Miss Marple maintains that the house is shrouded in gloom, a deep gloom that cannot be dispersed and makes her shuddder. The gloom extends even to the old greenhouse so densely overgrown with plants that might well conceal ugly secrets beneath their rich foliage. The reader, who has come to share Miss Marple's feelings, is now willing to share in her examination of the garden, which, she is sure, must hold clues to the riddles of the past. Intuition and feeling were qualities richly possessed by the heroines of the Gothic novel, dating back one hundred and fifty years or more. *Sleeping Murder* (1976), the last case Miss Marple solves, deals with a murder committed long ago and brought to light through memories and dreams of childhood.

It was Ngaio Marsh, a writer from New Zealand and devotee of Christie, who succeeded in combining psychological observation with the traditional hunt for clues and circumstantial evidence. For five decades she produced mystery novels, with her first rooted in the Golden Age and her last in the decade of the 1980s. Like Michael Innes, she managed a formidable output that spanned tremendous innovation and change in the mystery formula.

Her forte was in utilizing the tried-and-true elements of the country-house detective story, the English police procedural, *and* the psychological novel. And she did it in such a way that she *strengthened* the genre, rather than weakened it.

She began her career in London as a transplanted New Zealander, choosing a criminal investigator from Scotland Yard as her protagonist.

Roderick Alleyn, at the time of his debut in *A Man Lay Dead* (1934), is a Chief Detective-Inspector on the London force. Continuing the tradition of Dorothy L. Sayers in Lord Peter Wimsey, Alleyn is of aristocratic background, with one crucial difference: it is Alleyn's *brother* who has the title, not Alleyn. But he, like his forebears, is handsome, charming, witty, and erudite—what more could be wanted in a hero of such an Edwardian caste?

If he is a snob, he is an honest snob who knows his literary quotations and is familiar with cultural details of English life. But he is an expertly conceived combination of the amateur aristocrat and the professional policeman, a type that reaches back into the literary past and updates the French *roman policier* by means of all the modern methods of detection employed by Scotland Yard. Alleyn is a transitional character, a link between the turn of the century and the 1930s.

Basically, the early Marsh novels follow the conventions adopted by the Golden Age writers: specific isolated settings, interrogation of suspects, identification of murderer, and summation of murder methods. Yet she adds two specific backgrounds to her stories, gleaned from her own personal interests—the backgrounds of painting and of the theater.

In her enthusiasm for realism Marsh employed some of the most bizarre methods of murder yet encountered in mystery novels up to that time. For example, in *Vintage Murder* (1937), a jeroboam of champagne is dropped from the flies of a theater stage during a cast party onto the head of the unfortunate host. In *Overture to Death* (1939), the victim, a concert pianist, is shot to death by a handgun cleverly hidden in the piano. In *A Wreath for Rivera* (1949), the victim is stabbed with a poisoned needle hidden in an umbrella handle while he is playing an accordion in a crowded nightclub. In *Tied up in Tinsel* (1972), the victim's face is literally torn off by the blow of an iron poker. The murderer in *Grave Mistake* (1978) forces sleeping pills into the mouth of an already suffocated victim.

Others meet their fates in similarly ghastly manners: by walking into a pit of boiling mud; by being hacked with a sheep hook and then baled in wool; by being crushed under a six-hundred-pound drainpipe; by being skewered through the eye while sitting in an elevator. And so on.

Marsh's puzzles, while not quite so ingenious as Agatha Christie's, are well-constructed, and her clues—half an onion, trout scales, a dead cat, a druidic costume, a damp sheet of music—are cleverly selected to raise all sorts of questions in the reader's mind.

Her success in writing can be laid to her skilled use of dialogue, although some critics feel that she overused it. Nevertheless, her ear for the spoken word, fine-tuned by her theatrical background, is one of the best elements of her work.

There is little social criticism in Marsh's novels; her outlook is placidly middle-class and English, even though she was born in liberally oriented New Zealand and spent most of her life there. Even her attitude toward the police is of solid middle-class origin: they are the good guys; the criminals are the bad guys.

Although P. D. James's writing came along in the third and fourth decades of Marsh's, she too used psychology to provide motivation for evil deeds. Her debut occurred in 1962 with *Cover Her Face*, which she wrote while still employed as an administrator for the National Health Service. Her style is serious and sometimes almost ponderous, but her plots and story lines have a muscularity that succeeds in sustaining the entire superstructure.

James is a successor to Dorothy L. Sayers and Margery Allingham. She is of a later English generation than either of her predecessors, whose detectives were titled, and perhaps that is the reason hers is not. Even so, her first book, set in a country house named Martingale, centers around a traditional locked-room puzzle, and its plot dynamics are conventional. Upon the discovery of a house guest dead in a locked bedroom, Detective Chief-Inspector Adam Dalgliesh is called in, first of all interviews the suspects one by one, travels to London, returns, calls the principals together for a confrontation, and forces the murderer to confess.

In the follow-up novel, *A Mind to Murder* (1963), the setting is a London clinic in which an administrative officer is killed. Dalgliesh, now a Superintendent, interrogates all the principals, and unearths a number of conflicting motivations among the employees. The puzzle in this instance is once again a variation of the locked-room motif.

Unnatural Causes (1967) takes place in a writers' colony, near which Dalgliesh is on a holiday visit to a relative. Instead of the traditional country house, the writers' colony and its group of rather seedy literary types provides the background. Several brutal murders occur, almost dispatching Dalgliesh himself before he unmasks the murderer.

Shroud for a Nightingale (1971) won awards from the Crime Writers Association (Britain) and the Mystery Writers of America (United States). The setting is a nurses' training school, Nightingale House, where a series of poisonings takes place. James drops her quiet approach and features a grisly murder during a demonstration of intragastric feeding in which a murderer mixes lysol with the warm milk poured into the oesophageal tube. Dalgliesh must unravel the complex personal patterns of a number of the student nurses before identifying the murderer.

Ruth Rendell.

Following the lead of her mentor, Dorothy L. Sayers, who switched from Wimsey to Harriet Vane on occasion, James created the character of a female private detective in her fifth novel, *An Unsuitable Job for a Woman* (1972). The story line is faster paced; the writing is more terse; the attitudes are more urban; the entire work is a deliberate breaking out of the classic detective mold and utilizes the action-oriented, dramatic narrative structure of the American private-eye novel—feminine style.

Cordelia Gray becomes accidentally involved in private investigation work, but solves a murder case in the end, and in doing so, is even questioned in the office of James's other detective—Dalgliesh—at Scotland Yard!

After *The Black Tower* (1975), James produced a complex and difficult series of murders in *Death of an Expert Witness* (1977), set in a forensic laboratory in the countryside of East Anglia. The longest of her novels to date, it explores the tangled relationships of a large number of characters, all of them linked to the bureaucratic medical establishment and its day-to-day functions.

Then in 1980 came *Innocent Blood*, a surprise to everyone. It is not a mystery novel at all, but a psychological study of the relationship of a daughter and her natural mother. It is the story of a dual search:

one of a daughter for her unknown mother; the other of a father for the murderer of his daughter. Both lines converge at the crisis of the story. Although there are two deaths in the book, each forcefully and realistically described, it is not a standard detective novel per se, even though the two searchers become amateur detectives of a sort as they pursue their parallel goals.

James's writing is distinguished by the full characterizations given to spear-carriers who are neither main protagonists nor professional detectives. Although she does not mount a soap box to broadcast her sociological ideas, it is obvious that she is aware of the need for societal reform and for the acceptance and rehabilitation by the world of psychologically and physically maimed individuals.

Linked closely with the emergence of P. D. James as a major writer of detective fiction is Ruth Rendell, whose initial novel appeared two years after James's first. Her books fall into two categories: those in the classic mystery format, and those in the suspense or psychological format. Although the regular detective format provides Rendell with a good springboard for exciting mysteries, it is on the psychological level that she has produced her strongest work.

From Doon with Death (1964) features Detective Chief-Inspector Reginald Wexford, whose bailiwick is a small mid-Sussex town. Wexford is a fully realized character with a wife, children, friends, and a foil in the person of Inspector Michael Burden. Working in a classic form—the English version of the French *roman policier*—Rendell produces a leisurely paced English police procedural, with nice suburban touches, with interesting if sometimes eccentric characters, and embellished with neat plot switches. It is in these offerings that Rendell is able to provide the reader with excellently contrived surprise endings; she has a talent for working up believable but startling revelations.

In subject matter, she is light-years removed from Sayers and even James, with her plots treating of sexual repression and its fatal consequences, transvestism, lesbianism, and all manner of the modern psychological ills familiar to readers of Krafft-Ebbing. Rendell sees the world with modern eyes and treats her characters in like fashion. She is particularly interested in looking just under the surface of a personality to scrutinize the psychological irregularities that make the individual tick.

The Wexford novels recreate suburbia as it exists today in the modern English countryside, with a fine ear for dialogue, and with a fine eye for picking up the nuances of modern living.

The best of these conventionals? Probably *Shake Hands Forever* (1975) and *A Sleeping Life* (1978). Of course there are others. Rendell proves in these novels that she can handle the traditional, structured, classic detective novel effectively and competently.

It is in her non-series novels—those that do not feature Wexford—that many readers and critics believe she excels. It is in them that she explores the quirks in psychological behavior that make human beings into monstrous creatures, into forces of evil propelled to disrupt, destroy, and ruin those about them.

These novels are described by some as chillers, and they do certainly chill the reader. They do not adhere to any of the rules of the mystery genre as it was practiced by the Golden Age writers. Indeed the very first words of *A Judgement in Stone* (1977) reveal the murderer and the plot line: "Eunice Parchman killed the Coverdale family because she could not read or write." Despite this infraction of the rules of the Detection Club of London observed faithfully by the mentors of the Golden Age, the book itself is as suspenseful and as gripping as any story in which the killer's identity is deliberately withheld until the end.

In effect, Rendell probes into the *meaning* of the psychology of murder in these chillers. With the quirks of the mind in plain view, she then watches the maimed personalities wander through their wastelands much like Frankenstein's monster wandered about the countryside unable to realize the impending tragedy of which he was the central force.

Just one example: In *A Demon in My View* (1976), a protagonist with a psychological problem of submerged sexual repression keeps a clothing store dummy in a basement in order to work off his feelings of rage by strangling it from time to time. Then, one evening, as he passes a Guy Fawkes fire just beginning to burn in the street down the block he sees to his horror that his mannikin is slowly being consumed by flames!

The suspense from that point on is unbearable. The reader *knows* he will be forced to kill to satisfy his twisted urges; whom will he do in? How? When? A madman has been loosed on London, a time bomb walking the unsuspecting streets about to explode.

And with cool calculation and in full control of her material, Rendell follows the "demon" to ultimate rage and destruction.

She is certainly the most adept of the modern writers at handling the psychologically maimed—and, oddly enough, she handles them with compassion, with a kind of tenderness, and with heartfelt sympathy.

Writing in an entirely different vein, but essentially interested in the study of people and their psychological needs and outlooks, June Thomson is a contemporary of Ruth Rendell and P. D. James. Thomson's technique is quite different from Rendell's, although in some surprising instances story elements of both writers are the same: actions that result from twisted psychological motives and lead a person into crime.

Thomson hews to the classic detective formula, writing her novels in the tradition of the modern English police procedural. Inspector Finch appears as Inspector Rudd in the American version of all her books except the first. The American publisher who agreed to do her second book, Thomson says, insisted on the change of name because there already was an Inspector Finch on its publishing list.

The name Rudd, which Thomson chose as a substitute for Finch, symbolizes the English countryside, as does Finch. The inspector is a man of the soil, a man who comes from East Anglia, where he now works, a man who has risen in rank in the place he now solves crimes. He knows the country folk and he understands their inner motives.

Interestingly enough, Thomson is able to portray the countryside realistically, exploring the typical dweller in a tiny village with precision and believability. The first book *Not One of Us* (1971) depicts a small community that closes ranks on all outsiders. The leitmotif of alienation is prevalent throughout most of her work.

Yet there is much more to a Thomson novel than the countryside and the plowing up of clues to expose a murderer. She concentrates her energies on describing in detail the flowers, the grass, the trees, every bit of the scene as each character sees it. The houses, the buildings, the streets, the roadways, the sky—all enter into this picture. And yet somehow, under all these *quite ordinary things* there is something sinister, something evil, something *dead wrong* out there waiting ...

Dorothy Salisbury Davis.

And that something wrong is not necessarily a traditional motive for murder, like simple greed. Thomson explores such forbiddens as incest (twice), homosexualism, and other relationships, and even frequently eschews capturing and punishing the murderer. At times she will opt to leave him or her—thoroughly unmasked—to suffer the consequences of censure within the confines of a strictured social milieu. In the hands of June Thomson, such abnegation can be almost a fate worse than death.

Although she plays fair with the reader in the Golden Age sense, Thomson does not depend on the laborious uncovering of physical clues that instantly bring the truth into focus for the reader. Nor does she depend on a Freudian slip of the tongue, of the inadvertent use of a false word to tip off the detective. She uses the system of interrogation itself exactly the way it is used by the police.

Thus Inspector Finch/Rudd probes more and more deeply into each of his suspects from day to day, fitting the tiny facts that emerge together in logical pattern, until in the end, the case makes the most perfect sense. While the pace of the writing may seem leisurely, Thomson exerts a potent force on the reader's curiosity, and while not in the page-turning class of a Rendell, she can exert pressure on even the most apathetic of readers.

Nor does she allow herself to wander from the confines of the fictional countryside she has created. When Finch/Rudd travels to London, he sees it as an outsider. He thinks about whatever he sees in relation to East Anglia—the place where he was born and bred.

Thomson does not celebrate inhabitants of a country manor; rather she celebrates individuals who have always lived in small villages and *around* country manors, and who have always been in service to the wealthy and the leisured classes.

The American writer, Dorothy Salisbury Davis, named in 1984 a Grand Master by the Mystery Writers of America, works in the psychological vein in a manner similar to these three English writers, but she approaches her material a bit differently. She is concerned with the psychology of evil rather than with the unveiling of a murderer. Her stories tend to be studies of crises of faith, sexual conflicts, or identity problems. The fact that she was an adopted child, she once said, may account for her compelling interest in the search for one's true roots. *A Death in the Life* (1976) is generally considered her best book, telling the story of Julie Hayes and her struggle to cope in one of New York's seamier neighborhoods.

An American writer in the psychological vein who plays fair in a Golden Age way with her reader by presenting all the clues to the mystery as she goes along is Martha Grimes. She believes in the use of the psychology of insight and observation, making her detectives function accordingly. Even though American-born, Grimes sets all her novels in England, with Detective Chief-Inspector Richard Jury of Scotland Yard acting as her police detective, and the Earl of Caverness, Lord Ardry, Twelfth Viscount in the Ardry-Plant line—in other words, Melrose Plant—as her amateur sleuth. Grimes's titles are usually the names of real English pubs—*The Man with a Load of Mischief* (1981), *The Old Fox Deceiv'd* (1982), *The Anodyne Necklace* (1983), and so on.

The emotional mood Grimes frequently evokes is frightening enough, but it is not the stuff of horror associated with other more Gothic-oriented writers. Some of these authors, combining psychology with a strong accent on the emotions, have gone back to the props of the Gothic novel. Victor Gunn, pseudonym for Edwy Searles Brooks, hinted in his very titles at mysterious happenings. In *The Laughing Grave* (1955) a whole village is under the spell of an old legend, describing the terrifying laughter that comes from a grave and kills any passerby who hears it. Gunn's heroes, Chief Inspector Bill Cromwell of Scotland Yard and his assistant John Lister, are themselves a little shaken when in the dark of night they pass a cemetery in the eerie light of the moon and hear ghastly spine-chilling laughter. In the end the puzzle is solved and reason prevails. The murders turn out to have been committed by a Lady Haverford who used a loudspeaker system, taking advantage of the deep-seated superstition of the locals. Confronted with apparently irrational happenings, the reader must have a rational and convincing explanation. That is exactly what made *The Hound of the Baskervilles* a classic. Psychology and the blending of strange folklore motifs occurs also in other branches of literature.

Ira Levin, known through his modern horror stories, wrote *A Kiss before Dying* (1953), transferring the "Bluebeard" tale to modern times and a big American city. Hugh Pentecost wrote spy thrillers but in his Pied Piper title, *The Day the Children Vanished* (1976), set up a crime puzzle. Who had kidnapped the children, how, and why? Not long after its publication the plot of this novel became reality when a busload of children disappeared without a trace. Pentecost's writing nearly always finds a psychological solution. In the end all occurrences—the kidnapping, the turning up of caps, coats, and schoolbooks in the waterhole of a quarry—are only maneuvers to distract attention from a bank robbery.

Psychological thrillers by the Norwegian, Bernhard Borge, combine elements of detection with those of the horror tale. Borge sets his plots in the remote countryside where belief in the supernatural is common. As the demoniac may, of course, lie in man himself, a psychoanalyst plays an important role in the investigations. *Nattmennesket (Night People)* makes childhood experiences responsible for a murder. Borge stresses the melodramatic aspect of crime fiction by ironical remarks in which he maintains that in a really gripping story the first murder must happen if not at the bottom of page 2 at least on the beginning of page 3. The deaths must then follow rapidly one after the other. A crime story costing four *kroner* must not contain fewer than four murders! *De Dødes Tjern (Death at Sea)* is different. Old legends and the belief in ghosts lend atmosphere to the plot and the author continues in this vein with *Døde Menn*

Går i Land (Dead Men Go to Ground), using the theme of the Flying Dutchman. Here the end remains vague with the reader uncertain whether he is involved in actual crimes or in the acts of ghosts on the coast of Norway. The case is never solved.

The development of the psychological crime story was not restricted to one or two countries. In France the novels of Pierre Véry and of the literary collaborators Pierre Boileau and Thomas Narcejac followed this same trend. Véry offers many mysteries, but all have rational solutions in the end.

Together Boileau and Narcejac ("Narcejac" was the nom de plume of Pierre Ayrand) published twenty crime novels in which ancient superstitions play their part, motivating the deed and at the same

Martha Grimes.

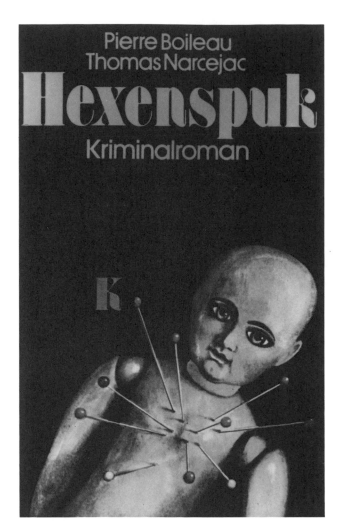

Cover design for *Witches' Spook* by Pierre Boileau and Thomas Narcejac.

ancestral home, making for a tale full of romantic horror. The second part relates how the descendants of the family who now own the ruined castle find the solution of these mysteries of the past. Criminals, not ghosts, were at the castle at one time, committing their foul deeds and carrying off their victims in a phantomlike coach. In *Maléfices (Spells of Evil)* (1961) the theme is a belief in wicked spells, whereas in fact a combination of arsenic and treacherous trapdoors are to blame for a variety of misdeeds. A woman in the Vendée, of strange and exotic appearance, becomes increasingly suspect and then in the end is the victim of a flood. Was her death murder? The question remains open without the story losing its tension. Rauchelle, attracted by two women, shares the

Cover design for Margaret Millar's *Beast in View*.

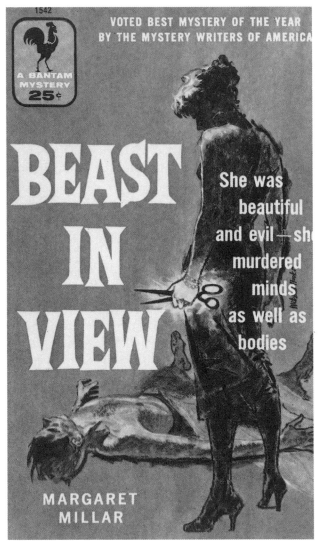

time hiding the crime. In *Celle Qui N'était Plus (The Woman Who Was No More)* (1954)—also known as *Les Diaboliques (The Fiends)* (1965) because of a film made of it under that title by Clouzot—a man who believes himself to be the murderer of his wife because he has planned to kill her becomes driven through fright and fear of the unknown into suicide. It then turns out that the whole weird situation has been set up by his wife who is, in fact, still alive. Although the case is solved, the murderess survives, apparently unscathed. *Au Bois Dormant (Asleep in the Woods)* (1956), published in two slim volumes, deals with the era following the French Revolution—the early nineteenth century in the first, the present in the second. The story tells of the mysterious experiences of the Seigneur de Muzillac who finds a family of ghosts in his

Still from film made from Patricia Highsmith's
The Talented Mr. Ripley, showing Alain Delon as Ripley,
Maurice Ronet as Philippe, and Marie Laforet as Marge.

fatal drive through rising floods; later he asks himself whether he is to blame for what happened, his mind going round in a mad whirl of unanswered questions.

Boileau and Narcejac introduced into their novels a great deal of subtle psychology. They maintained in an essay on the *roman policier* that their own work was closer to the mystery story than to the crime novel; at the same time they gave high praise to Georges Simenon in the development of that genre.

Chesterton with his *Father Brown* stories had drawn special attention to the human aspects of each case. In America Harry Kemelman worked along those lines in his novels concerning Rabbi David Small. The rabbi tracks down crime to protect the members of his community from wickedness and sus-

picion, as does the old priest in Fortune de Boisgobey's *Le Coup de Pouce (The Finishing Touch)* much earlier. *Friday the Rabbi Slept Late* (1964) was the first in a series of novels in which the rabbi, together with the chief of police, uses logic and human understanding to solve murders committed on the steps of the synagogue. Their joint effort helps stop an upsurge of antisemitism in the town. In his following novels, all arranged by the days of the week, Kemelman's idyllic description of small-town life almost overshadows the detective interest.

Patricia Highsmith is perhaps most convincing in her portrayal of man sliding into crime. Her attitude to the criminal varies as the motivation decides the measure of guilt. In *Strangers on a Train* (1950) two men meet; one is unstable and the other a criminal type planning a double murder. The unstable man can be forced into crime but cannot commit the deed without fear and self-blame. The hero of *Deep Water*

(1958) is a well-known printer and publisher, a good father, a friend, and neighbor. He remains that while his wicked, amoral wife whom the reader has come to hate pushes him into murdering her discarded lovers. One is drowned, apparently by accident, in a swimming pool during a party, while another disappears in a pond at a lonely quarry. A crime writer, a nosey man, disliked by his neighbors, trails the criminal but does not become the tale's hero in spite of his success as a detective. The reader's sympathy and understanding is focused on the unhappy husband and father driven into committing the crimes.

In *The Talented Mr. Ripley* (1955) criminal and victim face each other, although the plot makes it clear that the victim is not entirely without guilt and that the criminal is a victim in some ways too—psychologically scarred and forced into action. In the end Ripley turns to violence. In *Ripley under Ground*

Illustration for "The Red Chamber," a Poe-like short story by the Japanese writer, Edogawa Rampo.

(1970), however, he does not murder in cold blood—keeping a well-prepared alibi in readiness—but kills to save his profitable business in forged paintings. Possibly Highsmith had the real-life art frauds of van Megeeren in mind. Ripley eventually buries the murdered man in the cellar, and from then on, living in terror of being found out, ends his days in deceit and self-loathing.

An entirely modern method of dealing with the subject of crime is the historical detective novel, recreating the thoughts and behaviors of past centuries. Peter Lovesey, a philologist, relied on material culled from late nineteenth-century newspapers for his series of early novels of Victorian crime. In *Mad Hatter's Holiday* (1973) the young murderer is discovered and punished by his father while the police are said to require no further investigations. Obviously the police are anxious not to destroy the image of a respectable Victorian family.

Elizabeth Mackintosh wrote plays under the pen name of Gordon Daviot and crime novels as Josephine Tey. In her novel *The Daughter of Time* (1951), harking back to the fifteenth century, Inspector Grant, sick and bedridden, turns to the investigation of historical events. There are doubts that Richard III really instigated the murder of the young princes in the Tower and that he was the monster history and Shakespeare made him out to be. Her novel does not supply an answer to that question but it does paint a brilliant canvas of the period. In 1950 John Dickson Carr wrote the first of a series of historical novels—*The Bride of Newgate*—but his best was *The Hungry Goblin* (1972), in which the role of detective was played by Wilkie Collins. There are comparatively few historical crime novels; the moment a writer begins using facts and dates, the work seems to enter the realm of the Pitaval case history, leaving fiction altogether.

Ever since the seventeenth century a literary tradition of recording legal cases has existed in Japan. In the nineteenth century translations of Poe, Hoffmann, and Conan Doyle appeared, leading eventually to an interest in native crime fiction. The genre, however, never developed into a separate branch of literature, although it has grown in popularity through the years, producing scores of mystery works. There was a kind of Golden Age in the 1930s when Edogawa Rampo—born Hirai Taro—earned a wide and loyal readership with his thirty-odd mystery novels and numerous short stories in the genre. His pseudonym, incidentally, was a direct transliteration of the American name Edgar Allan Poe (pronounced *edoga-aran-po* in Japanese). Rampo argued successfully that the novel of crime had a definite function in the wide spectrum of writing, and that an important part of its function was to entertain. His *Nisendoka (The Two-Sen Piece)* (1923)—the title refers to a small Japanese coin—provides a good example of the author's work. Crime stories were often published in Japanese magazines before appearing in book form. *Shinseinen (Early Adolescence)* was a particular favorite with writers and public. Authors willing to experiment still took their cue from international trends. Their raw material, however, came from daily life in Japan, usually set in urban areas.

Seicho Matsumoto, a currently popular crime writer, uses as his vehicle the psychological thriller. His novel, *Ten to Sen* (*Points and Lines*, or *The Timetable Game*) (1957), concerns a skillfully disguised murder. All evidence points to the double suicide of a couple, but when studied from a psychological point of view, many questions remain unanswered and many facts seem debatable. Why did the man go to the dining car alone? Why was no hotel room booked for his mistress? Rail timetables and plane connections provide the killer with a false alibi. Nevertheless, police investigators trace the murderers—a sordid couple who commit suicide after the deed rather than face trial. The author gives the tale this rather insipid and unsatisfactory ending in order to provide the reader with food for thought as well as entertainment.

Writers on the subject of the psychological crime story have not fully appreciated the interesting contribution to the subgenre from the Soviet Union. Pavel Shestakov, a historian and teacher, defended his choice of the crime novel by maintaining that it allowed writers to describe how people choose to live their lives, what their aims are, and how they act to achieve them. Crime fiction, according to him, deals with what is permissible and what is not; it is both the best and the worst in man. The popularity of crime fiction played a large part in Shestakov's choice of writing, since it gave him a large readership. He knew English examples of the genre, perhaps through the work of Conan Doyle who was always popular in the Soviet Union and available in collected editions.

Seicho Matsumoto.

In Shestakov's novella *Strakh vysoty (Fear of Heights)* (1968) the suicide of Tykhmirov, a talented young student, turns out to have been an accident, caused by vertigo while standing on a balcony. At the same time the investigation considering the case establishes the fact that he passed sentence on himself. Anxious to succeed and make his way in the world quickly, he has secretly used results obtained by another scientist in the development of his own thesis. After getting his degree his old fear of heights seizes him again. The effect of looking down from a height coupled with the guilty knowledge of his undeserved success causes him to fall. The character of Tykhmirov confirms the fact that the author was not keen on portraying an outright villain. For Shestakov the question of guilt remains problematical.

Another of Shestakov's novellas, almost the length of a novel, *Tri dnya v Dagestane (Three Days in Dagestan)* (1968), combines psychological insight with murder in analyzing a crime within a small circle of suspects. One evening at a mountain resort locals and holidaymakers assemble in the house of an artist. There is a thunderstorm and the lights go out at the very moment the artist is murdered. Masin, a criminologist, by chance holidaying there, needs only three days to clear up the case. The culprit is an old criminal, now settled as a beekeeper nearby. Masin, giving the facts of the case in the end, tries to explain the psychology and thought patterns of an aged professional criminal who has shown decisiveness, ingenuity, and energy beyond the usual abilities of a frail old man.

In a Polish novella, concerned with family affairs, the culprit is not punished by the law, but falls into a trap he himself has set for an innocent person. In the end psychological considerations come near to obscuring the crime interest. *Ikony (The Icon Snatch)* (1978) by Waclaw Bilinski, is a case in point: a precious old icon is stolen and when the robbers make their escape they are involved in an accident, caused by the appearance of a ghost in the middle of the road. Eventually the robbery takes a back seat as the author finds it necessary to expose hypocrisy, egotism, greed, and unbridled sex in the characters. The icon ironically lies neglected in a bog by the roadside.

The atmosphere of horror often exploited in the psychological thriller may be limited to everyday happenings that cause fear and make the reader shudder—not vaults, ghosts, and subterranean passageways. Since the reader *wants* to shudder, albeit at a cozy distance, the hero must experience the same sensation so that the reader can identify with him.

Just as his predecessor in the Gothic novel, the hero is a frightened, hunted being, although he now lives in the practical world of today. It is important to the reader that in the end all evil should be defeated. In the novels by Ursula Curtiss rational thinking though taken into account, is often shown as being in conflict with the emotions. Curtiss does not employ ancient abbeys and castles to arouse tension, but exposes dark and threatening aspects of everyday life in the United States. Loneliness by itself is threatening. The action of her books usually takes place in quiet suburban streets or in old houses in the country. Gardens, trees, and shrubberies are natural objects, and play an important role. They seem both threatening and protective at the same time. The sense of danger may arise quite suddenly. *The Iron Cobweb* (1953) be-

gins characteristically with the heroine expressing sudden dreadful, unreasoning fear. Unlike Miss Marple, Curtiss's heroines often lack helpful intuition: in *Deadly Climate* (1954) the heroine, looking for protection, makes her way straight into the murderer's house, while earlier a harmless potting shed would have caused her apprehension and even terror. When eventually all puzzles are solved, the malignant force is seen not as a power in itself, not emanating from houses or trees, but a psychological evil developing in a human being who will eventually be brought to book or perhaps die while trying to escape.

The emotional experience is the fulcrum, the center from which tension arises; as a result this type of novel can safely be called a "thriller." As mentioned before, this subgenre is a direct descendant of the Gothic novel, clearly spelling out the sense of angst in the modern world arising from fears and doubts of the future.

The thriller has many faces and is not limited to crime fiction. It exploits the emotional, the mysterious, the strange—things scarcely or not at all explicable by reason. The thriller provides excellent material for film and television, more so than the traditional detective story, because it transforms emotion, together with fears and longings, into action, action that is readily conveyed on the screen.

There are two ways of creating tension and giving the reader an agreeable frisson—one is danger, the threat of an impending catastrophe that may occur in daily life with no special horror props, something that happens suddenly "on a day like any other." This is so in *The Desperate Hours* (1954) by Joseph Hayes. Three criminals on the run break into the house of a middle-class suburban family and hold it hostage for several hours, trying to extort money. Members of the family, helpless and confused to begin with, slowly face up to the situation and finally take positive action. The reader can easily identify with these everyday people. The other way of creating tension is to bring together as many horror motifs as possible, motifs beyond the modern world of glass, concrete, and comfortable apartments. With Margaret Millar's *A Stranger in My Grave* (1960) this method is obvious in the title itself as it is in her novel *Beyond This Point Are Monsters* (1970). In this latter work latent madness and hallucinations rule victim and criminal. *A Stranger in My Grave* reflects the fear and spiritual distress of the young heroine,

Still from the film *Rebecca*, from the Daphne du Maurier
novel. Joan Fontaine as the second Mrs. de Winter,
and Judith Anderson as the sinister housekeeper,
Mrs. Danvers.

who is driven inexorably towards suicide by her apparently loving and kindly husband. Here a rational
explanation of what seems irrational is very effective.

In *Rebecca* (1938) Daphne du Maurier paints the
portrait of a woman, the first Mrs. de Winter, who in-
tends to commit suicide. She tries to trick her husband into murdering her so that he, too, will be destroyed. Maxim de Winter survives with the guilt of
murder hanging over his head, even though happily
married again. Eventually the truth is discovered. In
some of her tales Daphne du Maurier gives no rational explanation of facts but simply relies on letting
unhappy forebodings turn into reality. In *Don't Look
Now* (1971) she relates how an artist and his wife go
to Venice after the death of their daughter. Following
a number of sinister and unexplained accidents the

man sees in his mind's eye a funeral gondola go down
the Grand Canal. On board, in mourning, are his
wife, since returned to England, and friends; he
knows without a doubt why they are there and what
the sad occasion is. He had meant to leave Venice
some time earlier because he had foreseen disaster,
but is compelled to stay, unable to escape his own
fate—death at the hands of a mad dwarf. Fate takes
over, an old motif, which, with the help of psychology, makes an unusually strong impact here.

The success of du Maurier's *Rebecca* pointed the
way for an almost spectacular rise in the popularity
of the romantic mystery thriller in the years following
World War II. In postwar England Victoria Holt, a
pen name for Eleanor Burford Hibbert, began producing a string of successful romantic thrillers in the
Gothic tradition that duplicated the unmistakable
highly charged emotional atmosphere of du Maurier's succès d'estime. Typical of Holt's works is *The
Shivering Sands* (1969), in which a quicksand becomes
a potential trap for the unwary heroine.

Phyllis A. Whitney.

These unabashedly emotional tales involve Gothic elements of murder, intrigue, threats of insanity, family skeletons a-rattle in the closet, and ghosts abroad in the moonlight. Yet in spite of these grisly aspects, Holt writes in a sunny, spare, yet colorful style. *The House of a Thousand Lanterns* (1974) takes place in Hong Kong, and contains finely wrought background descriptions, clues dropped along the way, and a sense of menace hovering over the protagonist. But the mayhem is genteel, and the writing itself more romantic than the malignant, muted hysteria of the real Gothic. The romantic thriller thus was becoming yet another face of the crime thriller subgenre.

Several American writers became best sellers following the trend, among them Phyllis A. Whitney. Whitney's books are not classic Gothics, yet she hews to Gothic elements: the isolation of the heroine in a house, residence, or structure of some kind; weird, sometimes supernatural, occurrences piling up one on top of another; strange events with no rational explanation, at least on the surface; the placing of the heroine in jeopardy; the atmosphere and mood of the old-fashioned ghost story.

Whitney was born in Yokohama. Perhaps because of this enforced interest in the exotic, she sets the majority of her romantic suspense novels in foreign locales. The setting to her is almost as important as characterization and plot. She thoroughly researches each place she writes about.

Blue Fire (1961) takes place in South Africa. *Black Amber* (1964) is set in Turkey. Japan is the scene of *The Moonflower* (1958), an English country house of *Hunter's Green* (1968), the Virgin Islands of *Columbella* (1966), and Norway provides the background for *Listen for the Whisperer* (1972).

Most of Whitney's novels revolve around the members of a family; essentially, she writes a "family mystery," and in doing so, favors two basic variations of this formula. One involves the return of the female protagonist to a home she has left many years before. Events occur that upset her. She cannot understand what is happening. A feeling of anxiety and unease is in the air. She begins to fear for her life. And with good reason. In another, a young bride settles into the home of her husband. In this brand new milieu strange, upsetting events occur. She does not understand why these unnerving things are happening, and tries to find out what is causing such obvious anxiety and distress. With dire results.

The typical Whitney offering usually involves an actual unsolved crime—probably murder—that has occurred sometime in the past. The arrival of the protagonist on the scene then sets off complications that place her life in jeopardy.

In many cases, the heroine is searching into her past. Usually she uncovers a criminal plot of some kind, and on its discovery achieves a sense of personal identity. She may be involved in a mother-daughter relationship, possibly one overlaid with competitive antagonism.

The story line rarely delves into detection or deduction, but there is a great deal of poking about, with few real secrets divulged in the course of the narrative action. This unsuccessful probing heightens suspense to an almost unbearable degree, until at the very end the villain is unmasked, the methodology of the crime is revealed, the motive is divulged, and the reward goes to the heroine. Only at this point does everything come clear in a blinding flash.

The evil is usually that of an ambiguous kind; the unease, the angst experienced by the protagonist is overall, pervasive, and amorphous at best. Yet it is nevertheless very real. Real enough to put Whitney's books frequently on the best-seller lists, constantly swelling her legions of faithful fans.

Mary Higgins Clark is another American who has molded the trappings of the romantic thriller to her own specific talents, much in the manner of Ursula Curtiss. Whitney utilizes most of the favorite elements of the nineteenth-century writers in the form without too much alteration; Clark does too, but after borrowing them she reshapes them until they are almost unrecognizable.

She came onto the scene in 1975, when her first novel, *Where Are the Children?* appeared to strong sales and solid reader interest. The second, *A Stranger Is Watching*, came out in 1978, and was immediately purchased for motion pictures, with MGM releasing in 1982. Her third, *The Cradle Will Fall*, appeared in 1980, and it too was purchased for filming, this time by CBS for a "Movie of the Week," broadcast in 1984. *A Cry in the Night* (1982) was filmed and opened in 1985.

Clark's romantic thrillers are tougher and scarier than most traditional Gothics. Unlike Whitney, she does not depend on an old house, a moldering residence, or an ancient castle for her backgrounds. She sets her stories in the everyday world with which her readers are well acquainted.

It is important to realize that the romantic thriller is in no way a detective novel. Only the protagonist—never a police officer and never an amateur detective—is at the center of the action. There are no clues of the type a policeman searches for in order to establish leads or to make deductions. The members of the police force who may be about are present for reasons not usually involving the heroine's problem per se.

In a Clark story, terror is always lurking very close to the surface of one's everyday experiences in life. Her characters are ordinary people, but unlike them, her protagonist is caught up quite suddenly and frighteningly in a situation fraught with evil—on a bus ride, in a crowded store, while vacuuming the living-room rug, or in another situation known to everybody. The familiar world about her suddenly takes on a sinister cast that quite soon becomes menacing, dangerous, and finally, life-threatening. Clark uses the elements of the mystery novel in the same way the English writer June Thomson uses them in her stories of the English countryside.

For example, the protagonist of *The Cradle Will Fall* inadvertently sees an unknown man placing what appears to be the body of a dead woman in the trunk of a car. Later on the heroine learns that her sister's neighbor—a pregnant housewife—has been murdered. The protagonist then learns the identity of the man with the body: he is a world-famous obstetrician known for his work with women unable to conceive. The fact that the heroine *knows* this world-famous obstetrician to be a killer means nothing. She has no proof, nor can she convince anyone that what she has seen is real. When the obstetrician finds out she knows, she is in deep trouble. From that moment on, it is a matter of survival by the moment.

From the beginning of a Clark book the salient facts are known, much in the manner of a Ruth Rendell non-Wexford novel. In spite of the fact that there are no secrets to spring at the end of the story, Clark manages to propel the reader through the pages of mounting suspense in the same manner that Rendell does. How can the heroine protect herself from this mad killer doctor? How can she bring him to justice? More to the point, how can she survive?

One trick Clark has mastered in her treatment of this type of novel is one the father of the suspense film—Alfred Hitchcock—understood instinctively from the beginning. So too, in fact, did the Greeks. That trick is to set a story or a narrative incident within a strict time frame. Hitchcock's bomb is going to go off in twenty minutes. The audience knows it; the hero or heroine does not. Or perhaps the hero or heroine *does* know it, which only increases the suspense and the dread.

Where Are the Children? takes place within the time frame of one day, *A Stranger Is Watching* in three days. The plots of these stories are carefully constructed so that by the time the story reaches its conclusion the suspense has become almost unbearable. The terror building in the reader is the dread of knowing that *something is going to happen* to the protagonist; will she discover the truth in time to do something about it?

Clark tries to establish a true sense of values in her work that will create a rapport between herself and her readers; she tries to delineate strong people who are able to confront the forces of evil surfacing to destroy them; she tries to show how individuals who are good can actually vanquish the multiple evils seeking to do them in.

Dick Francis.

For a Clark character fate never intervenes; it is up to the individual to fight her own battle for survival. In this manner, she manages a social commentary on the world about her, holding up a mirror to society, showing people how they *can* react to the wildly fictional situations she improvises for their amusement and occasional frisson.

Dick Francis utilizes many of the elements of the classic murder mystery, but he does not really write a detective story. He utilizes many of the elements of the private-eye novel, too, but his amateur sleuths are usually not investigators per se. What Dick Francis does is feature one more face of the "thriller"—call it the crime thriller if you will. Neither a puzzler nor a P.I.er, a Francis book nevertheless exploits tension to create suspense, working on the emotions of the reader for its emotional effects.

What is most exceptional about Francis is that he was successful at an entirely different profession (that of jockey) before he took up novel writing in 1962. He won 345 of 2,305 races, and placed and showed in 525, then retired from horse racing in 1957 to become a sports reporter for the London *Sunday Express*. Learning quickly how to rein in on excess ver-

biage in the same manner he reined in on an over-eager mount, Francis honed a rapid-fire style of writing that won him fans as a reporter.

In his off-time he wrote an autobiography of his days on the track, and after that appeared to an interested public, tried his hand at a mystery novel. *Dead Cert* came out in 1962, a fast-paced story about a steeplechase jockey who uncovers a race-fixing scheme at the same time he falls in love with a girl who turns out to be the daughter of the fixer. The novel winds up with a tremendously exciting horse chase through the wooded English countryside.

Even in his initial novel, Francis was unconsciously creating the prototype for a recurring protagonist, under whatever name he might appear. That hero was all of several most important things, and more: the independent loner, sometimes alienated emotionally from a wife or a family; the repressed male, perfectly ordinary on the outside, but propelled by deep emotion within; the individual somehow maimed to a degree by physical, psychological, or familiar problems.

Yet each Francis protagonist is a different person, with a different name, and a different life-style. The author's choice of professions for his protagonists is wide-ranging. The typical hero has been a jockey, a journalist, a pilot, a movie star, a bloodstock agent, a toymaker, an artist, an accountant, an envoy, a photographer, a financier, a kidnap consultant, a wine expert—almost anything imaginable under the sun. In only one exception does he appear in more than one book.

In 1965 Francis wrote *Odds Against*, the story of Sid Halley, a jockey whose arm is shattered in a fall, forcing him to abandon racing forever. He takes up the job of private inquiry agent—the English equivalent of a private eye. The book was received so well by the public that a one-hour television adaptation was made of it by Yorkshire Television, along with five other stories featuring Mike Gwilym in the role of Sid Halley, for the BBC series *Mystery!* The six shows were collectively titled *The Racing Game*. So much did Francis empathize with Gwilym that he found himself subconsciously plotting out a sequel to the original book, featuring the return of Sid Halley. That became *Whip Hand* (1979).

In turn, *Whip Hand* proved exceedingly popular with the public. By that time Dick Francis had proved to be an author whose works kept on selling well year after year. At about the time the television broadcasts of the *Mystery!* series appeared in America, his name began to surface in the best-seller lists. And once established there, each new title became a "sure thing," and he became that marvelous phenomenon—an author whose every work might expect to become a best seller.

Basically a Francis book is an action-crime thriller, usually oriented in some way, however remotely, to horse racing. Each Francis book has a specific crime of some kind, an intriguing type of murder or startling method of evil-doing; that is the crime that the protagonist must uncover. In some fashion the hero of each book becomes an amateur sleuth, not especially to find out the identity of a murderer, but to unmask the crime and apprehend the criminal.

Francis never had a formal education; his wife, the former Mary Brenchley, was university educated and became more or less his firmly guiding hand in matters literary. When it became time to begin the background research for a new project, she would always step in and do the nitty-gritty cut and paste for him.

By the very nature of the crime thriller, however, the surface values of diction and description have little to do with the ability of the story itself to grip the reader. What Francis brought to this type of psychological crime novel was something that was his exclusive province: he knew exactly how to *pace* his writing, when to let the action subside and even lag and when to pour on the pressure and push the reader into turning the pages.

Most critics appreciate Francis's clear and lucid writing style; it is hard not to when the prose that results is so crisp and even. But clarity sometimes sacrifices depth and psychological probing. Francis has been criticized for not getting into his characters all the way.

He finds himself also the target for critics who claim he indulges in too much sadism. True, he does subject his heroes to all kinds of horrendous physical torments. Francis's answer is a simple one: as a rider, he points out, he suffered dozens of falls, all painful, all requiring weeks and months to heal. He has lived with pain and he knows the human body can stand pain. Therefore, why not let his heroes suffer it too?

Whatever is to be said about his diction and his tendency to sadism, he understands not only the psy-

Herbert Resnicow.

chology of his characters, but the psychology of his readers as well. The fact that all his books are still in print at the time of this writing is proof of his ability to reach out and grip his readers. And it is his knowledge of psychology that, with each new title, makes them come back for more.

Reading a Dick Francis book is probably just about as exciting as watching Dick Francis, in his younger days, race a horse around a track. What more could one ask?

Literary interest in sports has not been confined to the race track, in spite of Francis's success in the field. One recent entry was *Murder at the Super Bowl* (1986), a U. S. thriller set in the world of professional football, written by Herb Resnicow, a recent arrival in the field of mystery writing, in collaboration with a retired football quarterback, Franc Tarkenton. The result was a readable crime thriller with some personal insight into the workings of professional sports, including player psychology and even "inside stuff" on betting, bookies, and possible manipulation of the point spread.

Antonia Fraser.

Simon Brett.

Another Briton, Lady Antonia Fraser, writes what might be called a crime thriller too, setting her series, as Francis does, in a specific milieu—not that of the race track, but that of the medium of television news. Although a relative latecomer to the field—1977—Fraser has created an arresting surrogate-detective character in Jemima Shore, a television investigative reporter in the Woodward/Bernstein tradition. Her books tend to be classic-type mysteries played out against a modern English background, sometimes oriented to the countryside, sometimes to today's London. Perhaps because she came to the field already an accomplished historical biographer, her writing is thoroughly professional and nicely combines readable dialogue and entertaining plot action.

Simon Brett also writes crime thrillers that take place in a specific milieu, in fitting with the Fraser-Francis tradition. Brett's books are set in the British theater, and star Charles Paris, an aging actor, no detective—amateur or professional—but a man who *does* manage to help unravel mysteries and crimes that take place in the theatrical world about him. Brett's style is studded with marvelously cynical observations about the world of entertainment—comments that could indeed as easily pertain to the world the rest of us inhabit.

Michael Gilbert started out as a lawyer in London—solicitor, in the British idiom—and has written in so many different subgenres of the crime thriller that he cannot really be categorized as a genre writer who sticks to any particular background, even that of the courts he knows best. He is, essentially, a Renaissance man. Espionage, police procedurals, intellectual puzzles, romances, thrillers, adventure novels—he has produced them all. And he is successful at short stories and plays as well. Every one of his offerings is spiced with a mordant wit and a humor that make him one of the most dependably enjoyable, exciting, and readable writers in the crime thriller genre.

Three American writers who worked in the genre of the crime thriller became important not for their written works but for the film classics that were modeled on their stories and books. The tremendous success of the filmed adaptations of their novels largely overshadowed the intrinsic value of their original works; they became known only obscurely and to the cognoscenti as suppliers of material for the cinema

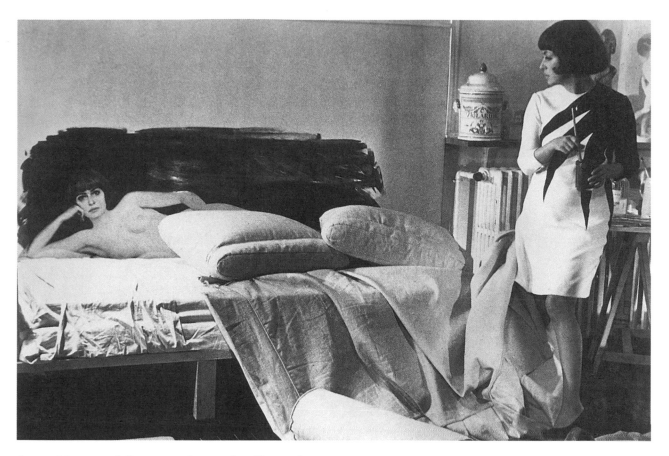

Jeanne Moreau as Julie contemplates nude self-portrait on
headboard of bed in François Truffaut's stunning version
of *The Bride Wore Black* (1968), adapted from the Cornell
Woolrich novel.

With her friend, Jean-Claude Brialy as Corey, Jeanne
Moreau learns how to use lethal bow and arrow in pursuit
of vengeance against murderer of her husband in *The Bride
Wore Black*.

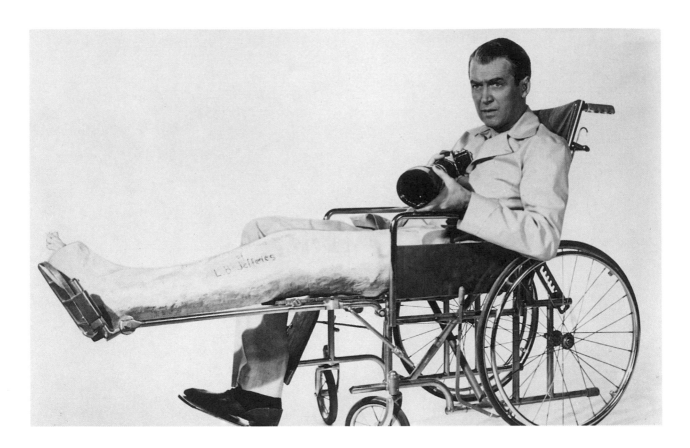

James Stewart plays L. B. Jeffries ("Jeff") a laid-up newspaper photographer who happens to witness murder in apartment across the way in Alfred Hitchcock's *Rear Window* (1954), smartly adapted from a Cornell Woolrich novelette.

art. They are Cornell Woolrich, James M. Cain, and W. R. Burnett.

Cornell Woolrich, who wrote under the pseudonyms of William Irish and George Hopley, had a particular flair for blending horror and suspense, even though his works are usually set in urban surroundings. One of his novels was *The Bride Wore Black* (1940), made into a famous François Truffaut motion picture. It was one of his short stories adapted into a motion picture scenario that became Alfred Hitchcock's classic *Rear Window*. Woolrich has accurately been called the "Edgar Allan Poe of the twentieth century."

James M. Cain's masterpiece is generally conceded to be *The Postman Always Rings Twice* (1934), although *Mildred Pierce* (1943) and *Double Indemnity* (1944) were both turned into excellent films as well. Cain's work has been considered the high point of hard-boiled prose writing—specifically because of his control of the hard-bitten, no-nonsense argot of the American Depression that even now simply leaps off the page at the reader. Cain worked in the action-suspense field of the crime thriller, and helped set the tone for what is now called the voguish "film noire."

Insurance money is only part of the prize for murder, Phyllis Dietrichson (Barbara Stanwyck) points out to Walter Neff (Fred MacMurray). Raymond Chandler lent a helping hand to the steamy screenplay of this film-noir classic made from James M. Cain's novel *Double Idemnity*.

Jessica Lange as Cora Papadakis, the lush temptress, and Jack Nicholson as Frank Chambers, the seedy drifter, in contemplative moment in *The Postman Always Rings Twice* (1981), made from James M. Cain's novel of seduction, murder, and retribution set against the background of the Great Depression.

In a mountain hideout Humphrey Bogart as "Mad Dog" Roy Earle plots a bank heist as Arthur Kennedy, with cigarette, and Ida Lupino look on with rest of henchmen in

High Sierra (1941), adapted with realistic intensity from the W. R. Burnett story by Burnett and John Huston.

Contemporary to Cain and Woolrich was W. R. Burnett, whose *Little Caesar* (1929) in its film version is usually credited with having begun the gangster film cycle of the 1930s. His *The Asphalt Jungle* (1949) became the high point of the straight "caper" novel, to be discussed later. The filmization of his novel *High Sierra* (1940) gave Humphrey Bogart a chance to hone his laconic tough-guy image into the unforgettable mold it assumed in the classic *Casablanca*.

Edward G. Robinson in the role of Rico, a trigger-happy mobster, set the tone for hypertense but deadly gangster heavies for decades to come in the 1931 version of W. R. Burnett's novel *Little Caesar*, the name Rico is tauntingly called by his rivals. Here he reasons with his best friend Joe, played by Douglas Fairbanks, Jr.

The *Roman Policier*

From the *Quai des Orfèvres* to *Petrovka*

In French literature the *roman policier* has for long portrayed the work of the police, a tradition that goes back to Vidocq. It was mainly Gaboriau who made the policemen of the Sûreté the heroes of his novels.

Leroux with his cheerful reporter-detective broke the tradition but the *roman policier* continued, eventually embracing the whole spectrum of crime fiction in France.

Georges Simenon

He could have kept in touch with some of his assistants if he had taken a radio car, but it would have been too conspicuous.

—Georges Simenon

Georges Simenon, perhaps one of the most internationally known of crime writers, created Inspector Jules Maigret of the Sûreté, portraying him and his colleagues in his own unique style. Though most of Simenon's work is connected with crime, he is equally concerned with the study of character, and is remarkably successful in the way he presents *real* men and women. Maigret is the head of a murder squad, although in the end it is the collaboration of all branches involved that solves the crime—a fact true to reality. Maigret is an amiable, understanding man who loves his pipe, his comfortable home, and his wife's excellent cooking. Equally he loves his office at 36 Quai des Orfèvres with the inspectors Lucas, Lapointe, Janvier, and Torrence. Of course, his inspectors make mistakes sometimes, and Maigret acts as something of a father figure to his colleagues. His many cases have made him a friend of reader and filmgoer alike. Simenon's novels have the special attraction of taking the reader into the heart of Paris to experience its day-to-day life, as well as into France's provincial towns and countryside. Only now and again does Simenon choose far-off regions for his plots: Arizona in *Maigret chez le Coroner (Maigret at the Coroner's Strange Case)* (1949), for example. Maigret is not interested in the mere facts of each case as such. He considers the whole human condition; in that sense he might well be linked to Balzac. From 1932 on, Maigret novels appeared in quick succession. In *Pietr-le-Letton (The Story of Peter the Lett)* (1933), Simenon introduced Maigret as experienced, slightly graying, and thoroughly professional. And he

has remained that way, not aging at all, even though from time to time he is sent into retirement. His inspectors and Madame do not get any older either as everything in the world around them changes, with the exception, of course, of the Quai des Orfèvres.

Georges Simenon.

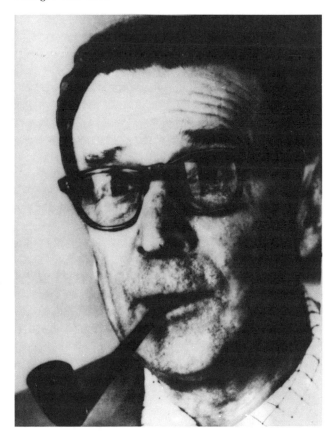

Maigret is always ready to understand the criminal, yet he does not tolerate crime or ever seek to excuse it. He investigates the environment in order to discover a criminal motive or sometimes the criminal himself. This environment is largely a family circle. In that way Simenon's work is closely related to the "family novel," continuing a literary tradition dating back to before Gaboriau. Some critics accuse Simenon of churning out too many books. Certainly he wrote at times under financial pressure—not just the Maigret novels but other crime fiction, stories, literary essays, and even "penny dreadfuls."

However, in his letters to André Gide and in some of his essays he makes it abundantly clear that he has literary ambitions although he never set out to write a "great" novel. He is a first-class storyteller who wants to entertain his public without pretentious moralizing.

With Maigret, spanning decades with undiminished liveliness, Simenon had created a happier figure than, for example, Nicolas Freeling with his inspector Van der Valk. The Freeling novels were set in Amsterdam, but came to an abrupt end when the hero was shot dead in *A Long Silence* (1970).

Still from the film *Maigret in Pigalle* with Gino Cervi.

Still from *Maigret und sein grösster Fall (Maigret and His Greatest Case)* with Heinz Rühmann.

Maj Sjöwall, Per Wahlöö, and Vic Suneson

*Crime squad officials together with police inspectors from the ninth district
knocked at the doors of all suspects and anybody
who might be a witness was interrogated.*

—Maj Sjöwall and Per Wahlöö

It would be unfair to writers in many countries to consider the *roman policier* only through the works of Simenon. The Maigret novels stand at the beginning of a general development that gained more and more ground as time went on. Maigret is a detective of the Sûreté, an experienced criminologist with sound ideas and a shrewd sense of observation. Other inspectors in literature may be somewhat inferior, not only in rank. They belong now to *teams*, in which crim-

inologists, forensic scientists, public prosecutors, and policemen work *together* to clear up a case. They all make mistakes, but all equally have good ideas; everybody, quite naturally, has good and bad qualities. The time of the old superdetective, the gifted amateur, is over. The new hero works with the whole police apparatus behind him, relying on the collaboration of scientific and technical departments. Thus the reader has contact with the progress of science, getting to know the results of forensic medicine, laboratory techniques, and the views of psychiatrists. This amazing apparatus was never dreamt of by the old master detective who simply asked questions. When popular writing on scientific subjects became widespread, the *roman policier* became in many ways related to it. In forensic medicine, research was concentrated on the identification of traces of blood, the analysis of blood and dust, the microscopic examination of the smallest detail, as well as the problems of poisoning, say, by arsenic. All these matters could not be treated in too much depth in a novel, since the author and reader must not be too confused, but must stay alert and interested enough to continue the search for clues. Yet the *roman policier* trends to be instructive as well as entertaining, encouraging the reader to give serious thought to the problems posed. Tension is no longer concerned with the question of "Whodunit?" Inquiries are not made in a circle of suspects whose number is whittled down in the course of the investigation. The main question now is: What trail is to be taken up? How can it lead to the culprit? Tracing him is a slow, cumbersome, but certain process, one that is completely realistic like the description of the social conditions under which culprit and victim live.

Experiments to establish the *roman policier* outside France were not very successful. Unlike Simenon in his Maigret novels, Swedish authors allowed no private romance to encroach on the lives of their detectives. Instead of the loving and understanding Madame Maigret, the commissioner of the Stockholm police, Martin Beck, created by the husband-and-wife team, Maj Sjöwall and Per Wahlöö, is married to a discontented, quarrelsome woman. Also, nobody in the Stockholm crime squad believes that the world will be a better place with yet another criminal out of the way.

"The crime squad consulted its registers, the government crime laboratory worked through the meager material found at the scene of the crime, and another department was frantically busy on all the data available. Crime squad officials together with police inspectors from the ninth district knocked at the doors of all suspects and anybody who might be a witness was interrogated."

These activities described by Sjöwall and Wahlöö take place when an unknown sex murderer threatens the streets and parks of Stockholm in their novel

Mannen på balkongen (The Man on the Balcony) (1967; U.S.: 1968). The criminal in the disguise of a "good uncle" lures little girls into parks and kills them. He might have been caught very quickly if the police had taken the telephone call of an old lady seriously. She believed that she had seen a man acting very suspiciously, but all he had done was stand on his own balcony and look down into the street. The telephone call is lightly dismissed. The police receive too many calls like that. Chance, however, keeps working, not without some irony. In the end the police search for and find the caller buying a cake at the baker's. A fourth child is saved only because a policeman is forced to leave his car to relieve himself in the shrubbery of a park. In spite of the occasional tone of mockery, the authors describe very seriously the hard, laborious routine of the crime squad. Crimes are cleared up, although the ending of each is never altogether satisfactory. The world and its social conditions produce further new crimes, and the detectives are right when at the end of the tale they believe that they have just completed another day's work.

Many evil deeds are committed in these novels, but the perpetrators seem more sick than wicked, though nobody actually recognizes their sickness. This is particularly so in *Roseanna* (1965; U.S.: 1967), the team's first novel. The presentation is close to that of the psychological thriller, the main interest being concentrated on the details of detection that range from the careful use of photographs to the planting of a decoy that leads to the arrest of the culprit.

Through their numerous novels the authors made their detectives familiar to a wide circle of readers. In *Den Vedervärdige Mannen från Säffle (The Abominable Man)* (1971; U.S.: 1972) victim and culprit belong to the police force and the motivation for revenge arises out of their work. Inspector Wyman, the "abominable" man from Säffle, abuses the power of his office, destroying the professional and private life of a young policeman. The everyday duties of policemen are monotonous and they often have to suffer indignities others would not tolerate. A combination of madness and mishaps amid the seemingly futile daily routine becomes a vicious circle that reaches its climax in a spectacular action by the police involving a helicopter, the fire brigade, and blasting operations—all for nothing in the end, and inhuman into the bargain. The culprit is a desperate man who goes mad

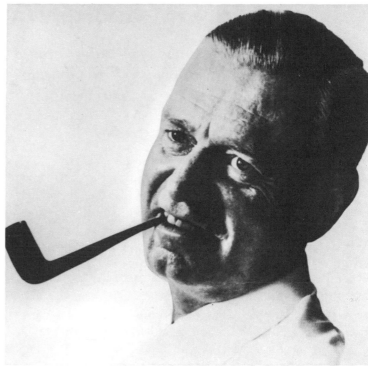

Per Wahlöö.   Vic Suneson.

when the first shots are fired. This kind of tale is loaded perhaps excessively in order to furnish a vehicle for social criticism.

In the novels of Sune Lundquist, an engineer writing under the pen name of Vic Suneson, the scene is Stockholm and the crimes are dealt with by the police there with the atmosphere of a large city providing wide scope for the writer. In contrast to Maj Sjöwall and Per Wahlöö, Suneson makes use of cases some years back that give him the opportunity of comparing the present with the past. The world keeps changing as does society, a society that again and again encourages criticism. *Fallet 44: An (Failure Number 44)* (1963) exposes the murder of a woman painter, committed years ago; it is a tale of simple legacy hunting. Other novels by the author skillfully combine th *roman policier* with the traditional detective story, and occasionally an element of the psychological thriller. Tangible evidence is no longer available and only the leading protagonists, their character, and their motivations remain to provide clues. One of seven classmates, a group to which some forty years ago detective O. P. Nilsson himself belonged, has murdered a poor second-hand book-seller. The culprit has prospered in his scientific career, but this began when he unlawfully adopted as his own discoveries those made by a decceased colleague. Eventually he kills so that this crime of the past will not destroy his hardgained social position. The end is bitter: he is unmasked by his own son and a detective.

In another novel a crime, apparently solved years ago, murder has also been committed by a killer for fear of lost position and prestige. There are proceedings in court when detective Nilsson and his men by their evidence accuse the daughter of one of their late colleagues. They are then forced to re-examine the case and their previous investigations. They do this as a professional duty, and also out of friendship. In the court scene the culprit ironically acts as a defense witness for the accused. The atmosphere created by the description of the surroundings and by police work itself is completely realistic, as is the establishment of the killer's motivation. This very realism gives the *roman policier* the opportunity to depict various aspects of the work of the police and to show how investigations vary widely in different countries.

177

Arkadi and Georgi Wainer and Others

"The most important thing," replied Vitali, shaking his head,
"is human life. There is nothing worse than murder.
That is a basic truth, if you want to know."

—Arkadi Adamov

When reading a novel like *Era Miloserdija (Time of Mercy)* (1976) by the Soviet authors Arkadi and Georgi Wainer, the reader is at once made aware that the criminal activities of a large gang, called "The Black Cat" cannot be cleared up by a lone master detective. What is needed is a big organization like the Moscow crime squad. The novel is set in Moscow, a few months after the end of World War II. Day-to-day life is hard. Conditions are made even worse for citizens through the activities of a ruthless gang that robs businesses and warehouses and then sells the goods on the Black Market with total disregard for human suffering. Criminals, violent or petty, fences, and aging slatterns group together; crime follows crime until this wicked network has spread all over the city where the rogues become well enough known to be called by their nicknames.

In the course of the story the reader is given a vivid picture of the dangerous work of the Petrovka, the crime squad, and also of the personal problems during the first winter after the war when even a small theft was a calamity.

> "The coupons, the coupons," Shura called in
> desperation. We are finished. They have
> been taken … the food coupons. Five small
> children … they'll die of hunger—the
> month has only just begun and they are the
> coupons for the whole month!"

Everything is done to catch the thieves. When at last the gang is rounded up, after first making fools of the police and leaving their trade mark—the drawing of a black cat at the scene of the deed—the sense of depression still lingers. In order to make the atmosphere seem real and to give a true picture of the period, which was by no means a comforting one, the authors pose the question: how much longer will it take to bring evildoers to justice and what further sacrifices will be required?

The brothers Wainer did not have to invent the material because, as legal men, they had come in their work across a variety of cases. In *Konets Khitrova Rynka (The End of the Khitrov Market)* (1967) Anatoli Bezuglov and Yuri Klarov wrote a parallel novel, based on extensive research in the local archives, about the seizure of the Yakov Koshelkov gang and the closing of the Khitrov market—a nest of swindlers that had frightened the citizens of Moscow for many long years. The action takes place in 1919, although it does not resemble a Pitaval case history. The facts from the files are of subordinate interest to the descriptions of the human condition and character. Bezuglov, a public prosecutor, and Klarov, a lawyer, were trying to continue in the tradition of the Russian literature of Tolstoy and Dostoyevski. They also knew a good deal about police investigations, including the language used.

> The large smoky-gray Alsation sat down.
> "Are you about to begin with Marcelushka?"
> I asked, stroking the dog gently. Khaletski
> unpacked the case carrying his instruments.
> Because of its size, it was called "Noah's
> Ark." "First take the blood spots on the
> floor," I said.

These words open the investigation concerning the theft of a precious Stradivarius in *Vizit k Minotravru (Visit to a Minotaur)* (1972).

The novels by Arkadi Adamov, a longtime member of a crime squad, concern not so much gangs as individual criminals who may employ accomplices. His criminals are not to be found among bandits, antisocial people, or those fallen by the wayside. They are well-respected citizens. The task therefore is not to fight against known bandits of ill repute or catch wanted criminals, but to expose cunningly hidden crimes in business and commerce and acts of violence—even murder—connected with them. This fact

Cover design for *Time of Mercy* (German edition).　　Georgi Wainer.

makes the comprehensive description of teamwork especially important; every member of the team and his particular task in clearing up the crime is vividly described as well as his home life and his circle of friends.

> My mother, still sleepy and in her dressing gown, got a goodbye kiss. She found time, however, to give me some good advice on how to conduct myself on the way.

This is how Vitali Losev starts his journey in *Slom Vetrom (Broken by the Wind)* (1975). *Petlya (The Slip-knot)* (1976) begins with the finding of a woman's body. The investigation must establish whether it was a murder, a suicide, or an accident. In time further crimes are discovered: theft, the receiving of stolen goods, fraud, corruption. The last hours of the dead woman are reconstructed, and still the investigators are unable to convict the main suspect. It

is suggested that the woman was forced into committing suicide.

> "You have to prove that," Kuzmich interrupted. "His wife will not testify against him."

In the event nothing can be proved, leaving the reader disappointed at seeing justice undone.

Adamov wrote an essay on the technique and value of crime fiction, maintaining that it, like other branches of literature in the Soviet Union, has the task of ideologically and morally educating the reader. To that end, he said, mastery of investigative technique and a thorough knowledge of the dangerous and exerting work of the police are necessary.

Adamov is fully conscious of the literary traditions of the classic English detective story represented by Conan Doyle and Chesterton. "Sherlock Holmes," he declares, "presents logic, wisdom, and scientific thought at one and the same time. Father

179

Arkadi Wainer.

Arkadi Adamov.

Brown, in contrast, knows human feelings. It is worthwhile to compare the two." Adamov made his young detective Vitali give an example: "He [Chesterton] suggests in one of his books that a lady might be visiting a woman friend's country house and asks her: 'Does anybody else live here?' Her hostess would never reply: 'Yes, of course, the butler, three menservants, the parlor maid, the cook, the groom and the gardener.' Even though the parlor maid has just tidied the room and the butler stands behind the lady's chair, she would certainly answer: 'No, I live alone.' However, if during an epidemic the doctor were to ask the same question, she would then name all the staff. And, thought Chesterton, this does show that questions have to be put carefully."

Kazimierz Kwaśnieski, the Polish writer, created a special type of *roman policier* in his novel *Zbrodniarz i Panna (The Murderer and the Maiden)* (1965). The crime squad is looking for a criminal who committed robbery and murder when attacking a security van. In

their investigations the police rely on a young woman employed by the bank who has witnessed the robbery and has recognized the murderer. Fully aware that she is exposing herself to danger, the young woman agrees to help the police by luring the murderer from hiding. This gesture brings Margareta Makowska, the girl, into the limelight and turns her into a pretty, confident young woman who after a chase in which the murderer is killed is happily wed to the chief of police.

In another novel, *Kaze Aktorom Powtorzyc Morderstwo (Her Part in the Murder Game)* (1965) the crime squad alone succeeds in clearing up the murder of a Warsaw professor, one Rudzìsky, by demolishing an alibi, carefully constructed by the culprit, the professor's wife, using railway timetables.

A series, D I E, appearing in the German Democratic Republic (East Germany), publishes novels dealing with the work of the police, particularly murder investigations, providing information, entertain-

180

ment, and tension while in the Federal Republic of Germany (West Germany) a former journalist, Friedhelm Werremeier, tries to imitate Maigret. However, his detective Trimmel never achieved the psychological impact of Simenon's novels. Werremeier dealt with actual cases of crime, but did not succeed in turning them into Pitaval case histories either. His greatest success came through work that was adapted for television.

In England there were many practitioners of the modernized *roman policier*, but probably none were read more widely than John Creasey, whose output during his lifetime was prodigious to the point of incredulity. At recent count, his production was tabulated at some number over six hundred titles, but unsold novels written earlier continued to be printed even after his death in 1973. His output between 1932 and 1973 appears to be almost fourteen books a year.

He wrote not only conventional mysteries but American Westerns, science-fiction novels, psychologicals, action-adventures, and thrillers of all kinds. Some were good, some were bad; but they were all surprisingly readable, brimful of energy, and virtually attentiongripping.

Probably his best were two series of police procedurals: those about Inspector West, and those about Commander Gideon. The latter were published under the pseudonym J. J. Marric (a fractured acronym synthesized from his own first initial, his first wife Jean's initial, and the first three letters each of his two sons, Martin and Richard).

It was in the Gideon *romans policiers* that Creasey hit his stride 1955, after more than a decade of preparation with Inspector West, who saw the first light of day in 1942. The West books helped Creasey more or less perfect a style of spinning a fast-paced, police-oriented, action-adventure yarn, with a minimum of literary trappings. A West story moves with rapidity, propelled by dialogue of a truncated nature, action described in as few words as possible, and plot twists thrown in quickly as soon as the frenetic pace settles down.

Characterization is at a minimum, with the names generally sufficing to identify the cast of good guys and bad. Written more like a motion-picture scenario than a novel, the typical West book is a riveting experience for the reader, with menace, physical violence, confrontations of all kinds, chases, and a variety of action elements strung together with Creasey's usual tireless energy. If there is any problem, it is the fact that the prose itself is stiff, colorless, and monotonous. (Creasey taught himself to write, not having had the advantage of a formal education.)

Nevertheless, the man was an inveterate, indefatigable researcher, who spent many hours at Scotland Yard and with the Metropolitan Police Force studying the methods used by homicide detectives in order to get the proper things done in the proper manner in his stories. This expertise is quite evident in many of the West stories. Creasey was quick to see the possibility of weaving together the best parts of the mystery formula with the best parts of the plodding, day-to-day details of ordinary police work.

As interest in the police procedural increased in Britain in the early postwar years, Creasey turned to a more in-depth study of the duties of the homicide detective. Thus George Gideon was born in 1955, appearing first in *Gideon's Day*. Several stories are relevant to Gideon's creation: a police friend of Creasey's suggested he "write it the way it *really* is"—and Creasey did so; an American editor wanted a series more balanced between a police officer's modus operandi and his family life—and Creasey produced just such a series.

Whatever, Creasey shuffled the old *roman policier* formula just a bit, focused at least as much attention on George Gideon's family—wife and two children—as he did on police methodology, cropped the cases into punchy, short takes, began running three or four cases simultaneously with parallel intercutting, and came up with a winning formula.

Critics were quick to point out that for those who liked the classic detective novel the typical Gideon would not suffice. Nevertheless, Creasey understood his reading audience probably as well if not better than the critics and suspected that not all of them were still irrevocably married to the classic puzzle mystery. To whet the appetite of newcomers to the mystery field, he managed to spice his product with any number of enticing criminous endeavors.

In addition to George Gideon, the Commander of the Criminal Investigation Division of Scotland Yard and his family—his wife Kate, and his sons Matthew and Thomas—the series also includes a number of subordinates and superiors, all of whom become fleshed out in a manner that Creasey had not attempted in his earlier Inspector West stories. There

Ed McBain.

is Chief Inspector Lemaitre, Superintendent Hemmingway, the Cockney Appleby, Superintendent Wragg, Superintendent Thomas Riddell, Deputy Commander Alec Hobbs, and dozens of others.

Nothing succeeds like success, and in New York the first Gideon book was greeted with raves from both critics and readers. In no time at all a rival series appeared, this one written by an American and featuring the homicide detectives of the 87th Precinct, a made-up number in a made-up city (Isola— Italian for "Island"; thus, "Manhattan").

Ed McBain, the author, was actually the writer Evan Hunter, a second pseudonym for a New Yorker who had been writing mystery stories under the Hunter byline and under a variety of bylines, including Richard Marsten. The subgenre of the American *roman policier* into which McBain entered with such enthusiasm with *Cop Hater* in 1956, one year after Gideon's first adventure appeared, was not entirely vacant at the time.

Early ground had been broken for the American police procedural just before and during World War II by Lawrence Treat—*D as in Dead* (1941), *H as in Hangman* (1942), *O as in Omen* (1943), *V as in Victim* (1945)—but it was Hillary Waugh who with *Last Seen Wearing* in 1952 set the postwar tone in America that McBain took up. The detailed procedure by which a small-town police chief and his detective sergeant in Connecticut solved the murder of an eighteen-year-old freshman coed at a nearby college is painstakingly chronicled, with the thoughts, conversations, and actions of the detectives the focus of the story. It is not speed and action that grips the reader, but the meticulous, frustrating, wearying details that must be dealt with to uncover the murderer.

To Waugh's quiet Connecticut countryside McBain added the drama and dynamism of the big city, created characters with memorable personality shticks, invented "homicide division-type" dialogue that amused the reader and moved the story forward at the same time, sprung plot twists that brought the reader up sharp, and finally, evoked an unforgettable atmosphere and smell of tension, frustration, hard work, cynicism, and compassion—components of the true New York scene.

The main character in the 87th Precinct is Steve Carella [McBain/Hunter was born Lombardino], a homicide detective, with a beautiful wife, Teddy, an intelligent and personable deaf mute; Carella works with a big cast of eccentric yet believable characters that become immediately unforgettable to the reader:

Cotton Hawes, the squad room sex symbol, whose parents have named him after the great witch-hunter of the seventeenth century, Cotton Mather.

Meyer Meyer, a Jewish detective brought up in a gentile neighborhood, who has learned patience the hard way.

Bert Kling, the youngest member of the department who has much to learn and learns by trial and error—usually error.

Arthur Brown, the squad room's visible black, who unlike Meyer, has never learned patience.

Andy Parker, the sadist of the division.

Lieutenant Peter Byrnes, who is the respected chief of the detective squad.

Dick Genero, probably the stupidest cop ever to don a uniform.

One of the most interesting features of the early novels was McBain's inclusion of completely filled out reports, newspaper clippings, documents of one kind or another, pieces of paper evidence that could be duplicated in the novel itself—a kind of throwback to Dennis Wheatley's "file" books of an earlier era—*File on Bolitho Blane* (1936), *File on Robert Prentice* (1937), and so on—but without many of the pieces of physical evidence thrown in. Shortly after the 87th Precinct became an established series, however, these "reports" and inserts became fewer and fewer, and soon tapered down to one or two at most.

The series began with *Cop Hater*, *The Pusher*, and *The Mugger* in 1956, and has continued unabated on into the middle 1980s.

McBain's strengths are his ability to write dialogue that reads like the clipped, ping-pong exchanges of 1930s movies, his talent for springing unlikely plot twists throughout his stories, and his genius at keeping the ball bouncing at all times where it cannot readily be seen.

Like Creasey, McBain deals in multiple story lines—usually three or four per book, each featuring a different type of case and sometimes different squad-room characters. In *Hail, Hail, the Gang's All Here!* (1971), he decided to let everyone in the 87th Precinct have a fling, with the result that he had at least fourteen different cases going, all completed at the end of the book!

An interesting feature of a typical McBain work is the manner in which he deliberately inserts pages and pages of dull textbook material taken verbatim out of some medical or forensic reference book by simply putting the words in the mouths of his characters and adding in appropriate grunts and exclama-tions to make it seem exciting. The same is true of his ability to insert an unimportant action—walking across the street to buy an egg cream at a stand—in the middle of an important and frustrating case, and make it seem as important as the unraveling of the mystery itself.

It was McBain's success with the formula that eventually led to the later success of Joseph Wambaugh, a Los Angeles police officer who began writing fiction based on the day-to-day action in which a policeman must involve himself such as *The New Centurions* (1970) and *The Blue Knight* (1972). In New York Dorothy Uhnak, after working on the police force for a number of years, wrote several novels based on her experiences, among them *The Ledger* (1970), *Law and Order* (1973), *The Investigation* (1977), and *False Witness* (1981).

One of McBain's most prolific imitators was Elizabeth Linington, a professional writer on the West Coast, who created a procedural series featuring Lieutenant Luis Mendoza of the Los Angeles homicide department (written under the pseudonym of Dell Shannon), a second series co-featuring Detective Vic Varallo of the Glendale police department and Jesse Falkenstein, a Jewish lawyer and amateur detective (under the pen name Lesley Egan), and a third procedural series featuring Sergeant Ivor Maddox (written under the pseudonym of Anne Blaisdell).

The *roman policier* will always be certain of a public somewhere, a public interested in the work of the police and in technical and scientific innovations in the realm of criminology.

Humor, Black and Otherwise, in the Crime Story

Sbirro with one hand kept the door invitingly open while his other hand almost tenderly rested on Laffler's plump shoulder.

—Stanley Ellin

Murder stories deal with very serious matters that leave little room for laughter. Most authors agree with this concept—particularly those who write murder mysteries—yet in the theater and in films there are stage tricks, exciting pursuits, disguises, and even frauds that may be introduced to amuse the audience.

A classic German comedy by Gerhart Hauptmann, *Biberpelz (Beaver Fur)*, deals with theft. There is no violence of murder, just a stolen fur. The sympa-

Gregory Mcdonald.

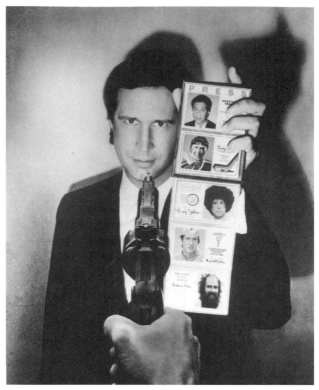

Chevy Chase as Fletch in motion picture *Fletch*, based on the Gregory Mcdonald novel.

thy of everybody is on the side of the thief, Mutter Wolffen (Mother Wolf). Her native wit triumphs, captivating even officialdom. Even so, on the whole humor in the crime story is rare.

Easily recognizable and entertaining is the humor in the American play *Arsenic and Old Lace* (1944), by Joseph Kesselring, with its amiable, murderous old ladies, perhaps best known through Frank Capra's film. Some crime writers tried to introduce comic or eccentric supporting characters in an effort to amuse, but this device is rarely successful.

A Swedish author, under the pen name of Bo Balderson, wrote of a murder in a small group of people in his novel *Statsradet och Döden (Death and the Minister)* (1968). The story is set among the inhabitants of several old villas on the Schären island of Lindo near Stockholm. Somewhat doubtful alibis are supplied and the culprit is caught in the end. Here the comic element is provided by the strange, even slightly manic actions of all involved. The reader is amused and able to exercise his powers of reasoning at one and the same time.

Margaret Scherf, the American writer, worked in

a different tradition. The background of her amateur detectives did not make them likely candidates for clearing up crimes. There is the minister, Dr. Martin Buell, whose way of life is closely watched by the female members of his congregation. Strange things happen to him wherever he goes. In *Gilbert's Last Toothache* (1960), for example, he returns from a wedding with a baby belonging to a colleague who has died suddenly. The next day his wife meets with an accident on a mountain road. Tension and tragicomedy are skillfully mixed. Other Scherf detectives, Emily Murdock and Henry Bryce, restaurant owners in New York, become closely associated in the course of a plot and their strange adventures combine comic incident with sustained tension. Scherf introduces a woman detective, Dr. Grace Severance, who as an anatomist finds nothing strange in murder and in sudden death.

Another American, Ron Goulart, has combined parody, satire, and slapstick humor in an impressive number of mystery, science-fiction, and fantasy novels, and is known to switch from realism to fantasy at will. Humor, in any of its aspects, is the keystone of

Members of mystery writers' round table: seated, Joyce Harrington, Bernard St. James, Mary Higgins Clark, Warren Murphy, and Whitley Strieber; standing, Bill Adler, Dorothy Salisbury Davis, Thomas Chastain, and Lucy Freeman.

this writer's output. A typical example is his choice of the name John Easy for his series character who specializes in searching out missing women.

One of the more popular writers of tongue-in-cheek humor in the crime novel is Gregory Mcdonald, whose series character Fletch—born Irwin Maurice Fletcher—established himself immediately in the 1970s as a light-hearted, wisecracking, ingenious investigative reporter for a Boston newspaper. With his nimble mind, as well as his nimble mouth, this surrogate private eye became an obvious prospect for the movies; the glib and artful Chevy Chase created the screen role in a bouncy, wry, and amusing motion picture.

The short story has always been a favorite vehicle for the crime writer, and is closely related to the anecdote reporting cases and court proceedings in which comic aspects exceed the crime interest. In the German Democratic Republic (East Germany) Joachim Dietrich wrote grotesque crime fiction under the pen name of Cobra.

Before black humor had become a definite concept, Richard Hull, a British writer, wrote novels that

seemed shocking at the time of their publication. In *The Murder of My Aunt* (1934), Hull successfully and artfully mixed the macabre with the theatrical.

As the crime novel became shorter and shorter, the short story itself also shrank considerably in size. The advent of television was being blamed for having brought about the all but complete demise of short magazine fiction. But it was not that the mystery story was vanishing; it was simply changing in its form. The essence of the typical half-hour or hour-long dramatic presentation on television is almost the same as that of the typical short story—particularly in the crime genre. The single incident, the single gimmick, the single surprise—this familiar triad proves to be the perfect springboard for such a story. The short mystery was turning from the print medium to the broadcast medium.

Yet crime writers love to write in the short form, and they continued to produce shorts even when there remained very little of the printed-word market left to them. Readers also liked the short form; it was a marvelous way to enjoy the drama of murder in miniature.

Edward D. Hoch.

One way of getting around the difficulty of the shrinking short-story market was to produce a collection of shorts in book form—which was tried most conspicuously by a group of New York mystery writers who had formed a "writers' round table" at a Manhattan restaurant to discuss the mystery as a genre.

Murder in Manhattan (1986), a collection of short stories, all set in New York, was the result of the club's monthly meetings. Packaged by author, editor, and publisher Bill Adler, the contributors included Thomas Chastain, Mary Higgins Clark, Dorothy Salisbury Davis, Lucy Freeman, Joyce Harrington, Warren Murphy, Bernard St. James, and Whitley Strieber, who had jointly produced over one hundred novels, including several best sellers and award winners.

One of the most prolific short-form writers in the mystery genre—Edward D. Hoch in America—turns out scores of stories every year, by one count in fact producing one of every twenty mystery short stories published annually in the U.S.!

Now the author of over 650 stories, Hoch writes under a half dozen pseudonyms, and has created at least two dozen series characters. He concentrates exclusively on clever plots. And he has come up with some dandies.

A carriage enters a covered bridge—and disappears. How?

A woman vanishes from a moving Ferris wheel leaving no trace. How?

A man leaps out of a window; his body lands on the ground four hours later. How?

A man steals the water out of a swimming pool in front of the owner's eyes. How? And why?

Hoch's most popular hero, and the one about whom he has written the most stories, is Nick Velvet, a reformed thief, in the vein of Raffles, who continues to perform outside the law for "good causes." The shtick Hoch exploits in this series is the absolute *valuelessness* of the objects stolen. Water. Why? And so on.

Simon Ark is another series hero in Hoch's huge cast of protagonists. Ark is a mystic, who is supposedly 2,000 years old, and generally utilizes his preternatural powers in carrying out investigations into puzzling enigmas.

In the subgenre of the espionage story, Hoch celebrates the exploits of Jeffery Rand, an ex-undercover agent, formerly a member of the "concealed communications" (cryptography) office of British Intelligence.

Captain Leopold is a Hoch-created policeman, a specialist in violent crimes, who solves various types of mysteries that come his way. Ben Snow is Hoch's "frontiersman" Westerner (is he really Billy the Kid?) who solves crimes that take place at the turn of the century in sagebrush America. Dr. Sam Hawthorne does not go back quite so far as Snow; he is a simple New England country doctor who operates in the 1920s and 1930s, solving locked-room puzzles, and other classic mysteries that his creator dreams up for him.

Hoch won an Edgar award for his Captain Leopold short story, "The Oblong Room," and has been nominated several times. Another short-story Edgar went to Stanley Ellin for "The Specialty of the House" (1948). Ellin's output of shorts is dwarfed by Hoch's, but his style and substance is specifically crafted with one response in mind—humor—an emotional reaction not generally associated with murder and mayhem. And black humor, at that. But black humor, it seems, is essentially compatible with the crime short story. The end of the short has to be sudden, has to come as a surprise, with the climax providing the humor, and, in fact, black humor seems to be the proper way to provide a wry, sardonic sort of twist ending to make the form meaningful.

As opposed to a detailed description of the scene of a crime in a Pitaval-type case history, for example, the use of black humor can leave much unstated, and the reader, prepared for wickedness and crime, has already guessed its essence. In the award-winning Stanley Ellin story mentioned above, collected in *Mystery Stories* (1956), there is talk of "lamb Amirstan," served from time to time as a *spécialité de la maison* in a strange gourmet restaurant. The reader *knows* with a shudder that now and again regular fat guests disappear—to be put into the pot and onto the menu! Yet the gourmet guests continue thoroughly to enjoy their meals, and no one is ever brought to justice. In other Ellin stories the irony of fate turns against the evildoer. The unexceptional Mr. Appleby can only carry on his beloved junk shop because he inherits a considerable sum—at suitable intervals—from his six wives. The seventh sees through his scheme and tries to protect herself with the help of her lawyers. However, when Appleby in the end goes out of his way to save her, she is so eager for revenge that she accidentally falls into the death trap she has set; and, ironically for Appleby too, his time is up.

In a story by Roald Dahl the investigating policeman happily eats the murder weapon, a frozen leg of lamb, thoughtfully defrosted and roasted by the murderous wife. She assures him that her Patrick—God rest his soul—would never forgive her if she ever failed to show hospitality to a guest at his house. His best known collection of macabre crime stories was published in 1960 under the title *Kiss, Kiss*.

With *Enter Murderers* (1960) and *A Crime for Mothers and Others* (1962) Henry Slesar is another American crime writer to introduce black humor into his work. Behind all his tales one can see the face of the *picaro*, the rogue who tries to make us understand the crime and not condemn it outright.

John Collier's "unlikely stories" are in a similar vein. Even the title strikes an ironical note: *Fancies and Goodnights* (1951) are about ordinary everyday events, like squabbling over an egg at breakfast, that may lead to murder. There is no detective to uncover the crime that often comes to light by almost ridiculous chance. The reader, taken to the very edge of ca-

tastrophe, can picture the consequences in the blackest of shades. The culprit is usually not a thoroughly wicked character, but a volatile one—perhaps also the most sensitive in his own circle.

Richard M. Webb and Hugh C. Wheeler, under the pen name Patrick Quentin, wrote in a similar vein, and were content to let the culprit go free even when the reader knew he was guilty. The authors almost managed to change values: the victim dispatched from this world is always a very unpleasant creature. He or she is egotistical and dangerous, in other words, a menace to society. *The Green-eyed Monster* (1960), one of the titles, speaks for itself. Another novel tells of a power-hungry mother who conveniently meets her death in a mountain torrent, so that, at long last, her poor son and his girl friend can begin a new and, one hopes, happier life.

Through curiosity, greed, and its gifts as a detective this cat solved a murder case and as a reward was given the status of crime reporter!

187

Donald Westlake.

It was Donald Westlake in America who really made a career out of humor in the mystery genre. While his humor was not quite so black as Henry Slesar's, it was slapstick and outrageous enough to satisfy large groups of people and make him a kind of cult figure in the genre. Writing under different names—Richard Stark and Tucker Coe were two of his most popular pseudonyms—Westlake in the 1950s produced several routine "tough guy" mysteries. He found his own way in the early 1970s, with what was to become his own light-hearted "caper" formula. In *The Hot Rock* (1970), Westlake unveiled Dortmunder, a stylized reincarnation of our old friend the rogue thief, the *picaro*, transported to the twentieth from the seventeenth century—but with one crucial difference. Dortmunder is a flake, a nerd, an inept.

Although the *picaro* tends to tempt the writer to discursive, plotless structure, Westlake eschewed this element and instead perfected the "inside" story of a specific "job"—in effect, he made each Dortmunder story a detailed caper in itself, a *Topkapi* or *Rififi*, but portrayed in a comic vein. Because of the popularity of the anti-hero during the 1960s, Westlake's books featuring Dortmunder were bought up by Hollywood, and were made into popular comic movies.

Westlake's caper novels include *The Hot Rock, Bank Shot* (1972), and *Jimmy the Kid* (1972), *Nobody's Perfect* (1977), *Why Me?* (1983), and *Good Behavior* (1986). While the serious caper works—Eric Ambler's *The Light of Day*, for example (the basis for the motion picture *Topkapi*); or, in America, W. R. Burnett's classic *The Asphalt Jungle*—create suspense by the detailed recounting of the planning, practicing, and final execution of a complicated criminal effort, in the typical Westlake story everything goes wrong at the crucial moment. The effect on the reader is one of laughter and hilarity rather than cold perspiration on the brow.

The key element that makes Westlake's anti-hero work is the milieu of the 1960s and 1970s in which his stories take place. The anti-hero is bent on pulling the tail of the lion (read, establishment); he robs because he is getting back at the fat cats whom he dislikes. Besides, the fat cats are, in his mind, just as dishonorable as he is, even though their actions may be within the letter of the law. When things fall apart, it is a big laugh to the reader. No one is going to kill the anti-hero; he is too inept and pitiable to deserve *that* kind of treatment. He is to be laughed off at the end; maybe, in fact, he might even get to keep the loot!

Just to show that the more things change, the more they remain the same, along came Elmore Leonard in the 1980s to show that the return of the *picaro* and the picaresque novel was not simply a fluke on the part of Donald Westlake, but was alive and well after having rested for several centuries. Although Leonard's methods parallel Westlake's in their focus on the criminal rather than on the investigator, he utilizes a much sharper and more acidy

George C. Scott as Walter Ballantine (Dortmunder in the novel) mounts a complex and intriguing campaign against a shopping center branch bank in *Bank Shot* (1974), adapted from the Donald Westlake novel.

Scott/Ballantine/Dortmunder studies a map by matchlight in his bunk to determine details of robbery and getaway.

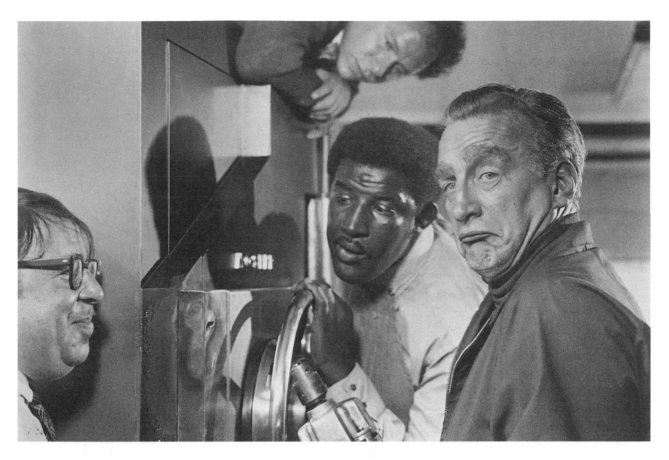

Nothing seems to work for Scott and his cohorts.

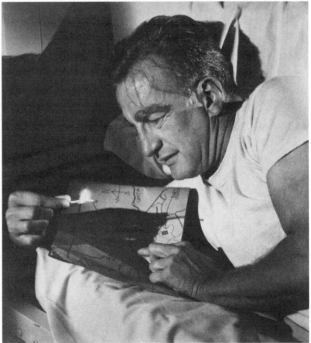

Elmore Leonard.

kind of humor than Westlake. Leonard's vision of the social milieu is not gray, but black. There is little that he likes when he looks about him. And his attitude comes out in the words he writes, particularly in the dialogue he patterns for his characters—for which he has become justly famous.

Leonard began writing the hard way. He worked for an advertising agency in Detroit. But since he wanted to sell fiction, he determined to write something that would fit a specific and viable market. He selected the Western, because there were at that time plenty of pulp Western magazines printing Western stories. Westerns were popular in the movies, too. This was in the 1950s.

As has been noted, the Western is a strictured form, in many ways remarkably similar to the mystery. The hero of the Western is almost interchangeable with the hero of the private-eye story: he is the

Burt Reynolds, center, as Stick, Dar Robinson as the albino killer, and José Perez as Rainy sail to collect money from a drug deal in *Stick* (1985), adapted from the Elmore Leonard novel.

knight errant who comes into an area where wrong has triumphed to dislocate the evildoers and set things right once again. Leonard sold Westerns to the pulps and finally to the American *Argosy*. Then he moved into the novel milieu, and the movies picked up and adapted *Hombre* (1961), which was released as a movie in 1967, starring Paul Newman.

Then in the 1970s and early 1980s Leonard began writing in the genre that was cousin to the Western—the mystery. Perhaps he felt confined by the strictures of the Western formula—the tight plot line, the overweening "good guy"/"white hat" attitude of the protagonist, the obligatory story elements demanded. Instead of throwing out all plot, however, he retained just a semblance of form, and began writing to his strength: dialogue. He had an ear not for what people actually say, but for what people would *like* to say—particularly, rough, tough, sleazy people.

And his style changed. *Split Images* (1982), *Cat Chaser* (1982), and *Stick* (1983) were far cries from the typical genre crime novel popular at the time. *Split Images* is about a crazy, homicidal multi-millionaire, and his sadistic chauffeur, an ex-cop. These two oddballs are trailed by a basically good cop, who is out to get them. The unforgettable feature of the story is the millionaire's sadistic penchant for killing people *and filming the murders as they occur! Cat Chaser* is more picaresque than its predecessor, and seems to go nowhere, although all the time it is *really* leading in a specific direction. It is filled with con artists of all stripes, plus a corrupt Central American politico, exiled in Miami, with enough money to move people about like hapless chessmen.

Stick is another change of pace. A rogue novel, paced in picaresque fashion, it is actually a tale of revenge, à la *The Count of Monte-Cristo*. But there is a fundamental difference. Monte-Cristo and heroes of the old-fashioned story of revenge worked within the social milieu, no matter how outlandish their machinations. *Stick* operates outside the social milieu, and it celebrates vigilantism as much as revenge. It borrows from two earlier novels—Joe Gores's *A Time of Predators* (1969) and its follow-up, Brian Garfield's *Death Wish* (1972)—one celebrating vengeance by a group of dedicated ex-servicemen to avenge the gang-rape and death of a buddy's wife, and the other vengeance by one half-crazy victim of hooliganism and depredation in a crowded city.

Stick is not plotted as tightly as its models, but it

Joe Gores.

is every bit as effective, moving through its confrontations in an eccentric but telling manner. It is a story related deadpan, narration as well as dialogue, hopscotching from one set of eccentric characters to another. From protagonist to minor hangers-on, everyone lives on the fringes of reality. "On the edge," as Ernest J. Stickley, Jr.—"Stick"—puts it.

La Brava (1983) has more of a conventional plot, plus the fact that its main character is a great deal more sympathetic than the nasties who inhabit the three books Leonard wrote before it. It won the Edgar Allan Poe Award from the Mystery Writers of America. Set in Miami, this story is a superb example of a master magician's ability to mix glitz and sleaze—and make the result compatible!

And, true to form, it was followed almost immediately by the bestseller (Leonard's first) *Glitz* in 1985. Both appeared almost simultaneously with the debut and surprising success of television's *Miami Vice*; the TV series parallels the spirit of Leonard's personal vision of the area and its weird denizens.

Leonard had now found his voice. And in doing so, he had returned to the roots of the picaresque novel, the rogue tale of trickery and survival. The formula he painfully worked out over the years came to combine the style and manner of the earlier picaresque romp with the twentieth century obsession for coping and making do.

Leonard sees, as many of his contemporaries do *not* see, that one must go one's way step by step, without the help of codes, of traditions, or of rules and regulations. Life is lived on an existential plane—where nothing much works, but where whatever works has *got* to be right.

This superimposition of the structure of the picaresque novel onto the philosophy of existentialism produces a strange union of unusually readable, sometimes puzzling, sometimes irritating, but always gripping material. There is no hero, no heroine. There are only spear-carriers, trotting about as minor background characters, men and women "on the edge," carrying the main story line along in a kind of "black hole"—swirling anti-matter—of alienation.

Leonard claims to be an innovator when it comes to the moral arena of crime fiction. In the Chandler-Hammett sense, he has no simplistic notion of good and evil. Such a concept is "sentimental" to Leonard, and shows that the earlier heroes are simply thick-skinned individuals with soft hearts and soft heads. Leonard goes one step beyond, pointing out in his work that there is no good and bad per se; ambiguity must just be accepted as the only workable moral code. In a Leonard story, there is usually some kind of crime or extralegal action under contemplation, and it is the *caper* that counts, not whether it's right or wrong. Most of the characters accept the fact that there is no black and white, that they must work it out for themselves. The hero, the man or woman "on the edge," is consciously an observer of the world and of the people in it. But then, once in a while, the protagonist must act.

When he does, he works it out on his own, and he thus establishes the morality of the moment as the action progresses. The Leonard hero is the existential hero of the world today. Instead of entering an upside down and tightly controlled milieu, rooting out the evil, and setting things to right again, the Leonard hero enters this upside down world, roots about, never pinning labels on anyone, and comes to terms with topsy-turvey land in whatever manner available to him. After all, whether or not the controlled world remains upside down or not is of no consequence.

"My heroes are just bumbling along," Leonard has said, "trying to make it."

It's the reader's job to decide whether they do so or not. Usually they do.

Postscript

Crime fiction has always been,
and will remain primarily an entertainment created by popular demand,
whether its form is that of detective story,
spy story, or crime novel.

—Julian Symons

As Julian Symons says, it is not at all surprising that crime fiction, though its demise has often been predicted, is as flourishing as ever today. The classic detective stories of the nineteenth and early twentieth century still remain popular. Parodies also stress the continued interest in crime fiction, and no parodies are better than those by the Polish writer, Jerzy Siewierski. In *Piec Razy Morderstwo (Five Times Murder)* (1976) he satirizes the style of various crime writers from many countries; the result amuses the reader and provides puzzles at the same time. Narcejac, too, tried his hand at parody. His novels written together with Boileau are a mixture of the grotesque and deep mysterious gloom.

The main reason for the existence and survival of the crime story is that it appeals to readers of all ages. Some organized themselves in clubs with their own magazines, as, for example, the *Baker Street Journal*, and this gives them a sense of kinship. The paper provides the *Baker Street Irregulars*, fans of Sherlock Holmes, with all kinds of information relating to their favorite subject. The *Armchair Detective* contains critical contributions, reviews, and reports concerning the genre, recommends books and publishes letters. In contrast Alfred Hitchcock's *Crime Magazine* is more of an anthology while *Ellery Queen's Mystery Magazine* contains book reviews and news for fans. Collections of stories and encyclopedias on the subject abound, providing a vast fund of information. Of special interest are: Ordean A. Hagen, *Who Done It? A Guide to Detective, Mystery and Suspense Fiction* (1969), Jacques Barzun and Wendell Hertig Taylor, *A Catalogue of Crime* (1971), Chris Steinbrunner and Otto Penzler, *Encyclopedia of Mystery and Detection* (1976), and Dilys Winn, *Murder Ink: The Mystery Reader's Companion* (1977).

The Crime Writers Association (1953) awards the Golden, Silver, and now Diamond Dagger every year to the best crime writer in English. In the United States the Mystery Writers of America (1945) awards eight categories of the Edgar, named after Edgar Allan Poe, for the best crime novel of the year, the best short story, the best review critical/biographical work, and even the best television program on the subject. The Private Eye Writers (1982) gives several awards annually for the best achievements in private-eye categories, and the Bouchercon (1970)—named after critic "Anthony Boucher," whose real name was William Anthony Parker White—an eclectic organization of writers, readers, and fans of the mystery, gives awards for best mystery selections chosen by the members of the group itself. There are several French awards: the *Prix du roman d'aventure*, the *Prix du Quai des Orfèvres*, the *Prix de littérature policière*, the *Prix Ciceron* and the *Prix Mystère*. In the Federal Republic of Germany (West Germany), the *Edgar-Wallace-Preis* is awarded, while Norwegian authors may receive the *Golden Revolver*. There is the *Berenice Prize* in Denmark and the *Nada Prize* in Spain.

Agatha Christie, perhaps the most successful of crime writers, was made a Dame of the British Empire in recognition of her work, when long before that she had been described by reviewers and journalists alike as the Queen of Crime or the Duchess of Death, which was an honor not just to the lady herself but an acknowledgment of the importance of crime writing, mirrored equally in all the international awards. Its universal popularity stems not least from its infinite variety, which caters to the intellect and to the emotions. The steady growth of scientific thought together with social and political changes brought about a new direction in public taste: Infor-

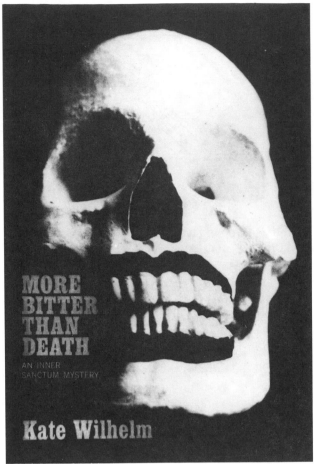

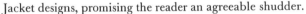

Jacket designs, promising the reader an agreeable shudder.

mation was demanded along with entertainment, confirming Brecht's theory that crime writing suits man in a scientific age.

The development of the genre naturally had a literary tradition. In some countries where this was lacking, translations, often pirated, had to fill the gap. Many writers, not always successfully, tried to imitate the Maigret novels. In Japan the development of indigenous crime writing was helped by historical tradition. In Spain the *picaro* was almost forgotten, and a new beginning had to be made. In the late sixties Francisco Garcia Pavon created a chief of police as his detective, assisted by a veteran in the role of Watson. Local color, description of countryside, and character sketches—particularly small-town types—distinguish these novels.

In Italy translations, mainly of British, American, and French writers have held the field for years,

gratefully received by readers who were starved of such books during the Fascist regime. Giorgio Scerbanenco, however, had a considerable success with his novels in which mobsters and gangs are the main subjects. If some scoundrels are caught, the worst often escape, leaving the reader contemplating a sad and gloomy world. This may well be realistic, but perhaps the reader would rather have reassurance.

Serious literary criticism has almost entirely ignored crime fiction in the Socialist countries, where its popularity among readers is actually on the increase. This is noticeably so in the Soviet Union. To begin with, translations from English, French, and Scandinavian authors dominated the market, with works by Collins, Gaboriau, Conan Doyle, Chesterton, Simenon, and Christie being well known. Films and television, too, used this material though in time native authors began to appear, continuing in their own tradition of story telling but now with added psychological insight. Today a new generation of authors is at work, writing and experimenting.

194

The development of the genre is international, and so is the wide circle of its readers with their variety of tastes and demands. In spite of a wealth of new publications to choose from, there is still a demand for the classic story; film and television in particular are fond of nineteenth-century themes. A result of the advent of television is a newly awakened interest for the book that inspired the film; this has led to new editions and reprints of old favorites. Historical cases are often turned into Pitaval case histories or novels, in which the author answers open questions as to suspect, motivation, and the like from his own point of view. Julian Symons with his *Sweet Adelaide* (1980) belongs to this category as does Günter Spranger, a writer from the German Democratic Republic (East Germany), with *Das Lügenspiel—Der Kriminalfall Grete Beier (A Game of Lies—The Case of Grete Beier)* (1980), while *Nalezeno Pravem (The Right Diagnosis)* (1971), by the Polish writer Vaclav Kaplicky, used court reports from the seventeenth century as a starting point.

To make a historical crime story ring true, it must be supported by factual elements that are especially apparent in the private-eye story and in the *roman policier*. Ample new possibilities exist. Popular paperbacks have deteriorated over the years into garishly presented material. Sex and crime are crudely, even lecherously presented, far removed from the literary manner of Chandler's *The Long Goodbye* (1953), *The High Window* (1942), or *The Big Sleep* (1939).

Unfortunately, television series sometimes tend to present violent action, and so help popularize "cheap" crime fiction. Horror stories, often disguised as psychological tales, continue to fascinate some readers, especially in providing an escape from the often ugly, boring or even dangerous world in which they live.

To sum up: this survey has led from the Greek oracle in a direct line to Scotland Yard, from antiquity to the present day. At the start it was difficult to unearth the scanty beginnings of crime fiction, but gradually and increasingly after 1800 the flood began to rise. The need for selection became clear with the result that it has only been possible to deal with literary landmarks. It is inevitable in this way that omissions have been made and somebody's favorite author left out. However, we trust we have done our best to inform and entertain and we defend our enterprise, meeting all charges with the reply: "Not guilty, milord."

The crime writer. Caricature from *V Mire Knig*, Moscow.

Appendix

Selected Bibliography

Achard, M. "Sophocle et Archimède, pères du roman policier." *Nouvelles Littéraires* (November 3, 1960).

Adamov, Arkadi. *Der Kriminalroman, mein Lieblingsgenre.* Moscow, 1980.

Alewyn, Richard. "Das Rätsel des Detektivromans." *Definitionen: Essays zur Literatur.* Adolf Frise, ed. Frankfurt/Main, 1963.

Alewyn, Richard. "Anatomie des Detektivromans." *Die Zeit* 47 (November 22, 1968) and 48 (November 29, 1969).

Anders, Karl. "Der Kriminalroman: Versuch einer Einordnung." *Bücherei und Bildung* 4 (1952).

Anderson, David R. *Rex Stout.* New York, 1981.

Arnold, Armin, and Josef Schmidt. *Reclams Kriminalromanführer.* Stuttgart, 1978.

Arnold, Armin, and Alois M. Haas, eds. *Sherlock Holmes auf der Hintertreppe: Aufsätze zur Kriminalliteratur.* Bonn, 1981.

Ball, John, ed. *The Mystery Story.* San Diego, 1976.

Bargainnier, Earl F. *12 Englishmen of Mystery.* Bowling Green, Ohio, 1984.

Bargainnier, Earl F. *10 Women of Mystery.* Bowling Green, Ohio, 1981.

Barnes, Melvyn. *Best Detective Fiction: A Guide from Godwin to the Present.* Hamden, Connecticut, 1975.

Barnes, Melvyn. *Dick Francis.* New York, 1986.

Barzun, Jacques, and Wendell Hertig Taylor, eds. *A Catalogue of Crime.* New York, 1971.

Benstock, Bernard. *Art in Crime Writing: Essays on Detective Fiction.* New York, 1983.

Benvenuti, Stefano. *The Whodunit: An Informal History of Detective Fiction.* New York, 1981.

Beyer, Hugo. "Kriminalnovelle, -roman." *Reallexikon der deutschen Literaturgeschichte.* 2 vols. Berlin, 1928-29.

Bien, Günter. "Abenteuer und verborgene Wahrheit: Gibt es den literarischen Kriminalroman?" *Hochland* 57 (1965).

Bloch, Ernst. "Die Form der Detektivgeschichte und die Philosophie." *Neue Rundschau,* 1960.

Bloch, Ernst. "Philosophische Ansicht des Detektivromans." *Verfremdungen I.* Frankfurt/Main, 1961.

Böckel, Fritz. "Kriminalgeschichten." *Monatsschrift für Kriminalpsychologie und Strafrechtsreform,* 1914-18.

Boileau, Pierre, and Thomas Narcejac. *Le roman policier.* Paris, 1964.

Brecht, Bertolt. "Über die Popularität des Kriminalromans." *Schriften zur Literatur und Kunst.* Vol. 2. Berlin and Weimar, 1966.

Bry, Karl Christian. "Verbrecherschwarten." *Das Literarische Echo.* 25th annual set (1922-23).

Buchloh, Paul Gerhard, and Jens Peter Becker, eds. *Der Detektiverzählung auf der Spur: Essays zu Form und Wertung der englischen Detektivliteratur.* Darmstadt, 1977.

Budd, Elaine. *13 Mistresses of Murder.* New York, 1986.

Caillois, Roger. *Le roman policier.* Paris, 1941.

Campos, Jorge. "Lo policiaco en la América hispana." *Insula* 231 (1966).

Carr, John C. *The Craft of Crime: Conversations with Crime Writers.* Boston, 1983.

Carr, John D. *The Life of Sir Arthur Conan Doyle.* New York, 1949.

Carter, John D. "Detective Fiction." *New Paths in Book Collecting.* London, 1934.

Cassiday, Bruce, ed. *Roots of Detection: The Art of Deduction before Sherlock Holmes.* New York, 1983.

Chandler, Frank W. *The Literature of Roguery.* Boston, 1907.

Chandler, Raymond T. *The Simple Art of Murder.* Boston, 1950.

Chassaing, H. *De Zadig au rififi on du roman policier.* Montpellier, 1959.

Chesterton, Gilbert Keith. "A Defense of Detective Stories." *The Defendant.* London, 1901.

Chesterton, Gilbert Keith. "Detective Story Writers." *Come to Think of It.* London, 1931.

Chesterton, Gilbert Keith. "On Detective Novels." *Generally Speaking.* London, 1929.

Christie, Agatha. *Meine gute alte Zeit.* Berne and Munich, 1977.

Dahnke, Walter. *Kriminalroman und Wirklichkeit.* Hamburg, 1958.

Depken, Friedrich. "Sherlock Holmes, Raffles und ihre Vorbilder: Ein Beitrag zur Entwicklungsgeschichte und Technik der Kriminalerzählung." *Anglistische Forschungen* 41. Heidelberg, 1914.

Dooley, Dennis. *Dashiell Hammett.* New York, 1984.

Eames, Hugh. *The Mystery Story.* New York, 1978.

Eckert, Otto. "Der Kriminalroman als Gattung." *Bücherei und Bildung* 3 (1951).

Egloff, Gerd. *Detektivroman und englisches Bürgertum: Konstruktionsschemen und Gesellschaftsbild bei Agatha Christie.* Düsseldorf, 1974.

Elgström, Jörge, and Ake Runniquist. *Svensk mordbok: Den svenska detektivromanens historia 1900–1950.* Stockholm, 1957.

Erné, Nino. "Whodunnit oder die Olive im Martini: Ein Plädoyer für den Kriminalroman." *Die Welt der Literatur* 16 (1965).

Ferri, Enrico. *Les criminels dans l'art et la littérature.* Paris, 1907.

Fischer, Peter. "Neue Häuser in der Rue Morgue." *Merkur* 23 (1969).

Fosca, François. *Histoire et technique du roman policier.* Paris, 1937.

Freeman, Lucy, ed. *The Murder Mystique: Crime Writers on Their Art.* New York, 1982.

Fürst, Rudolf. "Kriminalromantik." *Das literarische Echo* 10 (1908).

Gaillard, Dawson. *Dorothy L. Sayers.* New York, 1981.

Geherin, David. *The American Private Eye: The Image in Fiction.* New York, 1985.

Geherin, David. *John D. MacDonald.* New York, 1982.

Geherin, David. *Sons of Sam Spade: The Private Eye Novel in the 70s.* New York, 1980.

Gerber, Richard. "Verbrechensdichtung und Kriminalroman." *Neue Deutsche Literatur* 3 (1966).

Gerteis, Walter. *Detektive: Ihre Geschichte im Leben und in der Literatur.* Munich, 1953.

Gilbert, Michael, ed. *Crime in Good Company.* London, 1959.

Gribble, Leonhard. *Die grossen Detektive: 150 Jahre Kriminalistik.* Munich, 1965.

Hagen, Ordean A. *Who Done It? A Guide to Detective Mystery and Suspense Fiction.* New York, 1969.

Harper, Ralph. *The World of the Thriller.* Cleveland, Ohio, 1969.

Haycraft, Howard, ed. *The Art of the Mystery Story: A Collection of Critical Essays.* New York, 1975.

Haycraft, Howard. *Murder for Pleasure: The Life and Times of the Detective Story.* New York, 1941.

Haycraft, Howard. "Mystery and Detective Stories." *Encyclopaedia Britannica*, 1963.

Heissenbüttel, Helmut. "Spielregeln des Kriminalromans." *Trivialliteratur: Aufsätze.* Gerhard Schmidt-Henkel, ed. Berlin (West), 1964.

Highsmith, Patricia. *Plotting and Writing Suspense Fiction.* Boston, 1966.

Hollingworth, Keith. *The Newgate Novel 1830–1847.* Detroit, 1963.

Hügel, Hans-Otto. *Untersuchungsrichter—Diebsfänger—Detektive: Geschichte und Theorie der deutschen Detektiverzählung im 19. Jahrhundert.* Stuttgart, 1978.

Just, Klaus G. "Edgar Allan Poe und die Folgen." *Übergänge: Probleme und Gestalten der Literatur.* Berne and Munich, 1966.

Kaemmel, Ernst. "Literatur unterm Tisch: Der Detektivroman und sein gesellschaftlicher Auftrag." *Neue Deutsche Literatur* 10 (1962) 5.

Kaul, Karl. "Der Kriminalroman gestern und heute." *Neue Deutsche Literatur* 3 (1955).

Keating, H. R. F. *Whodunit? A Guide to Crime, Suspense, and Spy Fiction.* New York, 1982.

Knox, Ronald A. "Mystery Stories." *Encyclopaedia Britannica*, 1946.

Kracauer, Siegfried. "Der Detektivroman." *Schriften* 1. Frankfurt/Main, 1971.

Kruse, Hans-Joachim. "Introduction." *Die deutsche Kriminalerzählung von Schiller bis zur Gegenwart.* Herbert Greiner-Mai and Hans-Joachim Kruse, eds. 3 vols. Berlin, 1968.

Lacassin, Francis. *Mythologie du roman policier.* 2 vols. Paris, 1976.

La Cour, Tage, and Harald Mogensen. *The Murder Book: An Illustrated History of the Detective Story.* New York, 1971.

Lambert, Gavin. *The Dangerous Edge: An Inquiry into the Lives of Nine Masters of Suspense.* New York, 1976.

Langenbucher, Helmut. "Der Teufel spielt Verstecken oder Einiges zur Frage des gegenwärtigen Kriminalromans." *Die Buch-Besprechung* 3. Leipzig, 1939.

Lichtenstein, Alfred. *Der Kriminalroman.* Munich, 1908.

Madden, David, ed. *Tough Guy Writers of the Thirties.* Carbondale, 1968.

Mager, Hasso. *Krimi und Crimen.* Halle, 1969.

Mann, Jessica. *Deadlier Than the Male: Why Are Respectable English Women So Good at Murder?* New York, 1981.

Margolies, Edward. *Which Way Did He Go? The Private Eye in Dashiell Hammett, Raymond Chandler, Chester Himes, and Ross Macdonald.* New York, 1982.

Marsch, Edgar. *Die Kriminalerzählung: Theorie—Geschichte—Analyse.* Munich, 1972.

Messac, Régis. *The detective novel et l'influence de la pensée scientifique.* Paris, 1929.

Murch, A. E. *The Development of the Detective Novel.* Westport, Connecticut, 1958.

Murr, Stefan. "Krimi in Deutschland: Mordversuch an einem kultivierten Literaturzweig." *Das Antiquariat* 4 (1980).

Narcejac, Thomas. *Esthétique du roman policier.* Paris, 1947.

Nevins, Francis M. *The Mystery Writer's Art.* Bowling Green, Ohio, 1971.

Nolan, William F. *The Black Mask Boys: Masters in the Hard-boiled School of Detective Fiction.* New York, 1985.

Nusser, Peter. *Der Kriminalroman.* Stuttgart, 1980.

Ousby, Ian. *Bloodhounds of Heaven: The Detective in English Fiction from Godwin to Doyle.* Cambridge, Massachusetts, 1976.

Panek, LeRoy. *Watteau's Shepherds: The Detective Novel in Britain, 1915–1940.* Bowling Green, Ohio, 1979.

Penzler, Otto, ed. *Great Detectives.* Boston, 1978.

Peterson, Audrey. *Victorian Masters of Mystery: From Wilkie Collins to Conan Doyle.* New York, 1984.

Pfeiffer, Hans. *Die Mumie im Glassarg: Bemerkungen zur Kriminalliteratur.* Rudolstadt, 1960.

Pfeiffer, Hans. *Die Sprache der Toten: Die Gerichtsmedizin im Dienste der Wahrheit.* Berlin, 1968.

Pfeiffer, Hans. *Die Spur der Toten.* Berlin, 1977.

Pronzini, Bill. *Gun in Cheek: A Study of "Alternative" Crime Fiction.* New York, 1982.

Queen, Ellery. *The Detective Short Story: A Bibliography.* New York, 1969.

Queen, Ellery. *Queen's Quorum.* New York, 1969.

Reilly, John M., ed. *Twentieth-Century Crime and Mystery Writers.* New York, 1985.

Reinert, Claus. *Detektivliteratur bei Sophokles, Schiller und Kleist.* Kronberg, 1975.

Riley, Dick, and Pam McAllister, eds. *The New Bedside, Bathtub & Armchair Companion to Agatha Christie.* New York, 1979, 1986.

Rodell, Marie F. *Mystery Fiction: Theory and Technique.* London, 1952.

Routley, Erik. *The Puritan Pleasures of the Detective Story.* London, 1972.

Schulz-Buschhaus, Ulrich. *Formen und Ideologien des Kriminalromans: Ein gattungsgeschichtliches Essay.* Frankfurt/Main, 1975.

Scheper, George L. *Michael Innes.* New York, 1986.

Seesslen, Georg. *Mord im Kino: Geschichte und Mythologie des Detektivfilms.* Hamburg, 1981.

Sichelschmidt, Gustav. *Liebe, Mord und Abenteuer.* Berlin, 1969.

Siebenheller, Norma. *P. D. James.* New York, 1981.

Speir, Jerry. *Raymond Chandler.* New York, 1981.

Speir, Jerry. *Ross Macdonald.* New York, 1978.

Starrett, Vincent. "Mystery Stories." *Encyclopaedia Britannica,* 1946.

Steinbrunner, Chris, Charles Shibuk, Otto Penzler, Marvin Lachman, and Francis Nevins, Jr. *Detectionary.* Lock Haven, Pennsylvania, 1971.

Sutherland, Scott. *Blood in Their Ink: The March of the Modern Mystery Story.* London, 1953.

Symons, Julian. *Dashiell Hammett.* San Diego, 1985.

Symons, Julian. *The Detective Story in Britain.* London, 1962.

Symons, Julian. *A Pictorial History of Crime: 1840 to the Present.* New York, 1966.

Symons, Julian. *Mortal Consequences: A History from the Detective Story to the Crime Novel.* New York, 1972.

Thompson, H. Douglas. *Masters of Mystery.* London, 1931.

Thorwald, Jürgen. *Das Jahrhundert der Detektive.* Zurich, 1966.

Tschimmel, Irene. *Kriminalroman und Gesellschaftsdarstellung: Eine vergleichende Darstellung zu Werken von Christie, Simenon, Dürrenmatt, Capote.* Berne, 1979.

Van Dover, J. Kenneth. *Murder in the Millions: Erle Stanley Gardner—Mickey Spillane—Ian Fleming.* New York, 1984.

Vogt, Jochen, ed. *Der Kriminalroman.* 2 vols. Munich, 1971.

Watson, Colin. *Snobbery with Violence. Crime Stories and Their Audience.* London, 1971.

Winks, Robin W. *Modus Operandi: An Excursion into Detective Fiction.* Boston, 1982.

Wölcken, Fritz. *Der literarische Mord: Eine Untersuchung über die englische und amerikanische Detektivliteratur.* Nuremberg, 1953.

Würtenberger, Thomas. *Die deutsche Kriminalerzählung.* Erlangen, 1941.

Zmegac, Viktor, ed. *Der wohltemperierte Mord.* Frankfurt/Main, 1971.

Index of Crime Writers

This index lists the authors of crime fiction mentioned in the book as well as poets and other writers who in their work either tried their hand at the genre or otherwise showed a keen interest in literary criminality. Except in a few cases each individual is listed under his or her proper name, as opposed to the pseudonym. The italicized numbers refer to the illustrations.

Abele, Matthias von und zu Lilienberg (1616 or 1618–77) 27, 29, 61
After having studied philosophy and law he became secretary of the ironworkers' union in Steyr, Austria. In addition to his professional career he published short prose works and crime stories.

Abraham à San(c)ta Clara (1644–1709) 29
Real name Johann Ulrich Megerle. Famous Augustinian friar and preacher in Vienna whose popularity was due to his colloquial style of speech and his close affinity to the common people.

Adamov, Arkadi (born in 1920) 178, 179, 180; *180*
Soviet author who has been writing crime fiction for thirty years, author of *A Many-Colored Case* (1955), *Circles on the Water* (1973), *An Ill Wind* (1975).

Adams, Cleve F(ranklin) (1895–1949) 143
Contemporary of Hammett and Chandler, he wrote of the exploits of Rex McBride—a pre-Humphrey Bogart personality who came alive with Bogart's later success.

Adler, William (born in 1929) 186; *185*
American writer, editor, and publisher whose interest in the mystery inspired him to package a blockbuster best seller, Thomas Chastain's *Who Killed the Robins Family?*—a "contest" novel in which the *readers* wrote the solution, with $10,000 going to the contestant with the best solution.

Ainsworth, William H. (1805–82) 65
His stories, written in the manner of the historical novels of Walter Scott and Victor Hugo, included such novels as *Rookwood* (1824) and *Jack Sheppard* (1839), both providing romanticized portrayals of thieves, following the tradition of the Newgate novel.

Aeschylus (525–456 B.C.) 9
Famous dramatist in ancient Greece. Of his ninety trage-dies only seven have survived in theire intirety, including the great trilogy of the *Oresteia* (458 B.C.).

Alexis, Willibald, see Häring, Georg Wilhelm

Allain, Marcel (1885–1969) 103
Together with Pierre Souvestre (1874–1914) he invented the figure of the Fantômas, a criminal able to change his appearance almost at will. His Fantômas novels, which appeared between 1909 and 1965, exploited many elements of the thriller.

Allingham, Margery (1904–66) 152, 153
An English writer married to the editor of the *Tatler*, who helped her with her crime stories. In addition to novels such as *Mystery Mile* (1930) she also published short stories—for example, "Campion Criminologist" (1937).

Apuleius (born in A.D. 125, date of death unknown) 10, 12
Roman writer, lawyer and philosopher who lived most of his life in Africa and Rome. His main work was *Metamorphoses* or *The Golden Ass*.

Arnau, Frank (1894–1976) 130; *130*
A Swiss nationalist, journalist, and crime reporter who wrote textbooks on criminology and articles for the press. He also wrote detective stories and essays on contemporary criminal cases. Author of *The Eye of the Law* (1962), *The Perfect Murder* (1960).

Ayrand, Pierre, see Narcejac, Thomas

Bailey, H(enry) C(hristopher) (1878–1961) 123
English journalist and writer who initially worked for the London *Daily Telegraph*. As an author of crime fiction he invented the character of the scientific detective Reggie Fortune and the cunning lawyer Joshua Clunk.

Balderson, Bo 184
The nom de plume of a prominent Swedish personality who wishes to remain anonymous.

Balzac, Honoré de (1799–1850) 75, 173
Well-known French novelist who in his wide-ranging series of realistic novels often touched on the topic of crime. He also paid a literary tribute to Eugène Vidocq.

Barnes, Linda 142
American writer living in the Bay Area in Brookline, Mas-

sachusetts, with series character Michael Spraggue, a private investigator, debuting in *Blood Will Have Blood* (1981).

Barr, Robert (1850–1912)   116
A journalist of Scottish descent, he wrote a number of crime stories and novels featuring the French detective Eugène Valmont.

Bäuerle, Adolf (1784–1859)   80
Popular Viennese author of novels and comedies.

Beer, Johann (1655–1700)   28, 29
An Austrian composer and author of frequently satirical novels.

Bellem, Robert Leslie (1902–68)   143
U.S. author who combined the action of the private eye with the humor of the screwball comedies of the 1930s to produce his detective hero, Dan Turner. Stories in this offbeat series were set in Hollywood, and featured typical crazies of the time and the area.

Bentley, Edmund C. (1875–1956)   106
An English journalist and writer whose detective stories, though few in number, were very well received by his contemporaries.

Berkeley, Anthony, see Cox, Anthony Berkeley

Bezuglov, Anatoli   178
Soviet lawyer and legal expert who, together with former fellow student Yuri Klarov (see below)—later a public prosecutor—wrote detective stories based on their professional experiences.

Bierce, Ambrose (1842–1914)   92, 131
Took part in the American Civil War on the northern side. Later he worked as a critic and reporter. He is renowned for his realistic sardonic stories.

Biggers, Earl Derr (1884–1933)   126
A newspaper columnist and playwright, he began writing mystery novels in 1913, and in 1925 created Charlie Chan, a Chinese detective on the Honolulu police force, who made his debut in *The House without a Key*.

Bilinski, Waclaw   162
Polish writer.

Block, Lawrence (born in 1938)   143; *144*
U.S. writer and creator of Matthew Scudder and Bernie Rhodenbarr—Scudder an ex-cop P.I., and Rhodenbarr a witty ex-burglar and accidental detective.

Boileau, Pierre-Louis (born in 1906)   157, 159, 193; *158*
Collaborated with Thomas Narcejac (see below) on theoretical studies relating to the detective story. Author of psychological thrillers. *The Living and the Dead* (1956) was filmed by Hitchcock in 1958 and released as *Vertigo*. In 1965 his work *Et Mon Tout Est Un Homme (Choice Cuts)* was awarded the *Prix d l'humor noir* (the prize for black humor).

Borge, Bernhard   157
Norwegian writer of detective stories.

Borrow, George H. (1803–81)   62
English writer who translated Vidocq's memoirs and published *Celebrated Trials, and Remarkable Cases of Criminal Jurisprudence of 1825* (1825).

Braddon, Mary Elizabeth (1837–1915)   71
English novelist—*Lady Audley's Secret* (1862)—who later turned to the historical novel. *Lady Audley's Secret* introduced Robert Audley, one of the first amateur detectives in the novel.

Brentano, Clemens (1778–1842)   55
German poet of the Romantic era.

Brett, Simon (born in 1945)   168; *168*
British author whose series protagonist, the professional actor Charles Paris, knows his way around the theater. His tongue-in-cheek writing is quick-witted, humorous, and extremely readable.

Brooks, Edwy Searles (1889–1965)   156, 157
British crime writer who wrote books under the pseudonym of Victor Gunn and Berkeley Gray.

Browne, Howard (born in 1908)   143
U.S. writer and editor who wrote novels, short stories, novelettes, and screenplays; series detective, Paul Pine.

Bulwer-Lytton, Edward George (1803–73)   62, 63, 65
Graduate of Cambridge University, Member of Parliament and diplomat who also made a name for himself as a writer.

Burnett, W(illiam) R(iley) (1899–1982)   170, 172, 188; *172*
U.S. writer who produced novels that created various film trends—*Little Caesar* (1929), *High Sierra* (1940), and *The Asphalt Jungle* (1950)—and screenplays that made unforgettable films—*This Gun for Hire* (1941), and *Action in the North Atlantic* (1943).

Butler, John K.   143
A master of plot and story line in the early hard-boiled school. His series character was Steve Midnight, a cab driver who prowled the dark streets of Los Angeles, righting wrongs.

Caesarius, Abbot of Heisterbach   13
Abbot of the monastery of Heisterbach from *c.* 1180 to almost the middle of the thirteenth century. His writings included short stories and biographies.

Cain, James M. (1892–1977)   170, 172; *170*
U.S. author of hard-boiled school of writing whose works reflect the Great Depression in realism, grimness, and hard-bitten humor. Films of his works—*Mildred Pierce* (1945), *Double Indemnity* (1944), and *The Postman Always Rings Twice* (1946)—still evoke the gritty days of 1930s America.

Čapek, Karel (1890–1938)   129
Czech novelist and dramatist of international repute.

Capote, Truman (1924–84)   131
Leading U.S. writer, author of *In Cold Blood* (1966).

Capra, Frank (born in 1897) 184
U.S. film director, producer, and author of Italian extraction mainly renowned for his light comedies, but occasionally known to experiment in crime and black humor: as in *Arsenic and Old Lace.*

Carr, John Dickson (1906–77) 125, 160; *127*
U.S. author who under his proper name and the pseudonym Carter Dickson wrote over eighty detective stories and created a whole range of fictional detectives such as Dr. Gideon Fell, Sir Henry Merrivale, Henri Bencolin, and Colonel March. In 1949 he wrote a biography of Conan Doyle: *The Life of Sir Arthur Conan Doyle.*

Cassiday, Bruce (born in 1920) 143
U.S. writer and editor (the American *Argosy*) who produced radio dramas of psychological suspense and stories for magazines and books in the film noir vein, featuring series character Johnny Blood and mystery genre novels with various heroes.

Chandler, Raymond (1888–1959) 115, 131, 132, 133, 135, 137, 138, 140, 141, 146, 192, 195; *137, 138, 170*
American detective story writer who helped to develop the new, realistic form of the tough "hard boiled" story. Spent his early years in England and found occasional work as a journalist. After losing his job during the depression he started writing, at first short stories; then he turned to the socially critical detective story.

Chastain, Thomas 186; *185*
Newspaperman and editor who wrote the best-selling *Who Killed the Robins Family?* as a mystery with the solution to be written by the reader for $10,000 award for the best. Also wrote police procedurals.

Chekhov, Anton Pavlovich (1860–1904) 90
The Russian writer began his literary career by writing short stories before taking up drama later on. The theme of crime occurs only in his novels and in one story.

Chesterton, G(ilbert) K(eith) (1874–1936) 8, 80, 109, 110, 111, 125, 159, 179, 180, 194; *109*
English journalist, critic and writer. He was converted to Catholicism and later introduced the figure of Father Brown into his detective stories. Altogether he wrote fifty Father Brown stories.

Childers, Erskine (1870–1922) 108
Born in London, he embraced the cause of Irish nationalism, went to sea, joined the Irish Republican Army, was condemned by a military court, and shot. His one novel, *The Riddle of the Sands* (1903), is regarded as the first spy story in world literature.

Christie, Agatha (1890–1976) 7, 90, 111, 113, 115, 116, 117, 118, 120, 121, 122, 125, 128, 150, 151, 152, 153, 193, 194; *116, 117*
Born Agatha Mary Clarissa Miller in Devon, England, she married A. Christie, an officer, in 1918. During the war she worked as a nurse and wrote her first detective story in her spare time. But her literary breakthrough did not come until 1926 with the publication of *The Murder of Roger Ack-*

royd. In her second marriage she wed the archeologist M. Mallowan, continuing to write under the name Christie. She spent several months each year with her husband at archeological excavations in the Middle East. It is estimated that her books—some eighty novels and collections of short stories—have sold a total of 400,000,000 copies over the years.

Clark, Mary Higgins (born in 1929) 165, 166, 186; *185*
U.S. writer of popular novels usually exploiting suspense and terror in ordinary places. Although Gothic in concept, they are fundamentally crime-related stories rooted in murder, kidnapping, and blackmail.

Cicero, Marcus Tullius (106–43 B.C.) 10
Famous Roman statesman, writer and orator.

Clemens, Samuel Langhorne, see Twain, Mark

Cody, Liza 143
British author whose series protagonist Anna Lee is a private investigator in the classic tradition, operating out of London.

Cole, George Douglas Howard (1889–1959) 123
An English economist and Oxford professor who wrote a number of detective stories together with his wife Margaret Isabel, partly as a relaxing contrast to his academic work and partly in order to earn money.

Collier, John (1901–80) 187
He was born in London but later emigrated to the U.S. He has written numerous short stories spiced with black humor.

Collins, Michael 143
Pseudonym for Dennis Lynds (born in 1924). Novels under the Collins byline feature Dan Fortune, a one-armed P. I. Lynds under the William Arden byline produces Kane Jackson; under the Mark Sadler byline, Paul Shaw. He also writes novels under the name John Crowe, and straight novels under his own name.

Collins, William Wilkie (1824–89) 67, 68, 69, 70, 91, 92, 160, 194; *68*
English novelist. Author of the first Victorian detective stories.

Cooper, James Fenimore (1789–1851) 56, 76
After much traveling the U.S. writer settled down on his estate at Coopertown and wrote the Leather-Stocking Tales about American Indians.

Coryell, John Russell 94

Cox, Anthony Berkeley (1893–1971) 111, 123, 124, 148, 152
An English writer and journalist who, partly under the pseudonym of Anthony Berkeley and Francis Iles, wrote detective stories and novels.

Coxe, George Harmon (1901–84) 143
Author of scores of short stories and novels, many featuring Jack "Flashgun" Casey and later, Kent Murdock. Writer of radio plays, television plays, and screenplays.

Creasey, John (1908–73) 181, 183
Wrote under his name and dozens of pseudonyms, the most famous of which was J. J. Marric, author of the Commander George Gideon books, a top police-procedural series. Became long-running British TV series. Author wrote some 560 novels.

Crofts, Freeman Wills (1879–1957) 90, 111, 115
Born in Dublin, went to college in Belfast, and worked as a senior engineer on the railways. During a lengthy illness he wrote his first detective story—*The Cask* (1920)—and subsequently became a full-time writer.

Cross, Amanda 148, 149, 150, 151; *150*
Pseudonym for Carolyn G. Heilbrun (born in 1926). She writes from a background of academia about that milieu, with her academic detective, Kate Fansler. The novels feature lively intellectual dialogue, witty discussions on all subjects, and a feeling for the contemporary college scene.

Curtiss, Ursula (born in 1923) 162, 165
Born Ursula Reilly, and married to John Curtiss, she lives in New Mexico, U.S., and since 1948 has written more than twenty detective stories marked by psychological analysis and often containing spine-chilling elements.

Dahl, Roald (born in 1916) 187
A Welsh free-lance writer who has also produced some crime fiction interlaced with black humor.

Daly, Carroll John (1889–1958) 141
Early practitioner in the hard-boiled P.I. school of writing in *Black Mask*—some say its "originator." Creator of Race Williams, the fictional cowboy transplanted to the urban milieu, the gunman who makes wrongs right.

Dannay, Frederic (1905–82) 126, 149; *127*
Under the pen name of Ellery Queen the Brooklyn-born writer (real name, Daniel Nathan) wrote a great many detective stories, novels, and radio scripts, together with his cousin Manfred B. Lee. From 1941 onwards, he also published *Ellery Queen's Mystery Magazine*.

Davis, Dorothy Salisbury (born in 1916) 156, 186; *156, 185*
U.S. author and Grand Master of the Mystery Writers of America, whose series protagonist Julie Hayes appears in several of her books. She has had seven Edgar nominations for four novels and three short stories. The author deals with the difficulties of modern life and examines the stresses that make people turn to crime.

Davis, Norbert (1909–49) 143
Early master of the hard-boiled short story genre, inclined to overlay every piece of action with humor and wit, usually couched in wisecracks by the hero. Heroes include Max Latin and sometimes the twosome of Doan and Carstairs.

Defoe, Daniel (1660–1731) 30, 46
English journalist and writer who was also actively involved in politics. Best known for his work *Robinson Crusoe*.

Dewey, Thomas B(lanchard) (1915–77) 143

U.S. writer of crime fiction, creator of "Mac," a P.I. out of Chicago.

Dickens, Charles (1812–70) 65, 66, 67, 68, 92, 93; *64, 67*
Well-known English author of novels full of social criticism.

Dickson, Carter, see Carr, John Dickson

Dietrich, Joachim (born in 1927) 185
A contributor to *Eulenspiegel*, a satirical magazine in the German Democratic Republic (East Germany), who uses the pen name Cobra.

Dine, S. S. Van, see Wright, Willard Huntington

Dostoyevski, Fyodor Mikhailovich (1821–81) 8, 178
Russian writer whose novels are counted among the works of world literature.

Doyle, Arthur Conan (1859–1930) 7, 90, 91, 92, 97, 98, 99, 100, 102, 103, 107, 109, 115, 120, 132, 160, 161, 179, 194; *91, 92*
A Scottish doctor who studied medicine in Edinburgh before turning to authorship. Although he himself set more store by his historical novels and sketches, it was his detective stories featuring Sherlock Holmes and Dr. Watson, that brought him literary success.

Droste-Hülshoff, Annette von (1797–1848) 85; *86*
German novelist and poetess.

Dumas, Alexandre père (1802–70) 36, 75, 76, 82; *76*
French novelist and dramatist. His success was mainly due to his historical adventure stories but he was also editor of *Les Crimes Célèbres*.

Du Maurier, Daphne (born in 1907) 163; *163*
An English writer who has made a name for herself as the author of historical novels and romances. Her Gothic plots, particularly *Rebecca* (1938), abound in mystery and crime.

Dürrenmatt, Friedrich (born in 1921) 7, 147, 148; *148*
A Swiss writer known mainly for his plays. However, his prose works also include detective stories, such as *The Pledge* (1958).

Eberhart, Mignon G(ood) (born in 1899) 126, 131
A Grand Master of the Mystery Writers of America, this U.S. author began writing detective novels in 1929, and, six decades later, is still producing successful stories.

Ellin, Stanley (1916–86) 186, 187
Ex-steel worker from New York who, in his novels and particularly in his short stories, combined crime fiction and black humor in an intriguing mixture.

Euripides (484–406 B.C.) 9
Classic Greek tragedian.

Faulkner, William (1897–1962) 140, 141; *140*
Born in New Albany, Mississippi, his novels and short stories describe events and people in his area. In 1950 he was awarded the Nobel Prize for Literature.

Feuerbach, Paul Johann Anselm von (1775–1833) 58, 59; *60*
German philosopher and jurist who fought against feudal despotism and bureaucracy, author of *Kaspar Hauser* (1832), and *Narratives of Remarkable Criminal Trials* (1828–29).

Fielding, Henry (1707–54) 46, 66
Celebrated writer of the English Enlightenment.

Fish, Robert L(loyd) (1912–81) 143
U.S. author and creator of Captain José da Silva; also author of the "Schlock Homes" series of short stories. One of his novels under pseudonym of Robert L. Pike (*Mute Witness* [1963]) became hit film *Bullitt*.

Fletcher, J(oseph) S(mith) (1863–1935) 111, 123
An English writer who, in addition to poetry and biographies, produced about a hundred detective stories, some of them bordering on the thriller form, but all readable and unpedantic.

Fontane, Theodor (1819–98) 87, 89; *88*
Born into a German Huguenot family he worked as a journalist, theater critic, and novelist. In his search for critical realism his plots frequently dealt with criminal themes.

Francis, Dick (born in 1920) 166, 167, 168; *166*
Ex-jockey and ex-journalist, British writer Dick Francis has used the detective genre to write nongenre novels that are closer to mainstream than genre books, with each rooted in some way to the tradition of horse racing. No series hero, except for Sid Halley, who has appeared twice.

Fraser, Antonia (Lady) (born in 1932) 168; *168*
Biographer (*Mary, Queen of Scots* [1969]) and British author of a mystery series featuring a television investigative reporter, Jemima Shore. The mystery novels are refreshingly written and interlard plot with the name drops expected of a writer traveling in high London society.

Freeling, Nicolas (born in 1927) 174
Born in London, grew up in France, studied in Dublin, and worked in the Netherlands before he took to writing detective stories under his name and "F. R. C. Nicolas."

Freeman, Lucy (born in 1916) 131, 186; *185*
Ex-journalist who wrote best-selling book *Before I Kill More* (1955), and a series of mysteries with a psychoanalyst, Dr. Ames, as detective surrogate. Edited *The Murder Mystique* (1982).

Freeman, R(ichard) Austin (1862–1943) 110, 111
A London-born doctor who worked for a long time in Africa. His hero, Dr. John Evelyn Thorndyke, a forensic surgeon, first appeared in *The Red Thumb Mark* in 1907, and remains the most convincing scientific investigator in crime fiction.

Gaboriau, Emile (1832–73) 76, 77, 80, 90, 91, 95, 97, 98, 102, 106, 173, 174, 194
As secretary to F. Féval, a popular novelist, he had to visit prisons and courts and then write passages recounting his experiences for his employer's novels. Later he wrote novels of his own that were serialized in Parisian newspapers.

Gardner, Erle Stanley (1889–1970) 126, 132, 137, 138, 139
American lawyer and well-known defense attorney. In 1923 he began writing short detective stories for magazines. His first Perry Mason novel, *The Case of the Velvet Claws*, appeared in 1933. The climax of these novels is always a court scene that Gardner himself might have experienced.

Gault, William Campbell (born in 1910) 143
U.S. writer and creator of P.I.s Brock Callahan and Joe Puma—both of whom have run through dozens of cases. Gault also writes juveniles for teenagers.

Gay, John (1685–1732) 50
English poet renowned for his *Beggar's Opera* (1728).

Gerstäcker, Friedrich (1816–72) 82
German writer of travel sketches and adventure stories (for exemple, *The Mississippi Pirates*) who was also the author of one detective story. The subject of crime also features in his adventure stories.

Gilbert, Michael (born in 1912) 168
A British solicitor and author of scores of short stories and novels. His occasional heroes are Inspector Hazelrigg and Patrick Petrella. He has written radio plays and television plays, as well as plays for the London stage.

Godwin, William (1756–1836) 50; *45*
English political theorist who influenced leading Romantic writers and poets with fictional works such as *The Adventures of Caleb Williams* (1794).

Gores, Joe (born in 1931) 191; *191*
Ex-private detective infolved in repo cases (repossession of cars by dealers for nonpayment), he is screenwriter now for films and television, but wrote a number of novels and short stories in the crime genre. Did screenplay for *Hammett* (1978).

Goulart, Ron(ald Joseph) (born in 1933) 184
Prolific U.S. author of crime novels, science fiction novels, and straight novels, always in the humorous vein. Writes under the names Julian Kearny, Howard Lee, Kenneth Robeson, Frank S. Shaver, Con Steffanson, Josephine Kains, etc.

Grafton, Sue 143
U.S. author whose series mysteries feature Kinsey Millhone, a female private eye, working out of a pseudonymous Southern California town. Also writes screenplays for film and television.

Green, Anna Katharine (1846–1935) 95, 97, 106, 107
Her father was a well-known American defense attorney, an her first and most famous novel *The Leavenworth Case: A Lawyer's Story* (1878) likewise depicts a court case. Subsequently she wrote some forty detective stories.

Greenleaf, Stephen (born in 1942) 143; *144*
U.S. attorney and writer in the tradition of Hammett and

Chandler, with private investigator John Marshall Tanner, a hard-boiled California loner whose wisecracking cynicism masks the traditional hard-core idealism.

Grillparzer, Franz (1791–1872) 52
He trained as a lawyer and worked in this profession, mainly to ensure a regular income. He is one of Austria's foremost dramatists. Author of *The Poor Minstrel* (1848).

Grimes, Martha 156; *157*
Although she is American-born and a resident of the U.S., she writes crime novels that take place in England, featuring a police inspector, Richard Jury, and his aristocratic sidekick, Melrose Plant, the Earl of Caverness and Lord Ardry.

Gunn, Victor, see Brooks, Edwy Searles

Halliday, Brett 143
Pseudonym for Davis Dresser (1904–77). Creator of Mike Shayne, a hard-boiled private eye featured in over sixty novels and short stories; Shayne appeared in many films and in a television series.

Hammett, Dashiell (1894–1961) 7, 131, 132, 133, 134, 135, 137, 138, 139, 140, 141, 146, 192; *133, 134*
Began his career as a private eye with the Pinkerton Agency, his experiences reflected in detective stories he began to write in 1922. His most famous novels appeared between 1929 and 1934 and included *Red Harvest* and *The Maltese Falcon*. Along with Chandler he was a leading exponent of the "hard boiled" detective story.

Hansen, Joseph (born in 1923) 143
Creator of Dave Brandstetter, a homosexual P.I., who operates out of the Los Angeles scene with mysteries usually involving homosexual people and situations. He also writes mainstream novels and short stories under his name and under the name James Colton.

Häring, Georg Wilhelm (1785–1871) 59, 60
He was a lawyer at Berlin's Supreme Court. Later he became a journalist and writer, achieving a measure of fame under the pseudonym Willibald Alexis.

Harrington, Joyce 186; *185*
Public relations executive for a New York ad agency and writer of two detective novels and numerous short stories, one of which, "The Purple Shroud," won the Edgar Allan Poe Award.

Harsdörffer, Georg Philipp (1607–58) 21, 22, 23, 29, 31; *23*
Patrician, lawyer, and poet from Nuremberg. Cofounder of the Pegnitzschäfer Orden. Author of *Whispering Wenches*.

Hart, Francis (Newbold) Noyes (1890–1943) 126
Born in Silver Spring, Maryland, she achieved fame with her novel *The Bellamy Trial*, which appeared serially in the *Saturday Evening Post* in 1927.

Hauff, Wilhelm (1802–27) 55
Following an academic training at the University of Tübingen he worked as a journalist on Cotta's *Morgenblatt*.

This Romantic poet is best known for his *Fairy Tales* (in English: 1910) and *Caravan Tales* (in English: 1912).

Heliodorus (c. A.D. 400) 12
Born in Emesa (Syria), he was the father of the Hellenistic adventure story, with his romance *Aethiopica*.

Hensley, Joe L. (born in 1926) 143; *143*
U.S. judge in Indiana and novelist, with criminal lawyer Donald Robak as series character in some half dozen mystery novels. Features a mid-America setting that comes across as warm and authentic.

Higgins, George V. (born in 1939) 142
A lawyer by profession, this U.S. author made a name for himself with *The Friends of Eddie Coyle* (1972). His novels feature realistic dialogue, intricate plotting, and unrelenting exposure of the political, social, and criminal underpinnings of Boston.

Highsmith, Patricia (born in 1921) 159, 160; *159*
This U.S. writer achieved her literary breakthrough after moving to Europe—England and France. Her very first novel *Strangers on a Train* (1950) was a best seller and was filmed by Hitchcock.

Himes, Chester (born in 1909) 140
An Afro-American born in Jefferson City, Missouri. His detective stories take up the theme of racial discrimination. His detective heroes are Grave Digger Jones and Coffin Ed Johnson.

Hichtcock, Alfred (1899–1981) 125, 165, 170, 193; *123, 124, 170*
He achieved fame as a producer of thrillers, but he also published anthologies of crime fiction and *Alfred Hitchcock's Mystery Magazine*.

Hitzig, Julius Eduard (1780–1849) 59, 60
A Berlin lawyer at the Supreme Court who belonged to E. T. A. Hoffmann's circle of friends.

Hoch, Edward D. (born in 1930) 186; *186*
Prolific U.S. short story writer whose output is already in the 600s, and whose work appears under numerous pseudonyms: Pat McMahon, Mr. X., R. L. Stevens, Stephen Dentinger, and so on.

Hoffmann, Ernst Theodor Amadeus (1776–1822) 52, 53, 55, 56, 60, 160; *53*
German Romantic poet who was also a composer and painter. A lawyer at the Supreme Court in Berlin.

Holcroft, Thomas (1745–1809) 50
A Londoner who worked as a school teacher, actor, and journalist. In 1778 he started writing sentimental plays. His *Tale of Mystery* introduced melodrama to the English stage.

Holt, Victoria 163, 164
Pseudonym for Eleanor Alice Burford Hibbert. Holt's Gothic novels tend to be romantic mysteries, yet most have solid underpinnings of murder and other crimes.

Holtei, Karl von (1798–1880) 80

A German and man of many talents who worked as an actor, a dramaturge, and a writer.

Hornung, Ernest William (1866–1921) 107; *108*
Brother-in-law of Arthur Conan Doyle and himself a writer. After trying his hand at adventure novels he created Raffles, the gentleman burglar.

Hull, Richard, see Sampson, Richard Henry

Hume, Fergus(on Wright) (1859–1932) 93
An Englishman who emigrated with his parents to New Zealand where, after studying, he became a lawyer. Reading Gaboriau's novels inspired him to start writing detective stories himself. *The Mystery of the Hansom Cab* became an immense success in Australia, England, and in the U.S.

Iles, Francis, see Cox, Anthony Berkeley

Innes, Michael 148, 149, 151, 152; *149*
Pseudonym for J(ohn) I(nnes) M(ackintosh) Stewart (born in 1906). Innes's novels span five decades, from 1936 into the 1980s. John Appleby, an inspector of police, is his predominant hero, although Charles Honeybath is featured in some later books, sometimes with Appleby.

James, P(hyllis) D(orothy) 153, 154, 155
Pseudonym for Phyllis White (born in 1920). After service as a Red Cross nurse during World War II, this English-woman worked in the Home Office, then wrote *Cover Her Face* in 1962, which was immediately acclaimed and made her a top-rated writer.

Kästner, Erich (1899–1978) 123; *122*
Critical and humanistic German writer who particularly appealed to children and adolescents. Wrote *Emil und die Detektive* (1929) and *Die verschwundene Miniatur* (1936) (*The Missing Miniature* [1936]).

Kaul, Friedrich Karl (1906–81) 130
Legal expert and university professor who represented the German Democratic Republic (East Germany) in international political trials.

Kemelman, Harry (born in 1908) 159
A graduate of Harvard University in the U.S. who had a number of jobs before becoming a professor at Boston State College. In 1947 he made his literary debut with a short story, and began the Rabbi Small series with *Friday the Rabbi Slept Late* in 1964.

Kendrick, Baynard H. (1884–1977) 143
U.S. creator of the blind detective Captain Duncan Maclain, was inspired by his work with blind veterans after World War II.

Kisch, Egon Erwin (1885–1948) 128
Czech journalist and writer who wrote in German. He was a master of the art of reportage as in *The Rushing Reporter* (1925).

Klarov, Yuri 178
A. Bezuglov's coauthor (see above).

Kleist, Heinrich von (1777–1811) 52
He gave up his career as an army officer to concentrate on journalism and literature. He achieved fame with his dramas and novellas, for example, *Michael Kohlhaas* (1808). Increasing isolation finally drove him to suicide.

Knox, Ronald Arbuthnott (1888–1957) 111, 122, 125
Studied theology at Oxford University where he became an Anglican chaplain, then in 1917 became a Catholic, was ordained as a priest in 1919, and returned to Oxford. As a scholar and theologian he worked on a new translation of the Bible but also wrote detective stories and essays about detective stories; he drew up the ten rules of "fair play."

Kruse, Laurids (1778–1839) 80
Danish author who wrote his detective stories in German.

Kwaśniewski, Kazimierz (born in 1920) 180
Polish author who in addition to writing books for children and young readers has also produced some detective stories.

Langton, Jane (born in 1922) *142*
Boston-born writer whose mystery novels usually reflect her New England background; her detective surrogate, attorney Homer Kelly, is the typically laconic and dry New England eccentric. She also illustrates her novels with excellent pen and ink renderings.

Lathen, Emma 148, 151
Pseudonym for Mary J. Latsis and Martha Henissart. Latsis is an economist; Henissart is in corporate banking. With their protagonist, amateur detective John Putnam Thatcher, a banker by trade, they explore all manner of big-business enterprises, solving murders and exposing ambitious financial schemes.

Latimer, Jonathan (1906–83) 143
U.S. writer of the tongue-in-check hard-boiled P.I. school—creator of Bill Crane, an "alcoholic private detective" usually involved in bawdy, humorous adventures. Produced many screenplays, the best of which was for Dashiell Hammett's *The Glass Key*.

Latude, Henry Masers de (1725–1805) 32
In his memoirs he recalls his several lengthy spells of imprisonment.

Leblanc, Maurice (1864–1941) 107
A French writer who, after having studied jurisprudence, turned to writing dramas and short stories. He devised the character of Arsène Lupin, a French adaptation of Hornung's Raffles.

Lee, Manfred B. (1905–71) 126, 149; *127*
Cousin and coauthor of Frederic Dannay (see above).

Le Fanu, Joseph Sheridan (1814–73) 70, 71, 122, 129
An Irish author who wrote his first novels in the tradition of Walter Scott before helping to develop the Gothic novel; his most interesting works are probably "Carmilla" and *Uncle Silas* (1864).

Leonard, Elmore (born in 1925)   188, 190, 191, 192; *190*
U.S. author of crime novels, westerns, and mainstream stories. Screenplays include several of his own novels, and originals. Dialogue and mood are exceptionally effective in his crime works; his sense of morality and life-style is essentially existential.

Le Queux, William (1864–1927)   108
A Londoner who was a newspaper foreign editor, an artist, and also wrote novels, especially spy stories. His output of novels is in the hundred-odd.

Leroux, Gaston (1868–1927)   102, 103, 172; *103*
A lawyer by profession, he took up journalism and from 1907 onwards published novels which combined elements of the detective story, the adventure story, and the thriller. He wrote over thirty novels; his *The Phantom of the Opera* (1911) continues to be made into film thrillers.

Leskov, Nikolai Semyonovich (1831–95)   89
A Russian writer who began his career as a civil servant before devoting himself to literature. His novels and short stories—*Lady Macbeth of Mtsensk District*—reflect the social mores of the time.

Levitschnigg, Heinrich Ritter von (1810–62)   80
An Austrian journalist and writer whose novels often touched on criminal matters. *The Secret of Pest* appeared in 1852 and *The Thief Catcher*, an early detective story, in 1860.

Lewin, Michael Z. (born in 1942)   143
U.S. writer whose mysteries sometimes feature P.I. Albert Samson. Samson is no macho hero—almost the opposite. Lewin may be one of the few male P.I. writers to elucidate the feminist point of view.

Lewis, Matthew Gregory (1775–1818)   42, 44
After studying at Oxford he became a Member of Parliament. He also had a great interest in literature and sought contact with the great German classic writers of the day. He achieved fame with his Gothic romance *The Monk*, a prototype of the subgenre, for which he became known as "Monk" Lewis.

Lincoln, Abraham (1809–65)   58
The sixteenth president of the U.S. was originally a lawyer. In 1846 he wrote a novella based on one of his cases.

Linington, Elizabeth (born in 1921)   183
Created several series with different heroes. Writes under the pseudonyms of Dell Shannon, Lesley Egan, and Anne Blaisdell.

Lovesey, Peter (born in 1936)   160
An English author and teacher. Together with his wife he writes detective stories that have historical backgrounds and are usually based on reports in old newspapers.

Lowndes, Marie Belloc (1868–1947)   103, 106
An Englishwoman, sister of Hillaire Belloc, who wrote a series of detective stories marked by careful attention to the depiction of characters and settings. *The Lodger* (1913), a fictionalized view of Jack the Ripper, is a classic thriller.

Lundquist, Sune (1911–75)   177; *177*
A Swedish civil engineer who under the pen name Vic Suneson wrote more than twenty detective stories all set in Stockholm.

Lustgarten, Edgar (Marcus) (1907–78)   130, 131
After studying at Oxford he worked as a solicitor in Manchester before moving to the BBC in London. As well as writing detective stories he also compiled accounts of famous British court cases, known as *Prisoner at the Bar*.

Lyons, Arthur (born in 1946)   143
Recent exploiter of the Los Angeles area and the private-eye genre with detective Jacob Asch, a half-Jewish operator who inhabits an L. A. quite different from Philip Marlowe's.

MacDonald, John D(ann) (1916–86)   143, 144, 145; *144*
Prolific U.S. author, awarded Grand Master status in 1972 by the Mystery Writers of America, and creator of P.I. Travis McGee. He also wrote mainstream novels with crime overtones, and was known for his ability to combine action and character.

Macdonald, Ross, see Millar, Kenneth

Mackintosh, Elizabeth (1897–1952)   160
Scottish author who used the pseudonym Josephine Tey in her mystery novels. Having become well known through her historical dramas and one historical adventure story she had a good basis from which to develop a solidly crafted detective story. *The Franchise Affair* (1948) is one of her best.

Marek, Jiří (born in 1914)   128, 129; *128, 129*
A Prague-based journalist and lecturer on Czech literature who became a writer and also worked for television. He rose to prominence with his books that retell old criminal cases with affectionate irony.

Marlitt, Eugenie (1825–87)   80
Well-known German author of trivial literature.

Marsh, Ngaio (1899–1982)   152, 153
Born in Christchurch, New Zealand, she divided her time between New Zealand and England, working for the theater and writing detective stories.

Marsh, Richard (1858–1915)   103
An Oxford graduate who wrote horror stories and detective novels which often touch on the realm of mystery.

Mason, Alfred Edward Woodley (1865–1948)   111, 115
A Londoner educated at Oxford who later became a Member of Parliament. He wrote short stories and detective stories that have as their hero the French detective Inspector Hanaud—*At the Villa Rosa* (1910).

Masur, Harold Q. (born in 1909)   143
U.S. writer and lawyer who produced novels about P.I. Scott Jordan in the 1940s and 1950s. Also wrote mainstream novels featuring lawyers mainly to exploit the courtroom milieu and the big-business scene.

Matsumoto, Seicho (born in 1909)   161; *161*
The Japanese association of detective story writers awarded him a prize for his novel *Points and Lines* (1957), which became a worldwide success.

Maupassant, Guy de (1850–93)   89
The great French short story writer and novelist frequently examined the psychology of crime, particularly in his short stories.

May, Karl (1842–1912)   82, 84, 85; *84*
The son of a weaver in what is today the south of the German Democratic Republic (East Germany), he began by writing novels set in the local area that combined sensational elements with the documentation of social customs. Criminal matters featured frequently in these stories. The author's fame, however, derives from his later travel and adventure stories, especially his tales of American Indians.

McBain, Ed   182, 183; *182*
Pseudonym of Salvatore A. Lombino (born in 1926) whose most famous pseudonym is Evan Hunter. Also wrote under other names: Curt Cannon, Hunt Collins, Ezra Hannor, Richard Marsten, etc. McBain's 87th Precinct novels were made into a long-running television series in the U.S. He did the screenplay for Hitchcock's famed *The Birds* (1963).

Mcdonald, Gregory (born in 1937)   185; *184*
Popular U.S. mystery writer, using Boston as his background and "Fletch" Fletcher and Francis Xavier Flynn as his heroes—sometimes in the same book. Fletch is an investigative reporter, Flynn a hard-working detective inspector. Film *Fletch* appeared in 1985.

Meissner, August Gottlieb (1753–1807)   39; *36*
A churchman and director of higher teaching institutes in the German town of Fulda, he achieved recognition with his historical novels and his *Sketches*, which dealt with more contemporary problems.

Millar, Kenneth (1915–83)   141, 146; *141*
U.S. author who used the nom de plume of Ross Macdonald. Married to Margaret Millar (see below). He based his detective hero, Lew Archer, on the hard-boiled type developed by Hammett and Chandler. Archer debuted in *The Moving Target* (1949).

Millar, Margaret (born in 1915)   162; *158*
Born Margaret Sturm, she studied classical languages at the University of Toronto in Canada and later married Kenneth Millar (see above), a writer publishing under the name of Ross Macdonald. In 1941 she too started writing detective stories; full of apparently inexplicable mysteries, most are taut psychological thrillers. *The Invisible Worm* appeared in 1941.

Miller, Wade   143
Pseudonym for Bill Miller (1920–61) and Robert Wade (born in 1920). The team also wrote under the pseudonym of Whit Masterson, which Wade continued to use after Miller's death. Detective Max Thursday featured in many of the novels and short stories.

Milne, A(lan) A(lexander) (1882–1956)   115
Although the English author is famous for his children's books he also tried his hand—successfully—at crime fiction—*The Red House Mystery* (1922).

Möllhausen, Balduin (1825–1905)   82; *83*
After emigrating to the U.S. he returned to Germany in 1854 and settled in Berlin as an author of novels and travel books.

Mostar, Gerhart Herrmann (1901–73)   129, 130
Writer and dramatist.

Muller, Marcia (born in 1944)   143
U.S. writer and creator of P.I. Sharon McCone, working out of San Francisco. McCone is an intelligent, persevering woman, whose adventures feature bright dialogue, artistic plots, and well-researched backgrounds.

Murphy, Warren (born in 1933)   186; *185*
Reporter, editor, public relations counselor, and speechwriter, he collaborated with Richard Sapir in writing *The Destroyer* series, featuring Remo Williams, and took over the series in 1981. Also wrote paperback originals.

Murray, Max(well) (1901–56)   124
An Australian writer and producer for the BBC, he wrote a dozen detective stories instilled with spine-chilling atmosphere. *The Voice of the Corpse* was published in 1947; all his mystery titles feature the word "corpse."

Narcejac, Thomas   157, 159, 193; *158*
Pseudonym for Pierre Ayrand (born in 1908). A French author who in addition to working as a schoolteacher has published novels and works of literary criticism. In 1948 he was awarded the *Prix du roman d'aventure*. Since 1950 he has collaborated with Pierre Boileau (see above) in detective story writing and on theoretical studies of this genre.

Nebel, (Louis) Frederick (1903–67)   143
Writer of the hard-boiled school, creator of Tough Dick Donahue in the magazine *Black Mask*.

Neville, Margot   127
Pseudonym for Anne Neville Goyder Joske and Margot Goyder. Joske (born in 1893) and Goyder (born in 1903) are Australians who began their collaboration in 1922 with *Marietta Is Stolen*. Their Inspector Grogan debuted in 1943 in *Lena Hates Men*.

O'Donnell, Lillian (born in 1926)   143
U.S. writer of suspense and police-procedural works, featuring Mici Anhalt, as a female P.I., and Norah Mulcahaney as a policewoman.

Paretsky, Sara   143; *142*
U.S. author whose series protagonist is V. I. Warshawski, a truly female private eye in the original sense of the word; writes in the hard-boiled style. Warshawski operates out of Chicago.

Parker, Robert B(rown) (born in 1932)   146; *145*
U.S. author and ex-academic who blends the realism, hu-

mor, and reality of the hard-boiled crime school with the social consciousness and ambience of the 1980s. Said to be the "modern voice" of the 1930s American private eye.

Pavon, Francisco Garcia (born in 1919) 194
Born in Castile, he was a professor at the National Drama Academy. In the field of literature he has carved a niche for himself as a theater critic and author of detective stories.

Pentecost, Hugh, see Philips, Judson

Pfeiffer, Hans (born in 1925) 130
A writer and lecturer on drama at the Johannes R. Becher Institute in Leipzig, he has written some detective stories but has devoted his attention mainly to historical criminal cases and to the history of criminology.

Philips, Judson (born in 1903) 157
After studying at Columbia University he started writing for pulp magazines, switched to slicks, and then to the novel form, and has since published more than ninety detective novels, and scores of short stories—under the nom de plume of Hugh Pentecost and under his own name.

Pinkterton, Allan (1819–84) 94, 98, 99, 131, 133
U.S. detective and founder of a highly successful private detective agency. Published several books describing his life and experience as a detective.

Pitaval, François Gayot de (1673–1743) 7, 24, 31, 32, 36, 39, 46, 53, 55, 59, 62, 76, 110
Famous French legal expert.

Poe, Edgar Allan (1809–49) 7, 55, 56, 57, 58, 71, 74, 75, 82, 91, 92, 102, 106, 109, 125, 160, 161, 170; *56, 58*
Born in Boston, he was orphaned at an early age and then rejected by his foster parents, after which he experienced extreme poverty. He started writing and in 1833 won a short-story competition and became a newspaper editor. He enjoyed literary success but continued to have financial problems. His "The Murders in the Rue Morgue" effectively established the detective story as a genre.

Post, Melville Davisson (1871–1930) 123, 132
A U.S. attorney born in Virginia who later became a writer.

Prather, Richard S(cott) (born in 1921) 143
U.S. writer of mystery genre fiction known for his comic vitality and ingenuity of action. Shell Scott, his hero, is a wisecracking ex-Marine who works in Hollywood and conducts his business in an insouciant, breezy, casual fashion.

Prodöhl, Günter (born in 1920) 130
A journalist living in the German Democratic Republic (East Germany) who also covered court cases, he turned to the writing of detective stories and the publication of interesting criminal cases.

Pronzini, Bill (born in 1943) 143; *143*
U.S. writer and anthologist who features a nameless detective in his series works. Is prolific short-story writer. Excels at situations in which terror stalks a person or group of persons.

Queen, Ellery, see Dannay, F., and M. B. Lee

Quentin, Patrick 187
A pseudonym under which two Englishmen, Richard W. Webb and Hugh Callingham Wheeler (born in 1912), jointly wrote detective stories. Another pseudonym used by the two is Jonathan Stagge. Wheeler has also written on his own under the nom de plume Patrick Quentin, showing a propensity to use black humor in his work. The partnership broke up in 1952.

Raabe, Wilhelm (1831–1910) 89
German novelist characterized by a realistic attention to detail and an epic narrative style; wrote under the pseudonym of Jakob Corvinus. Wrote *Stopfkuchen* (1891) and *Des Reiches Krone (The Imperial Croner)* (1873).

Radcliffe, Ann (1764–1823) 44, 129; *43*
Born in London as Ann Ward, she married W. Radcliffe, a lawyer who later edited *The English Chronicle*. Her novels— such as *The Mysteries of Udolpho*—were in the Gothic tradition but included criminal matters.

Rampo, Edogawa (1894–?) 160, 161; *160*
Japanese mystery writer whose real name was Hirai Taro. Name Edogawa Rampo is Japanese transliteration of famed U.S. mystery writer Edgar Allan Poe. Credited with starting mystery fiction trend in Japan in 1920s and 1930s, and establishing it as literary genre.

Rhode, John, see Street, Cecil J. C.

Richer, François (1718–90) 31, 32
A French advocate who revised F. G. de Pitaval's *Causes Célèbres et Intéressantes*, which appeared in Paris from 1734 onwards.

Rendell, Ruth (born in 1930) 154, 155, 156, 165; *154*
British writer producing series novels featuring Detective Chief-Inspector Reginald Wexford and nonseries novels featuring various quirky characters on the verge of breakdown. Plots for both types of writing are complex, involuted, but always satisfying in the denouement. Won Edgars for stories in 1975 and 1984.

Resnicow, Herbert 167; *167*
Newcomer in the mystery field with *The Gold Solution* (1983), this ex-construction project manager has written a number of mysteries of all types, including "sports-crime" subgenre in collaboration with ex-quarterback Franc Tarkenton.

"Richmond" 66
The pseudonym under which a three-volume novel—*Richmond, or Scenes from the Life of a Bow Street Runner*—appeared in 1827. The identity of the author is unknown.

Rinehart, Mary Roberts (1876–1958) 106, 107
She was born in Philadelphia as Mary Roberts and married a doctor. In 1903 she began writing short stories and then moved on to novels. She was the author of over thirty detective stories. Her *The Circular Staircase* (1908) was filmed in 1915.

Roosevelt, Franklin Delano (1882–1945) 126
The President of the U.S. from 1933 to 1945, who was an avid reader of detective novels, requested a novel in which a number of different authors would each write one chapter. It appeared in 1935 under the title *The President's Mystery Story*.

St. James, Bernard (born in 1932) 186; *185*
Born Bernard William Treister in Berlin and raised in Paris, "St. James" became naturalized citizen in U.S.; *April Thirteenth* (1978) was his first detective novel. Mysteries feature Chief Inspector Blanc, of the Paris police; settings are in France.

Sampson, Richard Henry (1896–1973) 185
An Englishman who wrote under the name Richard Hull. From the early thirties onwards he published detective stories often designed to shock the reader.

Sayers, Dorothy Leigh (1893–1957) 8, 70, 111, 113, 115, 120, 121, 122, 135, 148, 150, 151, 152, 153, 154; *120*
After leaving Oxford with a Master of Arts she worked for a time in an advertising agency, writing detective stories predominantly for financial reasons—*Murder Must Advertise* (1933) and *The Nine Tailors* (1934). In addition she wrote religious dramas and poetry and tried her hand as a translator.

Scerbanenco, Giorgio (1911–69) 194
He was born in Kiev but moved to Italy with his parents. He worked in various professions before finally becoming a crime writer.

Scherf, Margaret (1908–79) 184
After completing her studies she worked in publishing before beginning her career as a writer in 1939. She is the author of some twenty detective stories, the first of which was *The Corpse Grows a Beard* (1940).

Schiller, Friedrich von (1759–1805) 30, 36, 39, 40, 85
Although the great classical German poet is remembered chiefly for his plays, he also had a strong interest in the criminal mind and made his own contributions to crime fiction.

Shakespeare, William (1564–1616) 20
The world-famous English dramatist often made use of criminal characters and activities in his plays—*Hamlet, Macbeth, Othello*, etc.

Shestakov, Pavel 161
A Soviet writer.

Shkliarevski, Alexander Andreyevich (1837–83) 90
He trained as a teacher but following the success of his first detective story worked as a free-lance writer in St. Petersburg. The successful author was invited by the authorities to take part in criminal investigations.

Siewierski, Jerzy 193
A Polish author.

Simenon, Georges (born in 1903) 7, 159, 173, 174, 175, 176, 181, 194; *173*

Belgian author of crime stories who published his first novel in 1920. In 1930 he settled in Paris and began writing short stories under various pseudonyms. His first Inspector Jules Maigret book appeared in 1932. After emigrating to the U.S. he became a Swiss resident. He stopped writing crime fiction in 1973. Of particular interest is his exchange of letters with André Gide.

Sjöwall, Maj (born in 1935) 7, 176, 177
A Swedish journalist and the wife of the novelist Per Wahlöö (see below) with whom she has jointly written detective stories strongly colored by social criticism. *Roseanna* (1967) was their first joint effort.

Slesar, Henry (born in 1927) 187, 188
A New Yorker who worked in an advertising agency and was awarded an Edgar for his first crime novel, *The Gray Flannel Shroud* (1959). His detective novels and short stories are often tinted with black humor, as is evident from one title, "A Crime for Mothers and Others."

Smith, Julie 143; *142*
A journalist turned mystery author, she features a female private eye, Rebecca Schwartz, operating out of the San Francisco Bay Area. First mystery was *Death Turns a Trick* (1982).

Sophocles (c. 496–406 B.C.) 9
A Greek tragedian who took the themes for his plays, including *Oedipus the King*, from the world of mythology.

Spicer, Bart (born in 1918) 143
U.S. writer and creator of P.I. Carney Wilde, and author of a number of mainstream novels crafted in the hard-boiled tradition, and later in the action-oriented world of international adventure.

Spiess, Christian Heinrich (1755–99) 46
A former itinerant actor who turned to writing knightly dramas, ghost and horror stories and was dubbed the "father of the horror story."

Spillane, Mickey (born in 1918) 138, 139, 140, 146; *139*
Brooklyn-born author who first wrote scenarios for comic magazines before adopting stylistic elements of the "hard boiled" detective story to write novels of revenge and violence. Over 160,000,000 copies of his books have been sold. His work is not popular with critics or reviewers; only with the public.

Spranger, Günter (born in 1921) 195
A German Democratic Republic (East Germany) novelist who has also written detective stories.

Stagge, Jonathan 187
Pseudonym used by Richard W. Webb and Hugh Callingham Wheeler (see Quentin, Patrick, above).

Stemmle, Robert Adolf (1903–74) 129
Coeditor with Gerhart Herrmann Mostar of the West German *Neuer Pitaval*, a collection of crime stories.

Stendhal (1783–1842) 89
Henri Beyle, a French essayist and novelist, chose the name

of the town Stendal (the birthplace of the German archeologist Winckelmann) as his pen name. One of his best-known works is *La Chartreuse de Parme (The Charterhouse of Parma)*.

Stevenson, Robert Louis (1850–94)   71, 74; *71, 72, 73*
The Scottish writer was particularly fascinated by psychological problems, with which he dealt in *The Strange Case of Dr. Jekyll and Mr. Hyde*, and by tales of adventure, as in *Treasure Island*.

Stout, Rex (1886–1975)   126
A U.S. writer who had a number of jobs before he began writing crime novels featuring Nero Wolfe and Archie Goodwin. Some of these appeared in serialized form in magazines before appearing in book form.

Street, Cecil J. C. (1884–1965)   123
An ex-army officer who turned to crime fiction.

Strieber, Whitley (born in 1945)   186; *185*
Born in San Antonio, Texas, and later writer for a New York ad agency, he produced *The Wolfen* (1978) and *The Hunger* (1981), both made into movies. Writings veer toward the occult and the supernatural.

Sue, Eugène (1804–57)   39, 75, 77, 82, 100, 129; *76*
French journalist who with his 2,000-page *Les Mystères de Paris (The Mysteries of Paris)* helped develop the serialized novel.

Suneson, Vic, see Lundquist, Sune

Symons, Julian (born in 1912)   140, 193, 195
A London journalist with a reputation as a writer in various literary fields, including the genre of the detective story. His *Bloody Murder* (1972) (U.S.: *Mortal Consequences*) dealt with the history of crime fiction. He took over the running of the Detection Club from Agatha Christie.

Temme, Jodocus Donatus Hubertus (1798–1881)   60, 80; *61*
Deputy director of Berlin's criminal court between 1839 and 1843. A libertarian and democrat, he was accused of high treason in 1849, acquitted but nevertheless dismissed from public service. In 1852 he was appointed professor at Zurich University. In addition to his professional career he also achieved some success as a writer of fiction, particularly of crime stories.

Tey, Josephine, see Mackintosh, Elizabeth

Thackeray, William Makepeace (1811–63)   62, 63, 65
The books of the English writer, who was gifted with a shrewd knowledge of people and a faculty for critical observation, contain a detailed picture of contemporary society.

Thomson, June (born in 1930)   155, 156, 165
British writer with series character Inspector Finch in all her books. In the U.S., Finch appears as Rudd, except in the first. She excels at the countryside milieu, where Rudd/Finch slowly clears up the murky outlines of the characters until their true personas—and motives—shine through,

with the solution grasped finally through persistence and intelligence and not through trick endings.

Tieck, Ludwig (1773–1853)   40
Known as the King of the Romantic Age his favorite literary form was the novella; wrote, among others, *Phantasus* (1812–14).

Treat, Lawrence (born in 1903)   182
U.S. writer and one of the founding fathers of the Mystery Writers of America. Considered "father" of police procedural novel—from which sprang *Dragnet* on radio and TV, Maigret in France, and the 87th Precinct in the U.S. Wrote many short stories and puzzles.

Twain, Mark (1835–1910)   94, 95; *96*
His real name was Samuel Langhorne Clemens. The North American writer won recognition chiefly through his humorous novels as well as his books about Tom Sawyer and Huckleberry Finn.

Uhnak, Dorothy (born in 1933)   183
After working on the police force of New York for some years Dorothy Uhnak wrote a number of books based on her experiences.

Upfield, Arthur W(illiam) (1888–1964)   127
At the age of nineteen he was sent away from England by his family to Australia where he worked as a cook, shepherd, farmworker, gold prospector, and trapper. From 1926 onwards he wrote detective stories; series character is Inspector Napoleon "Bony" Bonaparte, a half-caste aborigine, who debuted in *The House of Cain* (1928).

Vance, Louis Joseph (1879–1933)   107
U.S. author whose novels centered on the crime adventures of Michael Lanyard, alias the "Lone Wolf." There are eight Lone Wolf novels.

Véry, Pierre (1900–60)   157
French author and scriptwriter who saw his detective stories as "fairy tales for adults." He achieved fame with his *L'Assassinat du Père Noël*.

Vidocq, Eugène François (1775–1857)   56, 68, 74, 76, 92, 107, 173; *75*
Born in Arras, he became a soldier during the French Revolution. Then he fell in with a gang of villains, was captured and sentenced to the galleys. He escaped and offered his services to Napoleon, was very successful at combating crime, and headed the Sûreté, the new criminal investigation department in Paris until forced to resign. His *Memoirs* appeared in 1828–29.

Vollert, Anton   60
Author in Berlin in the nineteenth century who succeeded Hitzig and Häring as the editor of the *Neuer Pitaval* collection of crime stories.

Vulpius, Christian August (1762–1827)   40
A librarian in Weimar and the brother-in-law of Goethe, he achieved fame through his novel about a highwayman, *Rinaldo Rinaldini* (1797).

Wahlöö, Per (1926–75) 7, 176, 177; *177*
A Swedish journalist and novelist who, together with his wife Maj Sjöwall (see above) wrote detective stories featuring Martin Beck, a Stockholm detective, containing strong elements of social criticism.

Wainer, Arkadi (born in 1931) 178; *180*
A Soviet writer who is a lawyer by profession. Together with his brother Georgi (see below) he has written numerous crime stories that have been translated into several languages.

Wainer, Georgi (born in 1938) 178; *179*
Beginning his career as a correspondent with the Tass news agency, he pooled forces with his brother Arkadi (see above) to write detective stories, short stories, and scripts for radio and television.

Wallace, Edgar (1875–1932) 7, 40, 111, 113, 123, 126, 128; *113, 114*
He spent a long time working in South Africa as a reporter. After his return to England he published his first crime story, *The Four Just Men* (1906). In the following years he wrote 172 novels and 17 plays. His income amounted to around $250,000 a year. His books were filmed right up to the 1960s.

Walpole, Horace (1717–97) 42; *42*
At his home in Strawberry Hill the English writer of letters and memoirs assembled a valuable collection of old books, papers, and works of art. His interest in both history and fiction was reflected in the first Gothic novel, *The Castle of Otranto* (1764).

Waugh, Hillary (born in 1920) 182
U.S. author of several series in the police procedural subgenre, one set in Connecticut, others in New York City. Also writes under the pseudonyms of H. Baldwin Taylor and Elissa Grandower.

Webb, Richard W. 187
English author who collaborated with Hugh Callingham Wheeler using the joint pseudonyms Patrick Quentin and Jonathan Stagge (see above).

Wells, Carolyn (1869–1942) 125
A U.S. librarian who turned to writing novels, including crime stories, and wrote *The Technique of the Mystery Story* (1913).

Werner, Zacharias (1768–1823) 51
After a checkered life he wound up as a cathedral canon; he became known through his plays in which the tragedy is brought about by the hand of fate; founded the "fate tragedy" school. Wrote *Attila* (1808) and *Der vierundzwanzigste Februar (The 24th of February)* (1844).

Werremeier, Friedhelm (born in 1929) 181
West German journalist and writer of detective stories, some in the vein of the Maigret stories.

Westlake, Donald (born in 1933) 188, 190; *188*
U.S. writer of humorous mysteries, including the Dortmunder series, and the Alan Grofield and Parker series under the pseudonym of Richard Stark. As Tucker Coe, Westlake writes the Mitch Tobin books. His stories have been turned into many successful movies.

Wheeler, Hugh Callingham (born in 1912) 187
English author who, together with Richard W. Webb, wrote under the pseudonyms Patrick Quentin and Jonathan Stagge (see above).

White, Phyllis, see James P. D.

Whitfield, Raoul (1898–1945) 143
Early writer of hard-boiled detective fiction, and creator of Jo Gar. Known for novels *Green Ice* (1930) and *Death in a Bowl* (1931).

Whitney, Phyllis A. (born in 1903) 164, 165; *164*
Author of romantic mysteries and juvenile mysteries, all in the Gothic vein. Her novels hew to the classic Gothic formula: confined area with murder in the past causing discomfort to the heroine.

Wickram, Jörg (born c. 1505 or 1520, died before 1562) 19
Founded a school for meistersingers in Kolmar in 1549, acted as town clerk in Burgheim, and in 1555 published a collection of humorous tales and short stories, *Das Rollwagenbüchlein*.

Wilde, Oscar (1854–1900) 90
Irish writer most famous for his plays; parodied ghost stories in *The Canterville Ghost* and murder stories in "Lord Arthur Saville's Crime."

Woolrich, Cornell (1903–68) 170, 172; *169, 170*
Prolific U.S. author of short stories, novelettes, and novels in the suspense genre, whose works translate well into the film medium—*Rear Window* (1954), *The Bride Wore Black* (1967), and *Phantom Lady* (1944). Wrote also under the pseudonyms William Irish and George Hopley.

Wright, Willard Huntington (1888–1939) 125, 126, 149
A U.S. art critic who began writing crime stories in 1925 aimed at an elite sector of the reading public. He wrote under the pen name of S. S. Van Dine in order, as he thought, not to jeopardize his reputation as an art critic. His detective creation, Philo Vance, appeared in some twelve novels, starting with *The Benson Murder Cox* (1926).

Zola, Emile (1840–1902) 89; *87*
In planning *Les Rougon-Macquart*, a series of novels intended to paint a portrait of life under the Second Empire, the celebrated French novelist necessarily had to include the depiction of criminal characters and occurrences. An early novel *Thérèse Raquin* (1867) also deals with the subject of crime but cannot be regarded as a true detective story.

Acknowledgments

ADN Berlin   124, 130, 148
Archiv des Fernsehens der DDR   72 above, 73
Archive of the author   14, 18 left, 23 left, 28, 38, 77 left, 83, 84, 93, 96
Avon Books   150
Bantam Books   158 right
Bauer, Jerry   154, 168
CBS Television Network   139
Dell Books   103, 123
Deutsche Fotothek, Dresden   15, 16, 17, 29
Deutsche Staatsbibliothek Berlin   19, 35 above, 36 below, 41, 51, 53, 56, 57, 58, 60 above left, 63, 67, 68, 71, 76, 91, 98, 109, 116, 120, 121, 134 left, 140
Dodd, Mead   149
Dressler, Marjory   185
Estate of Bertolt Brecht/Helene Weigel   117, 127, 137, 194
First National   172 below
Francis, Mary   166
Gerson, Mark   168
Gleasner, Bill   164
Gores, Dori   191
Greenleaf, Ann   144
Grimes, Bill   157
Henkel, Thea, Berlin   12 left
Herbert, Rosemary   142
Hunter, Mary Vann   182
Karger-Decker, Heinz, Berlin   11, 12 right, 26 above, 27, 32, 33 below, 36 above, 44, 65, 92, 95, 97
Kuwata, M.   160
Laragy, Jim   186
Leni   167

Leonard, Joan   190
Lopert Pictures   169 (2)
McManus, Jay   142
Museum der bildenden Künste, Leipzig/Joachim Petri   45, 47, 48, 49
Paramount Pictures   72, 138, 170, 171 (2)
Pirtle   143
Pocket Books   134 right
Progress Publishers, Moscow   119 below right
Ravid, Joyce   188
Sassier, Jacques   144
Savage, Sally   156
Skorpianski, Peggy   142
Staatliche Galerie Moritzburg, Halle   25
Staatliche Museen zu Berlin, Kupferstichkabinett und Sammlung der Zeichnungen   22, 34
Staatliches Filmarchiv der DDR, Dokumentensammlung   54, 88 above, 99, 101, 112, 113, 114, 118, 119 above and below left, 136, 159, 163, 174, 175
Twentieth Century-Fox   100
United Artists   189 (3)
Universal City Studios   190
Universal Pictures   184 right
Verlag Das Neue Berlin   108
Verlag Volk und Welt, Berlin   128, 129, 158 left, 161, 173, 177, 179, 180
Warner Books   184 left
Warner Brothers   141, 172 above
Victor, Thomas   145
Weiman, Jon   144
Wright, S. C.   142

215